Imaginación y fantasía

CUENTOS DE LAS AMÉRICAS

Imaginación y fantasía

CUENTOS DE LAS AMÉRICAS

Fifth Edition

DONALD A. YATES
Emeritus, Michigan State University

JOHN B. DALBOR
Pennsylvania State University

HOLT, RINEHART & WINSTON, INC.

New York   Chicago   San Francisco
Philadelphia   Montreal   Toronto
London   Sydney   Tokyo

Publisher: Vince Duggan
Associate Publisher: Marilyn Pérez-Abreu
Developmental Editors: Irwin Stern, Teresa Chimienti
Project Editors: Danielle J. Khoriaty, Julia Price
Production Manager: Priscilla Taguer
Design Supervisor: Kathie Vaccaro
Text and Cover Design: Grafica
Cover Photograph: Reginald Wickam

Permissions and acknowledgements appear at the end of this book.

Library of Congress Cataloging-in-Publication Data
Imaginación y fantasía: cuentos de las Américas / Donald A. Yates.
  John B. Dalbor [editors].—[5th ed.]
    p.   cm.
  ISBN 0-03-006947-5
  1. Spanish language—Readers. 2. Short stories, Spanish American.
3. Fantastic fiction, Spanish American. I. Yates. Donald A.
II. Dalbor, John B.
PC4117.I39 1988   88–15588
468.6′421—dc19   CIP

ISBN 0-03-006947-5

Printed in the United States of America

9 0 1 2 090 9 8 7 6 5 4 3 2 1

Holt, Rinehart and Winston, Inc.
The Dryden Press
Saunders College Publishing

To the Memory
of
Jorge Luis Borges

(1899 – 1986)

CONTENTS

PREFACE TO THE FIFTH EDITION

When the first edition of IMAGINACIÓN Y FANTASÍA appeared in 1960, our aim was to expose intermediate college-level students of Spanish to stories of a type not widely available then—tales of imagination and fantasy. In the second edition (1968), we eliminated three stories and added five new ones, raising the total number to fourteen. We were searching for new prose selections that would increasingly challenge students' abilities and stimulate their thinking. In the third edition (1975), we decided to replace five of the stories, based on the results of a survey of teachers who had used this text. Finally, in the most recent edition of this text (1983), we replaced five more stories with others we believed would successfully engage the attention of current college-level students.

Now, nearly three decades after the first appearance of this text, we have decided to subject IMAGINACIÓN Y FANTASÍA to its most extensive revision. Numerous carefully considered suggestions from users of this text have made us realize that this reader has gradually become too difficult for its intended audience. Therefore, in this fifth edition we have retained six of the selections from the previous revision and added eight additional stories. With these fourteen tales we believe we have fashioned a text that more closely suits the interests and abilities of today's students. There are fables, parables, tales of humor, fantasy and suspense, detective stories, psychological narratives, and even a touch of science fiction.

We have also modified the accompanying exercises. We have kept the idea of designating a series of Key Expressions for each story, which are listed beforehand and should be studied in preparation for reading each selection. Moreover, most of the language exercises following each story will draw on these highlighted expressions. These exercises have been prepared with definite purposes in mind. Exercise A, Questions and Opinions, is not only a series of questions, but also a review designed to lead to a full comprehension of the most significant features of each story. At the end of each of these sections a few additional questions have been provided that inquire more directly into the individual student's reaction to the story. These questions, a new feature in this edition, are preceded by a bullet (•). They may be handled in several different ways: as simple queries to be answered concisely; as more probing questions that explore the student's interpretation and evaluation of the story; or as topics that could be assigned for a brief essay or theme.

Exercise B, Verb Practice, deals with verbs that have been defined and explained in the Key Expressions listing. Students are free to compose original sentences using these verbs. The sentences can either parallel those found in the story itself or they can be spontaneous and creative.

Exercise C, Vocabulary Practice, involves the verbs and expressions from the Key Expressions not included in Exercise B. Again, students are encouraged to use these items in sentences of their own design.

Exercise D, Communication Practice, is presented as a new way of encouraging one's individual expression in Spanish. There is no single "correct" response here: students are urged to "think themselves into" the contexts described and to find, on their own, an appropriate way of expressing the given idea, without the inhibiting limitation of a specific translation being called for.

Finally, presented under the heading of Exercise E are various additional and self-explanatory Review Exercises, included at the end of the odd-numbered stories. After even-numbered stories, Exercise E has the form of a Completion Exercise, wherein sentence fragments involving highlighted verbs from the story are given, and for which students are asked to provide any appropriate and original concluding clause in Spanish.

It is our hope that these exercises will increase the value of this text as a language-learning tool and that they will successfully complement its main purpose of serving as an entertaining introduction to the reading of Spanish American imaginative fiction.

D.A.Y.
J. B. D.

A PREFATORY NOTE TO THE READER

There are not many things that can seriously delay you from developing, early in your acquaintanceship with the Spanish language, a considerable ability in reading Spanish prose. The stories that follow are presented with the purpose in mind of demonstrating this point. The first story, «Los dos reyes y los dos laberintos» by the Argentine writer Jorge Luis Borges, provides an excellent illustration of certain immediate advantages that the English-speaking student enjoys.

The author, Borges, who received his education in Europe, was one of his country's most cultured literary figures. His prose is by nature quite formal, and his vocabulary is notable for the use of many "learned" words. You will find that words of this type are among the easiest to comprehend on sight, for a large number of them are English cognates—they resemble their corresponding terms in English.

Thus it is that we start off with a story written in Spanish by a cultured Argentine that has the promise of being quite easy to understand. The story has approximately 300 words. Of these, roughly one-fifth are nouns. Of the 56 individual nouns, 23 are recognizable cognates. In addition, you probably already know many of the remaining nouns. The balance will be new nouns to be learned and retained for future readings.

More than a tenth of the words are verb forms. Of the roughly 30 individual verbs, a third are cognates; and it is likely that you will already know another third.

The great majority of the remaining words will be familiar to you. Therefore, we feel that you may turn to the Borges story with some feeling of confidence.

As you will see, there are numerous other ways besides spotting cognates of rapidly building up a reading vocabulary in Spanish. In the exercises following several of the stories these techniques will be discussed and utilized.

We are confident that you will find ahead of you much pleasurable and rewarding reading in this collection.

LOS DOS REYES
Y LOS DOS
LABERINTOS

JORGE LUIS BORGES

JORGE LUIS BORGES (1899–1986) was born in Argentina and educated in Europe. He returned to Buenos Aires in 1921 to begin forging one of the most respected literary reputations ever attained by a Spanish American writer. A leading poet in his early years, in the 1930s and 1940s he turned to prose expression with essays and stories that firmly established him as one of the finest literary stylists ever to write in the Spanish language. He was appointed Director of the National Library in Buenos Aires in 1955, the same year in which he lost his sight. But he continued to compose prose and poetry up until the time of his death, more than three decades later.

Of the numerous themes that run through the writings of Borges, one of the most striking is that of the maze, or labyrinth. A maze is, of course, a system of winding paths designed to confuse all who set foot in it. In Borges, however, the labyrinth becomes a symbol of the universe, an image of what the design of human existence might be. In «Los dos reyes y los dos laberintos» the author has conjured up one more labyrinth, proposing for it a new form — perhaps the most surprising form it may ever acquire.

A PRELIMINARY LOOK AT KEY EXPRESSIONS

The expressions listed below are found in the story and are used in the exercises and activities that follow. By studying these expressions before you read the story, you will facilitate your comprehension of the story and thus increase your enjoyment in reading it. This preliminary study will also help you do the assignments that follow more quickly and accurately, since all constructions and terms used in the activities and exercises appear here first with definitions and, in some cases, with further explanation and examples. The expressions are listed in the same order in which they occur in the story and with page and line numbers.

1. (4: 3) **mandar** + *infinitive* When there is no indirect object, the expression means *to have* + *past participle.* For example, **El rey mandó construir un laberinto.** *The king had a labyrinth built.* But if there is an indirect object, the English wording changes: **El rey les mandó construir un laberinto.** *The king ordered them to build (made them build) a labyrinth.*
2. (4: 7) **hacer burla de** *to make fun of, make a fool of*
3. (4: 8) **hacer** + *infinitive* This expression is similar to Number 1: **El rey hizo construir un laberinto.** *The king had a labyrinth built,* but **El rey les hizo construir un laberinto** is *The king had (made) them build a labyrinth.*
4. (4: 9) **dar con** *to find, come across, hit upon, run into* (usually by accident)
5. (4:11) **dar a conocer** *to make known* For example, **Te lo daré a conocer.** *I'll make it known to you.*
6. (4:12) **algún día** *someday Any day* (at all) is **cualquier día.**
7. (4:12) **luego** *then, next* **Luego** refers to a point in time; **entonces** means *then* in the sense of *at that time, in those days,* etc. Compare **Luego le desaté las ligaduras.** *Then (next) I untied his bonds* with **Entonces yo no era más que un niño.** *Then (at that time) I was just a child.*
8. (4:15) **llevar** *to take, carry* This verb is used when something or someone is taken or transported from one place to another. **Tomar,** on the other hand, means *to take into one's possession:* **Tome Ud. este libro y devuélvalo a la biblioteca.** *Take this book and return it to the library.*
9. (4:16) **querer** *(in preterit)* + *infinitive to try* + *infinitive* **Querer** in the preterit indicates that an effort was made to carry out some action: **Me quisiste perder en tu laberinto.** *You tried to get me lost in your labyrinth.* However, in the imperfect **querer** expresses only the desire,

2

whether an attempt was ever made or not: **Yo quería protestar, pero no dije palabra.** *I wanted to protest, but I didn't say a word.*

10. (4:17) **tener a bien** *to see fit*   This phrase is followed by an infinitive with no change of subject: **Dios ha tenido a bien terminarlo.** *God has seen fit to end it.* But it is followed by the subjunctive when there is a change of subject: **Dios ha tenido a bien que yo lo termine.** *God has seen fit that I end it.*

LOS DOS REYES
Y LOS DOS LABERINTOS

Cuentan los hombres dignos de fe (pero Alá[1] sabe más) que en los primeros días hubo un rey de las islas de Babilonia que congregó a sus arquitectos y magos y les mandó construir un laberinto tan perplejo y sutil que los varones más prudentes no se aventuraban a entrar, y los que entraban se perdían. Esa obra era un escándalo, porque la confusión y la maravilla son operaciones propias de 5 Dios y no de los hombres. Con el andar del tiempo vino a su corte un rey de los árabes, y el rey de Babilonia (para hacer burla de la simplicidad de su huésped) lo hizo penetrar en el laberinto, donde vagó afrentado y confundido hasta la declinación de la tarde. Entonces imploró socorro divino y dio con la puerta. Sus labios no profirieron queja ninguna, pero le dijo al rey de Babilonia que él en 10 Arabia tenía un laberinto mejor y que, si Dios era servido, se lo daría a conocer algún día. Luego regresó a Arabia, juntó sus capitanes y sus alcaides y estragó los reinos de Babilonia con tan venturosa fortuna que derribó sus castillos, rompió sus gentes e hizo cautivo al mismo rey. Lo amarró encima de un camello veloz y lo llevó al desierto. Cabalgaron tres días, y le dijo: «¡Oh, rey del tiempo y 15 substancia y cifra del siglo!, en Babilonia me quisiste perder en un laberinto de bronce con muchas escaleras, puertas y muros; ahora el Poderoso ha tenido a bien que te muestre el mío, donde no hay escaleras que subir, ni puertas que forzar, ni fatigosas galerías que recorrer, ni muros que te veden el paso.»[2]

Luego le desató las ligaduras y lo abandonó en mitad del desierto, donde 20 murió de hambre y de sed. La gloria sea con[3] Aquél que no muere.

EXERCISES

A. Questions and Opinions*

1. ¿Qué mandó construir un rey de las islas de Babilonia?
2. ¿Por qué era un escándalo esa obra?

---

[1]*Alá:* Allah (the Moslem name for God)   [2]*que te veden el paso:* that block your way   [3]*La gloria sea con:* Glory be to
*Opinion questions are indicated throughout the book by a bullet preceding the number.

3. ¿Quién vino a la corte del rey?
4. ¿Con qué propósito hizo penetrar en el laberinto a su huésped?
5. ¿Qué hizo el rey árabe antes de pedir socorro?
6. ¿Qué dijo el rey árabe que tenía en Arabia y que le daría a conocer algún día al otro rey?
7. ¿Quién hizo cautivo al rey de las islas de Babilonia?
8. ¿Hasta dónde llevó al rey después de amarrarlo encima de un camello?
9. ¿Es el desierto un laberinto de veras?
10. ¿Quién es «Aquél que no muere»?
●11. ¿Cree Ud. que Dios era servido en este cuento?
●12. ¿Conoce Ud. algún laberinto?

B. Verb Practice

Here are some of the story's most important and most common Spanish verbal phrases — already presented in the preceding Key Expressions section with a brief explanation where necessary. Use each one in an original Spanish sentence — either similar to the one found in the story or, preferably, something completely different and personal. For example, **hacer burla de: El rey de Babilonia hizo burla de la simplicidad de su huésped** (based on the story) or **Nunca hago burla de nadie** (your own). Be prepared to explain the meaning of your sentences.

1. **mandar** + *infinitive*
2. **hacer** + *infinitive*
3. **dar con**
4. **llevar**
5. **querer** *(in preterit)* + *infinitive*

C. Vocabulary Practice

Listed in the right-hand column are lexical (vocabulary) items that figure among the Key Expressions for this story. Complete the sentences below, matching the expressions on the right with the italicized English words on the left. Be sure to use the correct form of each verb. Then use each expression in an original Spanish sentence and indicate in English what your sentence means.

1. *Next,* llamé a mi compañero.   **hacer burla de**
2. ¿Piensas ir a Arabia *someday?*   **tener a bien**
3. El jefe *did not see fit* darme un aumento de sueldo.   **algún día**
4. En ese caso, ¿por qué *don't you make known* tus quejas en la oficina del presidente?   **luego**
5. Creo que los otros *would make fun of me.*   **dar a conocer**

D. Communication Practice

The following sentences also involve the Key Expressions in the story. Express in Spanish the ideas suggested here, avoiding wherever possible a word-for-word rendering. The purpose here is to encourage you to think in Spanish and arrive at your own way of communicating the idea. For example, say that God saw fit that the King of Arabia show his own labyrinth to the King of Babylonia. (Remember to use the subjunctive.) **Dios tuvo a bien que el rey de los árabes (Arabia) le mostrara su laberinto al rey de Babilonia.**

1. Say that you, too, are going to have a labyrinth built some day.
2. Explain where the King of Arabia took the King of Babylonia.
3. Suggest that maybe tomorrow someone will hit on the solution.
4. Indicate that they have already made known the names.
5. Express the idea that no one saw fit to show you the staircase.

E. Review Exercise

The following words from the story are cognates that you may have been able to recognize because of their resemblance to familiar English words. Review them now and see if you can give their meanings on sight. Check the end vocabulary if necessary.

Nouns: **islas, arquitectos, laberinto, escándalo, confusión, maravilla, operaciones, corte, árabes, simplicidad, capitanes, fortuna, castillos, camello, desierto, substancia, cifra, bronce, galerías, gloria, Babilonia, Alá**

Verbs: **congregar, construir, aventurarse, entrar, penetrar, implorar, forzar, abandonar**

Adjectives: **perplejo, sutil, prudente, confundido, divino**

Can you now make any generalizations on how certain groups of English words appear in Spanish? What form, for example, do many English words with the following endings take in Spanish: *-tion, -ty, -nce, -ent?*

Can a Spanish word begin with *sc-, sl-, sm-, sp-,* or *st-?* What is characteristic of the form of the Spanish equivalents of many English words of this type?

EL BUEN EJEMPLO

VICENTE RIVA PALACIO

VICENTE RIVA PALACIO (1832–1896) was born in Mexico City, became a lawyer at the age of twenty-two, entered politics, then the army, and rose to the rank of general in 1865. After the victory over the French at Juárez, he retired from his active public career to write. From his pen came numerous historical novels dealing with the colonial era in Mexico in general and with the influence in the New World of the Spanish Inquisition in particular. His short stories are highly regarded today, constituting what many critics feel to be the most valuable part of his literary endeavors. In 1886 he returned to his country's service as Mexico's ambassador to Spain.

It is generally thought that the author is best represented in the volume of short stories entitled *Los cuentos del general,* which was published shortly after his death in 1896. In these stories he is relating, essentially, anecdotes, in a light and ingratiating style that is as pleasing in itself as the amusing tales he recounts. Under the author's pen these anecdotes become stories set off in little worlds of their own. Riva Palacio's art is nowhere more delightfully demonstrated than in «El buen ejemplo», a light-hearted satire that may still find a target in today's educational world.

A PRELIMINARY LOOK AT KEY EXPRESSIONS

Be sure to study these expressions before you read the story.

1. (10: 2) **tener razón** *to be right* **No tener razón,** then, is *to be wrong.*
2. (10: 3) **referirse a** *to refer to*
3. (10:17) **faltar a** *to be absent from, to miss* This expression can be used with things as in the story: **Jamás faltaba al cumplimiento de su obligación.** *He never missed doing his duty,* or places: **¿Por qué faltaste a clase?** *Why were you absent from (did you miss) class?*
4. (10:18) **necesitar** *to need*
5. (10:21) **una especie de** *a type of* This is used when the speaker is comparing one thing to another in a rather imprecise way, as in the English *"sort of . . .":* **Era una especie de orfeón.** *It was sort of like a singing society.*
6. (10:25) **soportar** *to stand, endure, bear*
7. (10:29) **dar** + *clock-time* *to strike* + *clock-time* All times, except for one o'clock, require a plural verb, which precedes the time: **Dieron las ocho.** *The clock struck eight.*
8. (11: 3) **disfrutar de** *to enjoy*
9. (11:16) **de arriba abajo** *up and down, from top to bottom:* **Me miró de arriba abajo.** *He looked me up and down.*
10. (11:21) **transcurrir** *to go by, elapse* The time expression normally follows this verb: **Transcurrieron así varios años.** *Several years went by this way.*
11. (11:21) **llegar a** + *infinitive* *to come, get* + *infinitive* This expression uses **llegar** *to arrive* in a special way: **Llegué a tener confianza en él.** *I came to have confidence in him.*
12. (11:24) **Serían como** + *clock-time* *It must have been (probably was)* + *clock-time* This shows how the conditional can be used in Spanish to express probability or conjecture in the past. This usage occurs many times throughout this collection of stories. Watch for it.
13. (11:24) **casualmente** *by chance, coincidentally* This is an example of a deceptive cognate. *Casually* is expressed in Spanish with a wide variety of expressions, such as **informalmente, de manera despreocupada,** etc., none of which involves the word **casual.**
14. (11:27) **a lo lejos** *in the distance*
15. (11:28) **cuanto antes** *without delay, as soon as possible, immediately*
16. (11:33) **volver a** + *infinitive* *verb* + *again* **Volvió a ocupar su asiento.** *He took his seat again.*
17. (11:34) **acabar de** + *infinitive* *to have just* + *past participle* **Acaban de comer.** *They have just eaten.* The expression in the imperfect has the same meaning: **Cuando llegamos, acababan de comer.** *When we ar-*

rived, they had just eaten. However, in the preterit the best English rendition is *to finish + present participle:* **Por fin acabaron de comer.** *They finally finished eating.*

18. (12: 2) **despedirse de** *to say good-by to*
19. (12:16) **al principio** *at first*
20. (12:23) **volver** + *direct object   to turn + direct object*   This is used for turning one's face, head, back, or the pages of a book, or even to turn or roll up one's sleeves.

EL BUEN EJEMPLO

Si yo afirmara que he visto lo que voy a referir, no faltaría, sin duda, persona que dijese[1] que eso no era verdad; y tendría razón, porque no lo vi, pero lo creo, porque me lo contó una señora anciana, refiriéndose a personas a quienes daba mucho crédito y que decían haberlo oído[2] de una persona que llevaba amistad con un testigo fidedigno, y sobre tales bases de certidumbre bien puede darse fe[3] 5 a la siguiente narración:

En la parte sur de la República Mexicana, y en las faldas de la Sierra Madre, que van a perderse en las aguas del Pacífico, hay un pueblecito como son en general todos aquéllos: casitas blancas cubiertas de encendidas tejas o de brillantes hojas de palmera, que se refugian de los ardientes rayos del sol tropical a 10 la fresca sombra que les prestan enhiestos cocoteros, copudos tamarindos y crujientes platanares y gigantescos cedros.

El agua en pequeños arroyuelos cruza retozando por todas las callejuelas, y ocultándose a veces entre macizos de flores y de verdura.

En este pueblo había una escuela, y debe haberla todavía;[4] pero entonces la 15 gobernaba don Lucas Forcida, personaje muy bien querido por todos los vecinos. Jamás faltaba a las horas de costumbre al cumplimiento de su pesada obligación. ¡Qué vocaciones de mártires[5] necesitan los maestros de escuela de los pueblos!

En esa escuela, siguiendo tradicionales costumbres y uso general en aquellos 20 tiempos, el estudio para los muchachos era una especie de orfeón, y en diferentes tonos, pero siempre con desesperante monotonía, en coro se estudiaban y en coro se cantaban lo mismo las letras y las sílabas que la doctrina cristiana o la tabla de multiplicar.

Don Lucas soportaba con heroica resignación aquella ópera diaria, y había 25 veces que los chicos, entusiasmados gritaban a cual más y mejor;[6] y era de ver[7] entonces la estupidez amoldando las facciones de la simpática y honrada cara de don Lucas.

Daban las cinco de la tarde; los chicos salían escapados de la escuela, tirando pedradas, coleando perros y dando gritos y silbidos, pero ya fuera de las aguas 30 jurisdiccionales de don Lucas, que los miraba alejarse, como diría un novelista, trémulo de satisfacción.

---

[1]*no... dijese:* without a doubt there would be someone who would say   [2]*decían haberlo oído:* said they had heard it   [3]*bien puede darse fe:* one can well give credence   [4]*debe haberla todavía:* it must still be there   [5]*¡Qué vocaciones de mártires:* What a calling for martyrdom   [6]*a cual más y mejor:* to see who could do it the loudest and the best   [7]*era de ver:* you should have seen

Entonces don Lucas se pertenecía a sí mismo: sacaba a la calle una gran butaca de mimbre; un criadito le traía una taza de chocolate acompañada de una gran torta de pan, y don Lucas, disfrutando del fresco de la tarde y recibiendo en su calva frente el vientecillo perfumado que llegaba de los bosques, como para
5 consolar a los vecinos de las fatigas del día, comenzaba a despachar su modesta merienda, partiéndola cariñosamente con su loro.

Porque don Lucas tenía un loro que era, como se dice hoy, su debilidad, y que estaba siempre en una percha a la puerta de la escuela, a respetable altura para escapar de los muchachos, y al abrigo del sol por un pequeño cobertizo de hojas
10 de palma. Aquel loro y don Lucas se entendían perfectamente. Raras veces mezclaba sus palabras, más o menos bien aprendidas, con los cantos de los chicos, ni aumentaba la algazara con los gritos estridentes y desentonados que había aprendido en el hogar materno.

Pero cuando la escuela quedaba desierta y don Lucas salía a tomar su choco-
15 late, entonces aquellos dos amigos daban expansión libre a todos sus afectos. El loro recorría la percha de arriba abajo,[8] diciendo cuanto sabía[9] y cuanto no sabía; restregaba con satisfacción su pico en ella, y se colgaba de las patas, cabeza abajo, para recibir la sopa de pan con chocolate que con paternal cariño le llevaba don Lucas.
20 Y esto pasaba todas las tardes.

Transcurrieron así varios años, y don Lucas llegó a tener tal confianza en su querido *Perico,* como lo llamaban los muchachos, que ni le cortaba las alas ni cuidaba de ponerle calza.

Una mañana, serían como las diez, uno de los chicos, que casualmente estaba
25 fuera de la escuela, gritó espantado: «Señor maestro, que[10] se vuela Perico». Oír esto y lanzarse en precipitado tumulto a la puerta maestro y discípulos, fue todo uno;[11] y, en efecto, a lo lejos, como un grano de esmalte verde herido por los rayos del sol, se veía al ingrato esforzando su vuelo para ganar cuanto antes refugio en el cercano bosque.
30 Como toda persecución era imposible, porque ni aun teniendo la filiación del prófugo podría habérsele distinguido[12] entre la multitud de loros que pueblan aquellos bosques, don Lucas, lanzando de lo hondo de su pecho un «sea por Dios»,[13] volvió a ocupar su asiento, y las tareas escolares continuaron, como si no acabara de pasar aquel terrible acontecimiento.
35 Transcurrieron varios meses, y don Lucas, que había echado al olvido[14] la ingratitud de Perico, tuvo necesidad de emprender un viaje a uno de los pueblos circunvecinos, aprovechando unas vacaciones.

---

[8]*recorría... abajo:* went up and down his perch   [9]*cuanto sabía:* all that he knew   [10]*que:* should not be translated   [11]*Oír... uno:* No sooner had they heard this when the teacher and pupils charged forward to the door in a wild rush   [12]*podría habérsele distinguido:* could one have picked him out   [13]*«sea por Dios»:* it's God's will   [14]*había echado al olvido:* had forgotten

Muy de madrugada[15] ensilló su caballo, tomó un ligero desayuno y salió del pueblo, despidiéndose muy cortésmente de los pocos vecinos que por las calles encontraba.

En aquel país, pueblos cercanos son aquéllos que sólo están separados por una distancia de doce o catorce leguas, y don Lucas necesitaba caminar la mayor 5 parte del día.

Eran las dos de la tarde; el sol derramaba torrentes de fuego; ni el viento más ligero agitaba los penachos de las palmas que se dibujaban sobre un cielo azul con la inmovilidad de un árbol de hierro. Los pájaros enmudecían ocultos entre el follaje, y sólo las cigarras cantaban tenazmente en medio de aquel terrible 10 silencio a la mitad del día.

El caballo de don Lucas avanzaba haciendo sonar el acompasado golpeo de sus pisadas con la monotonía del volante de un reloj.

Repentinamente don Lucas creyó oír a lo lejos el canto de los niños de la escuela cuando estudiaban las letras y las sílabas. 15

Al principio aquello le pareció una alucinación producida por el calor, como esas músicas y esas campanadas que en el primer instante creen oír los que sufren un vértigo; pero, a medida que avanzaba, aquellos cantos iban siendo más claros y más perceptibles; aquello era una escuela en medio del bosque desierto.

Se detuvo asombrado y temeroso, cuando de los árboles cercanos se despren- 20 dió, tomando vuelo, una bandada de loros que iban cantando acompasada-mente *ba, be, bi, bo, bu; la, le, li, lo, lu;* y tras ellos, volando majestuosamente un loro que, al pasar cerca del espantado maestro, volvió la cabeza, diciéndole alegremente:

«Don Lucas, ya tengo escuela.» 25

Desde esa época los loros de aquella comarca, adelantándose a su siglo,[16] han visto disiparse las sombras del obscurantismo y la ignorancia.

EXERCISES

A. Questions and Opinions

1. ¿Quién le refirió al autor la historia que él cuenta?
2. ¿Dónde enseñaba el maestro don Lucas Forcida?
3. ¿Cómo estudiaban los alumnos de la escuela de don Lucas?
4. ¿Cómo se divertía don Lucas todos los días después de la clase?
5. ¿Con quién partía don Lucas su modesta merienda?

---

[15]*Muy de madrugada:* At daybreak   [16]*adelantándose a su siglo:* getting ahead of their own century

6. ¿Por qué no le cortó don Lucas las alas a su compañero?
7. ¿Qué llegó gritando una mañana uno de los chicos?
8. ¿Adónde tuvo que ir don Lucas varios meses después?
9. A medida que avanzaba por el camino, ¿qué oyó don Lucas a lo lejos?
10. ¿De qué se componía esa escuela en medio del bosque?
•11. ¿Cree Ud. que la repetición en coro es una buena manera de enseñar?
•12. ¿Por qué abandonó Perico a su buen amigo don Lucas?

B. Verb Practice

Use each of the following verbal phrases in an original sentence in Spanish, either based on the story or of your own design. Be prepared to explain the meaning of your sentences. (If necessary, refer to Key Expressions to check the meaning of each phrase and the way in which it is used.)

1. **tener razón**
2. **referirse a**
3. **faltar a**
4. **necesitar**
5. **soportar**

6. **disfrutar de**
7. **llegar a** + *infinitive*
8. **volver a** + *infinitive*
9. **acabar de** + *infinitive*
10. **despedirse de**

C. Vocabulary Practice

Match the lexical expression on the right with the italicized English words on the left. Put the verb in the correct form. Check Key Expressions, if necessary. Then use each expression in an original Spanish sentence and explain what your sentence means.

1. Luego *went by* tres o cuatro días.
2. Se podía oír al loro *in the distance.*
3. Don Lucas tomaba *sort of a* merienda.
4. Al oír al loro, don Lucas *turned* la cabeza.
5. Uno de los chicos *by chance* volvía de la escuela.
6. *The clock struck five.*
7. Don Lucas quería encontrar a su loro *as soon as possible.*
8. El loro parecía mirarnos *from head to foot.*
9. *It must have been around four* cuando desapareció el loro.
10. *At the beginning* no creía que el loro volviera nunca.

una especie de
dar + *clock-time*
de arriba abajo
transcurrir

serían como + *clock-time*

volver + *direct object*
casualmente

a lo lejos

al principio

cuanto antes

D. Communication Practice

1. State that you and your best friend have always enjoyed good health.
2. Say that you know it was a type of bird and not an animal.
3. Indicate that you are going to need more milk tomorrow.
4. Say that you understand exactly what she was referring to.
5. Express the idea that your teacher cannot stand it when students are late.

E. Completion Exercise

Complete the following sentence fragments with your own ideas. Be sure to use the appropriate mood and tense with verbs you introduce.

1. A don Lucas siempre le gustaba...
2. Serían como las nueve anoche cuando...
3. Yo me detuve temeroso porque...
4. Volvimos a decirle a Carlos que...
5. El chico nos gritó que...

EL LEVE PEDRO

ENRIQUE ANDERSON IMBERT

ENRIQUE ANDERSON IMBERT (1910–   ) is a native
Argentine who came to the United States more than four decades ago to continue a successful and fruitful career as teacher,
author, literary critic and historian. His novels *Vigilia* (1934)
and *Fuga* (1953) and his collection of short stories *Las pruebas
del caos* (1946) established him as one of his country's most
gifted writers. In 1954 he published his *Historia de la literatura
hispanoamericana*, a valuable work that has since been revised
and translated. Professor Anderson has been one of the most
frequent and respected contributors to the pages of the principal
Argentine literary newspapers and magazines, and is now a
distinguished member of the Argentine Academy of Letters.

«El leve Pedro», taken from *Las pruebas del caos,* is that
book's opening story. It is the first suggestion the author gives of
the form that chaos might take in our comfortable, everyday
world—if some imperceptible malfunction of one of the numerous simple "laws of nature" were to occur. If just one
infinitesimal impossibility did happen, then, as he proposes
elsewhere in his book, a cigarette could smoke a man. Or, in a
like manner, we might have the case of—«El leve Pedro».

Be sure to study these expressions before you read the story.

1. (17: 1) **asomarse a** *to peek at, to get a glimpse of; to lean out of* This verb is used to express the position one takes when looking around a corner, leaning out of a window, peeking from a doorway, etc.
2. (17: 3) **solito** *all alone, all by oneself* The diminutive ending **-ito** emphasizes the meaning of the adjective **solo** *alone* in a variety of ways. Like most adjectives in Spanish it changes in form to modify a feminine noun: **La chica estaba solita.** *The girl was all by herself.*
3. (17:13) **animarse a** + *infinitive* *to get up the energy, courage, nerve to* + *verb*
4. (17:17) **costarle poco (mucho) a uno** *to be easy (hard) for someone* The subject is usually an infinitive: **Le cuesta poco subir la escalera de cinco en cinco.** *It's very easy for him to go up the stairs five at a time.*
5. (17:27) **en cuanto** *as soon as* When the action referred to has not yet occurred, the subjunctive is used: **En cuanto llegue, hablaremos con ella.** *As soon as she gets here, we'll speak with her.*
6. (18: 5) **casi** + *present tense* *almost* + *past tense* **¡Casi me caigo!** *I almost fell!*
7. (18: 5) **caerse** *to fall down*
8. (18:17) **dejar(se) de** + *infinitive* *to stop* + *present participle*
9. (18:17) **dar un paso** *to take a step*
10. (18:23) **quitarse** + *article of clothing* *to take off* + *article of clothing*
11. (18:24) **alcanzar a** + *infinitive* *to succeed in, get, manage to* + *verb*
12. (18:33) **mañana (hoy) mismo** *tomorrow (today) for sure, without fail* **Mismo** emphasizes the time word and is rendered in a variety of ways in English: **ahora mismo** *right now,* **mañana mismo** *tomorrow at the latest,* **ayer mismo** *just yesterday.*
13. (18:36) **sentirse** + *adjective* *to feel* + *adjective*
14. (18:37) **tener ganas de** + *infinitive* *to feel like* + *present participle*
15. (19: 1) **dar las buenas noches (los buenos días,** etc.**)** *to say goodnight (good morning,* etc.**)**
16. (19: 2) **al otro día** *(on) the next day*
17. (19: 6) **al fin** *at last, finally*
18. (19: 9) **tener que** + *infinitive* *to have to* + *verb*
19. (19:11) **ponerse a** + *infinitive* *to start, begin* + *infinitive* This expression usually implies voluntary action or sudden movement: **Se puso a tirar de la cuerda.** *She began to pull on the cord.* **Comenzar a** or **empezar a** is used for a more static or passive situation: **Comenzó a leer el cuento.** *He began to read the story.*
20. (19:19) **hacerse** + *noun* *to become, turn into* + *noun*

EL LEVE PEDRO

Durante dos meses se asomó a la muerte. El médico murmuraba que la enfermedad de Pedro era nueva, que no había modo de tratarla y que él no sabía qué hacer... Por suerte el enfermo, solito, se fue curando. No había perdido su buen humor, su oronda calma provinciana. Demasiado flaco y eso era todo.
5 Pero al levantarse después de varias semanas de convalecencia se sintió sin peso.[1]

—Oye —dijo a su mujer— me siento bien pero no sé... el cuerpo me parece... ausente. Estoy como si mis envolturas fueran a desprenderse dejándome el alma desnuda.[2]

—Languideces —le respondió su mujer.

10 —Tal vez.

Siguió recobrándose. Ya paseaba por el caserón, atendía el hambre de las gallinas y de los cerdos, dio una mano de pintura verde[3] a la pajarera bulliciosa y aun se animó a hachar la leña y llevarla en carretilla hasta el galpón. Pero según pasaban los días[4] las carnes de Pedro perdían densidad. Algo muy raro le iba
15 minando, socavando, vaciando el cuerpo. Se sentía con una ingravidez portentosa.[5] Era la ingravidez de la chispa y de la burbuja, del globo y de la pelota. Le costaba muy poco saltar limpiamente la verja, trepar las escaleras de cinco en cinco,[6] coger de un brinco[7] la manzana alta.

—Te has mejorado tanto —observaba su mujer— que pareces un chiquillo
20 acróbata.

Una mañana Pedro se asustó. Hasta entonces su agilidad le había preocupado, pero todo ocurría como Dios manda.[8] Era extraordinario que, sin proponérselo, convirtiera la marcha de los humanos en una triunfal carrera en volandas sobre la quinta.[9] Era extraordinario pero no milagroso. Lo milagroso
25 apareció esa mañana.

Muy temprano fue al potrero. Caminaba con pasos contenidos porque ya sabía que en cuanto taconeara iría dando botes por el corral.[10] Arremangó la camisa, acomodó un tronco, cogió el hacha y asestó el primer golpe. Y entonces, rechazado por el impulso de su propio hachazo, Pedro levantó vuelo.[11] Prendido

---

[1]*sin peso:* weightless [2]*Estoy... desnuda:* I feel as if my skin were peeling off, leaving just my naked soul. [3]*dio... verde:* he applied a coat of green paint [4]*según pasaban los días:* as the days went by [5]*Se sentía... portentosa:* He felt himself to be marvellously free of gravity. [6]*de cinco en cinco:* five at a time [7]*de un brinco:* with one leap [8]*todo... manda:* nothing out of the ordinary happened [9]*convirtiera... quinta:* he turned a normal human's walk into a triumphal series of soaring flights over the small farm [10]*en... corral:* as soon as he put his heels down, he would start bouncing all over the yard [11]*levantó vuelo:* took off

todavía del hacha, quedó un instante en suspensión, levitando allá, a la altura de los techos; y luego bajó lentamente, bajó como un tenue vilano de cardo.

Acudió su mujer cuando Pedro ya había descendido y, con una palidez de muerte, temblaba agarrado a un rollizo tronco.

—¡Hebe! ¡Casi me caigo al cielo! 5

—Tonterías. No puedes caerte al cielo. Nadie se cae al cielo. ¿Qué te ha pasado?

Pedro explicó la cosa a su mujer y ésta, sin asombro, le reconvino:

—Te sucede por hacerte el acróbata.[12] Ya te lo he prevenido. El día menos pensado[13] te desnucarás en una de tus piruetas. 10

—¡No, no! —insistió Pedro—. Ahora es diferente. Me resbalé. El cielo es un precipicio, Hebe.

Pedro soltó el tronco que lo anclaba pero se asió fuertemente a su mujer. Así abrazados volvieron a la casa.

—¡Hombre! —le dijo Hebe, que sentía el cuerpo de su marido pegado al suyo 15 como el de un animal extrañamente joven y salvaje, con ansias de huir[14] en vertiginoso galope.— ¡Hombre, déjate de hacer fuerza, que me arrastras![15] Das unos pasos como si quisieras echarte a volar.

—¿Has visto, has visto? Algo horrible me está amenazando, Hebe. Un esguince, y ya empieza la ascensión. 20

Esa tarde Pedro, que estaba apoltronado en el patio leyendo las historietas del periódico, se rió convulsivamente. Y con la propulsión de ese motor alegre fue elevándose como un ludión, como un buzo que se había quitado las suelas. La risa se trocó en terror y Hebe acudió otra vez a las voces de su marido. Alcanzó a cogerlo de los pantalones y lo atrajo a la tierra. Ya no había duda. Hebe le llenó 25 los bolsillos con grandes tuercas, caños de plomo y piedras; y estos pesos por el momento le dieron a su cuerpo la solidez necesaria para tranquear por la galería y empinarse por la escalera de su cuarto. Lo difícil fue desvestirlo. Cuando Hebe le quitó los hierros y el plomo, Pedro, fluctuante sobre las sábanas, se entrelazó a los barrotes de la cama y le advirtió: 30

—¡Cuidado, Hebe! Vamos a hacerlo despacio porque no quiero dormir en el techo.

—Mañana mismo llamaremos al médico.

—Si consigo estarme quieto[16] no me ocurrirá nada. Solamente cuando me agito me hago aeronauta. 35

Con mil precauciones pudo acostarse y se sintió seguro.

—¿Tienes ganas de subir?

—No. Estoy bien.

---

[12]*Te sucede... acróbata:* It's happened because of your playing the acrobat. [13]*El día menos pensado:* One of these days [14]*con ansias de huir:* anxious to flee [15]*déjate... arrastras!* stop pulling, you're dragging me! [16]*Si consigo estarme quieto:* If I manage to stay still

Se dieron las buenas noches[17] y Hebe apagó la luz.

Al otro día cuando Hebe despegó los ojos vio a Pedro durmiendo como un bendito,[18] con la cara pegada al techo. Parecía un globo escapado de las manos de un niño.

5 —¡Pedro, Pedro! —gritó aterrorizada.

Al fin Pedro despertó, dolorido por el estrujón de varias horas contra el cielo raso. ¡Qué espanto! Trató de saltar al revés, de caer para arriba, de subir para abajo. Pero el techo lo succionaba como succionaba el suelo a Hebe.

—Tendrás que atarme de una pierna y amarrarme al ropero hasta que llames
10 al doctor y vea qué es lo que pasa.

Hebe buscó una cuerda y una escalera, ató un pie a su marido[19] y se puso a tirar con todo el ánimo. El cuerpo adosado al techo se removió como un lento dirigible. Aterrizaba.

En eso[20] se coló por la puerta un correntón de aire que ladeó la leve corporei-
15 dad de Pedro y, como a una pluma, la sopló por la ventana abierta. Ocurrió en un segundo. Hebe lanzó un grito y la cuerda se le escapó de las manos. Cuando corrió a la ventana ya su marido, desvanecido, subía por el aire inocente de la mañana, subía en suave contoneo como un globo de color fugitivo en un día de fiesta, perdido para siempre, en viaje al infinito. Se hizo un punto y luego nada.

EXERCISES

A. Questions and Opinions

1. ¿Qué dijo el médico de la enfermedad de Pedro?
2. ¿Cómo se sintió Pedro al levantarse después de varias semanas de convalecencia?
3. ¿Por qué dijo la mujer de Pedro que éste parecía un chiquillo acróbata?
4. ¿Qué ocurrió cuando Pedro dio un golpe con su hacha?
5. ¿Podría ser el cielo un precipicio de veras?
6. ¿Qué le pasó a Pedro una tarde cuando se rió convulsivamente?
7. ¿Con qué le llenó Hebe los bolsillos a su marido?
8. Al despertarse la mañana siguiente, ¿qué vio Hebe?
9. ¿Cómo se le escapó de las manos la cuerda?
10. ¿Hasta dónde subió el leve Pedro?
●11. ¿Qué le parece a Ud. la idea de que el cielo es un precipicio?
●12. ¿Ha tenido Ud. ganas alguna vez de echarse a volar? ¿Sería divertido?

---

[17]*Se dieron... noches:* They said goodnight to each other one"   [19]*ató... marido:* tied one of her husband's feet   [18]*un bendito:* a baby; literally a "blessed one"   [20]*En eso:* At that moment

B. Verb Practice

Use each of the following verbal phrases in an original sentence in Spanish, either based on the story or of your own design. Be prepared to explain the meaning of your sentences.

1. **animarse a** + *infinitive*
2. **costarle poco (mucho) a uno**
3. **caerse**
4. **dejar(se) de** + *infinitive*
5. **quitarse** + *article of clothing*
6. **alcanzar a** + *infinitive*
7. **sentirse** + *adjective*
8. **tener que** + *infinitive*
9. **ponerse a** + *infinitive*
10. **hacerse** + *noun*

C. Vocabulary Practice

Complete the sentences below, matching the expressions on the right with the English words on the left. Be sure to use the correct form of each verb. Then use each expression in an original Spanish sentence and indicate in English what your sentence means.

1. *Finally* Pedro empezó a aterrizar.   **asomarse a**
2. Cada vez que *he took a step* brincaba como un acróbata.   **solito**
3. Cuando la esposa de Pedro le quería *say good morning*, no lo veía en ninguna parte.   **ayer mismo**
4. No quiero de ningún modo *get a glimpse of* la muerte.   **casi** + *present tense*
5. Pedro *felt like* subir al cielo.   **dar un paso**
6. *Just yesterday* me asusté por mi propia agilidad.   **en cuanto**
7. Hebe, *as soon as* taconee levantaré vuelo.   **dar los buenos días**
8. Hebe prometió llamar al médico *the next day*.   **al otro día**
9. Déjame, que puedo aterrizar *all by myself*.   **tener ganas de** + *infinitive*
10. ¡*I almost went up* (**subir**) al techo!   **al fin**

D. Communication Practice

1. Ask a close friend how she feels today.
2. Say you don't feel like going to the city with the others.
3. Indicate that Pepe is becoming just a dot in the sky.

4. Say you began to clean your apartment at eight-thirty.
5. Ask your classmates if they managed to finish all the sentences.

E. Review Exercise

The following words, which appeared in the last two stories, carry the diminutive endings **-ito, -cito, -illo, -cillo,** and **-uelo**. What different translations can these words have? What do these diminutive suffixes suggest (1) with regard to the object itself and (2) about the point of view of the speaker or author?

pueblecito	**bolsillos**	**arroyuelo**
solito	**criadito**	**callejuelas**
casita	**vientecillo**	
carretilla	**chiquillo**	

Being aware of the widespread use of the various diminutive endings in Spanish is a valuable asset in recognizing new (and, at first glance, apparently unknown) words, and in expanding your own active vocabulary as well.

JAQUE MATE
EN DOS
JUGADAS

ISAAC AISEMBERG

ISAAC AISEMBERG (1919–   ) is one of the principal
Argentine cultivators of the detective story—a type of fiction
that for decades has enjoyed great popularity in the principal
cities of Spanish America. Thanks to Aisemberg and others of
his Buenos Aires colleagues, the detective story has had a
greater and more varied development in Argentina than in any
other Spanish-speaking country—including Spain. Aisemberg
brings an interesting background to the writing of detective
short stories and novels. He has studied law (with the intention
of entering politics), has worked on Buenos Aires newspapers,
and has done program planning for Radio Nacional in the
capital. He has also written for Argentine movies and television.
His *Tres negativos para un retrato* (1949) and *Manchas en el
Río Bermejo* (1950) are two of the most imaginative and well-
executed detective novels that have been written in Argentina.

«Jaque mate en dos jugadas» is an ironic tale of revenge, set
against the backdrop of Buenos Aires by night. One of Aisemberg's most successful stories, it has been published in translation in the United States and has appeared in other short-story
anthologies. Beginning with the story's first three words and
continuing on to the surprise climax, the reader is absorbed in
the thoughts of Claudio Álvarez and experiences with him the
elation and subsequent creeping doubt and terror of a man who
has committed a crime in the hope of going unpunished for it
before the law.

A PRELIMINARY LOOK AT KEY EXPRESSIONS

Be sure to study these expressions before you read the story.

1. (26: 1) **quedar** + *past participle* *to be, become* + *adjective* This expression is similar to **estar** + *past participle* except that **quedar** emphasizes the change or result. **Está liberado** means *He is free*, but **Queda liberado** means *He gets free* or *He is freed*.
2. (26:10) **acostumbrarse a** *to get used to*
3. (26:12) **a pesar de** *in spite of*
4. (26:13) **hacerse** + *adjective* *to become, get* + *adjective* This expression is used for relatively fundamental or important changes: **Se hizo intolerable.** *He became unbearable*, as opposed to **ponerse**, which is used for more superficial, temporary changes: **Me puse triste.** *I got sad.*
5. (26:19) **dedicarse a** + *infinitive* *to devote oneself to* + *verb*, or *to spend a lot of time* + *present participle*: **Se dedica a jugar al ajedrez.** *He spends a lot of time playing chess.*
6. (27:30) **tener inconveniente en** + *infinitive* *to mind* + *present participle* or *to object to* + *verb*: **El médico no tendría inconveniente en suscribir el certificado de defunción.** *The doctor would not object to signing the death certificate.*
7. (28: 1) **estar dispuesto a** *to be ready, disposed to* + *verb*: **Estamos dispuestos a revelarlo todo.** *We're ready to confess everything.* It also means *to be inclined toward* + *noun*: **Tú siempre estás dispuesto a la tragedia.** *You're always inclined toward tragedy* or *You always make things seem so tragic.*
8. (28: 4) **tomársela con** *to pick on, quarrel with, have a grudge against, have it in for*: **¿Por qué mi tío siempre se la toma conmigo?** *Why is my uncle always picking on me?*
9. (28:10) **resolver** *to solve*
10. (28:17) **resultar** *to turn out (to be)*: **El veneno resultaba rápido.** *The poison was turning out to be fast.*
11. (28:19) **en paz** *alone, "in peace"*: **¡Déjame en paz!** *Leave me alone!, Stop bothering me!*
12. (29: 5) **pensar en** *to think of, about*
13. (29:30) **de un trago** *in one gulp, swallow*
14. (29:36) **cerrar el paso** *to block the way* The person whose way is blocked is the indirect object: **El inspector le cerraba el paso.** *The inspector was blocking his way.*
15. (30:14) **a cargo de** *in charge of*
16. (30:33) **encontrarse con** *to meet, run into* This is either a planned or a chance meeting.

17. (31:14) **tener entendido** *to understand* in the sense of *be informed:*
Tengo entendido que ustedes jugaban al ajedrez. *I understand that you used to play chess together.*
18. (31:19) **como es de imaginar** *as you (one) can imagine*
19. (31:36) **con vida** *alive:* **¿Quién fue el último que lo vio con vida?** *Who was the last one to see him alive?*
20. (32: 4) **con toda mi (el, su,** etc.**) alma** *with all my (his,* etc.*) heart and soul*

JAQUE MATE
EN DOS JUGADAS

Yo lo envenené. En dos horas quedaría liberado. Dejé a mi tío Néstor a las veintidós.[1] Lo hice con alegría. Me ardían las mejillas. Me quemaban los labios. Luego me serené y eché a caminar tranquilamente por la avenida en dirección al puerto.

Me sentía contento. Liberado. Hasta Guillermo saldría socio beneficiario[2] en el asunto. ¡Pobre Guillermo! ¡Tan tímido, tan inocente! Era evidente que yo debía pensar y obrar por ambos. Siempre sucedió así. Desde el día en que nuestro tío nos llevó a su casa. Nos encontramos perdidos en el palacio. Era un lugar seco, sin amor. Únicamente el sonido metálico de las monedas.

—Tenéis[3] que acostumbraros al ahorro, a no malgastar. ¡Al fin y al cabo,[4] algún día será vuestro! —decía. Y nos acostumbramos a esperarlo.

Pero ese famoso y deseado día no llegaba, a pesar de que tío sufría del corazón. Y si de pequeños[5] nos tiranizó, cuando crecimos se hizo cada vez más[6] intolerable.

Guillermo se enamoró un buen día. A nuestro tío no le gustó la muchacha. No era lo que ambicionaba para su sobrino.

—Le falta cuna..., le falta roce...,[7] ¡puaf! Es una ordinaria... —sentenció.

Inútil fue que Guillermo se dedicara a encontrarle méritos.[8] El viejo era testarudo y arbitrario.

Conmigo tenía otra clase de problemas. Era un carácter contra otro. Se empeñó en doctorarme[9] en bioquímica. ¿Resultado? Un perito en póquer y en carreras de caballos. Mi tío para esos vicios no me daba ni un centavo. Tenía que emplear todo mi ingenio para quitarle un peso.

Uno de los recursos era aguantarle sus interminables partidas de ajedrez; entonces yo cedía con aire de hombre magnánimo, pero él, en cambio, cuando

---

[1]*a las veintidós:* In many parts of the world the 24-hour system of telling time is often used. "Twenty-two," therefore, is 10 P.M.　[2]*socio beneficiario:* partner in the profits　[3]*Tenéis:* the second-person plural form of the verb used with the subject pronoun *vosotros* (The uncle, who is a Spaniard, uses these forms since they are normal in Spain for the familiar form of address. The nephews, however, like all Spanish-Americans, use *ustedes* with its corresponding third-person plural forms to express the familiar plural.)　[4]*¡Al fin y al cabo:* After all　[5]*de pequeños:* when we were children　[6]*cada vez más:* more and more　[7]*le falta cuna... roce:* she has no breeding, no class　[8]*encontrarle méritos:* point out her good qualities　[9]*Se... doctorarme:* He insisted that I get a doctor's degree

estaba en posición favorable alargaba el final, anotando las jugadas con displicencia, sabiendo de mi prisa por salir para el club. Gozaba con mi infortunio saboreando su coñac.

Un día me dijo con tono condescendiente:

5 —Observo que te aplicas en el ajedrez. Eso me demuestra dos cosas: que eres inteligente y un perfecto holgazán. Sin embargo, tu dedicación tendrá su premio. Soy justo. Pero eso sí,[10] a falta de diplomas,[11] de hoy en adelante tendré de ti bonitas anotaciones de las partidas. Sí, muchacho, vamos a guardar cada uno los apuntes de los juegos en libretas para compararlas. ¿Qué te parece?

10 Aquello podría resultar un par de cientos de pesos, y acepté. Desde entonces, todas las noches, la estadística. Estaba tan arraigada la manía en él, que en mi ausencia comentaba las partidas con Julio, el mayordomo.

Ahora todo había concluido. Cuando uno se encuentra en un callejón sin salida, el cerebro trabaja, busca, rebusca. Y encuentra. Siempre hay salida para 15 todo. No siempre es buena. Pero es salida.

Llegaba a la Costanera.[12] Era una noche húmeda. En el cielo nublado, alguna chispa eléctrica. El calorcillo mojaba las manos, resecaba la boca.

En la esquina, un policía me hizo saltar el corazón.

El veneno, ¿cómo se llamaba? Aconitina. Varias gotitas en el coñac mientras 20 conversábamos. Mi tío esa noche estaba encantador. Me perdonó la partida.[13]

—Haré un solitario[14] —dijo—. Despaché a los sirvientes... ¡Hum! Quiero estar tranquilo. Después leeré un buen libro. Algo que los jóvenes no entienden... Puedes irte.

—Gracias, tío. Hoy realmente es... sábado.

25 —Comprendo.

¡Demonios! El hombre comprendía. La clarividencia del condenado.

El veneno producía un efecto lento, a la hora,[15] o más, según el sujeto. Hasta seis u ocho horas. Justamente durante el sueño. El resultado: la apariencia de un pacífico ataque cardíaco, sin huellas comprometedoras. Lo que yo necesitaba. 30 ¿Y quién sospecharía? El doctor Vega no tendría inconveniente en suscribir el certificado de defunción. ¿Y si me descubrían? ¡Imposible!

Pero, ¿y Guillermo? Sí. Guillermo era un problema. Lo hallé en el *hall* después de preparar la «encomienda» para el infierno. Descendía la escalera, preocupado.

35 —¿Qué te pasa? —le pregunté jovial, y le hubiera agregado de buena gana: «¡Si supieras, hombre!»

—¡Estoy harto! —me replicó.

---

[10]*eso sí:* keep in mind   [11]*a falta de diplomas:* since there'll be no diploma   [12]*la Costanera:* a riverside thoroughfare in Buenos Aires, officially named Avenida Costanera Rafael Obligado   [13]*Me perdonó la partida:* He excused me from the game.   [14]*Haré un solitario:* I'll play a game by myself   [15]*a la hora:* after an hour

—¡Vamos! —Le palmoteé la espalda—. Siempre estás dispuesto a la tragedia...

—Es que el viejo me enloquece. Últimamente, desde que volviste a la Facultad[16] y le llevas la corriente[17] en el ajedrez, se la toma conmigo. Y Matilde...

—¿Qué sucede con Matilde? 5

—Matilde me lanzó un ultimátum: o ella, o tío.

—Opta por ella. Es fácil elegir. Es lo que yo haría...

—¿Y lo otro?

Me miró desesperado. Con brillo demoníaco en las pupilas; pero el pobre tonto jamás buscaría el medio de resolver su problema. 10

—Yo lo haría —siguió entre dientes—; pero, ¿con qué viviríamos? Ya sabes cómo es el viejo... Duro, implacable. ¡Me cortaría los víveres!

—*Tal vez las cosas se arreglen de otra manera...* —insinué bromeando—. ¡Quién te dice...!

—¡Bah!... —sus labios se curvaron con una mueca amarga—. No hay esca- 15 patoria. Pero yo hablaré con el viejo tirano. ¿Dónde está ahora?

Me asusté. Si el veneno resultaba rápido... Al notar los primeros síntomas podría ser auxiliado y...

—Está en la biblioteca —exclamé—, pero déjalo en paz. Acaba de jugar la partida de ajedrez, y despachó a la servidumbre. ¡El lobo quiere estar solo en la 20 madriguera! Consuélate en un cine o en un bar.

Se encogió de hombros.

—El lobo en la madriguera... —repitió. Pensó unos segundos y agregó, aliviado—: Lo veré en otro momento. Después de todo...

—Después de todo, no te animarías,[18] ¿verdad? —gruñí salvajemente. 25

Me clavó la mirada.[19] Sus ojos brillaron con una chispa siniestra, pero fue un relámpago.

Miré el reloj: las once y diez de la noche.

Ya comenzaría a producir efecto. Primero un leve malestar, nada más. Después un dolorcillo agudo, pero nunca demasiado alarmante. Mi tío refun- 30 fuñaba una maldición para la cocinera. El pescado indigesto. ¡Qué poca cosa es todo![20] Debía de estar leyendo los diarios de la noche, los últimos. Y después, el libro, como gran epílogo. Sentía frío.

Las baldosas se estiraban en rombos.[21] El río era una mancha sucia cerca del paredón. A lo lejos luces verdes, rojas, blancas. Los automóviles se deslizaban 35 chapoteando en el asfalto.

---

[16]*la Facultad:* the University (really just a school, college, or division of a university)   [17]*le llevas la corriente:* you let him have his way   [18]*no te animarías:* you wouldn't have the nerve   [19]*Me clavó la mirada:* He fixed his gaze on me.   [20]*¡Qué... todo!* How easy it all is!   [21]*Las... rombos:* The paving stones stretched out in the shape of diamonds. (Frequently the sidewalks of Buenos Aires consist of diamond-shaped stones or sections of cement.)

Decidí regresar, por temor a llamar la atención. Nuevamente por la avenida hacia Leandro N. Alem.[22] Por allí a Plaza de Mayo.[23] El reloj me volvió a la realidad. Las once y treinta y seis. Si el veneno era eficaz, ya estaría todo listo. Ya sería dueño de millones. Ya sería libre... Ya sería..., *ya sería asesino.*

5 Por primera vez pensé en la palabra misma. Yo ¡asesino! Las rodillas me flaquearon. Un rubor me azotó el cuello, me subió a las mejillas, me quemó las orejas, martilló mis sienes. Las manos traspiraban. El frasquito de aconitina en el bolsillo llegó a pesarme una tonelada. Busqué en los bolsillos rabiosamente hasta dar con él.[24] Era un insignificante cuentagotas y contenía la muerte; lo
10 arrojé lejos.

Avenida de Mayo. Choqué con varios transeúntes. Pensarían en un borracho.[25] Pero en lugar de alcohol, sangre.

Yo, asesino. Esto sería un secreto entre mi tío Néstor y mi conciencia. Recordé la descripción del efecto del veneno: «en la lengua, sensación de hormi-
15 gueo y embotamiento, que se inicia en el punto de contacto para extenderse a toda la lengua, a la cara y a todo el cuerpo.»

Entré en un bar. Un tocadiscos atronaba con un viejo *rag-time*.[26] «En el esófago y en el estómago, sensación de ardor intenso.» Millones. Billetes de mil, de quinientos, de cien. Póquer. Carreras. Viajes... «sensación de angustia, de
20 muerte próxima, enfriamiento profundo generalizado, trastornos sensoriales, debilidad muscular, contracciones, impotencia de los músculos.»

Habría[27] quedado solo. En el palacio. Con sus escaleras de mármol. Frente al tablero de ajedrez. Allí el rey, y la dama, y la torre negra. Jaque mate.

El mozo se aproximó. Debió sorprender mi mueca de extravío, mis músculos
25 en tensión, listos para saltar.

—¿Señor?

—Un coñac...

—Un coñac... —repitió el mozo—. Bien, señor —y se alejó.

Por la vidriera la caravana que pasa,[28] la misma de siempre. El tictac del reloj
30 cubría todos los rumores. Hasta los de mi corazón. La una. Bebí el coñac de un trago.

«Como fenómeno circulatorio, hay alteración del pulso e hipotensión que se derivan de la acción sobre el órgano central, llegando, en su estado más avanzado, al síncope cardíaco...» Eso es. El síncope cardíaco. La válvula de escape.
35 A las dos y treinta de la mañana regresé a casa. Al principio no lo advertí. Hasta que me cerró el paso. Era un agente de policía. Me asusté.

---

[22]*Leandro N. Alem:* a main street in downtown Buenos Aires, near the waterfront   [23]*Plaza de Mayo:* main square of Buenos Aires   [24]*hasta dar con él:* until I found it   [25]*Pensarían en un borracho:* They must have thought I was drunk.   [26]*rag-time:* syncopated American music, mainly composed by blacks and popular in the early years of this century   [27]*Habría:* He must have   [28]*la caravana que pasa:* the "passing parade"

—¿El señor Claudio Álvarez?

—Sí, señor... —respondí humildemente.

—Pase usted... —indicó, franqueándome la entrada.

—¿Qué hace usted aquí? —me animé a murmurar.

—Dentro tendrá la explicación —fue la respuesta.   5

En el *hall,* cerca de la escalera, varios individuos de uniforme se habían adueñado del palacio. ¿Guillermo? Guillermo no estaba presente.

Julio, el mayordomo, amarillo, espectral trató de hablarme. Uno de los uniformados, canoso, adusto, el jefe del grupo por lo visto, le selló los labios con un gesto. Avanzó hacia mí, y me inspeccionó como a un cobayo.   10

—Usted es el mayor de los sobrinos, ¿verdad?

—Sí, señor... —murmuré.

—Lamento decírselo, señor. Su tío ha muerto... asesinado —anunció mi interlocutor. La voz era calma, grave—. Yo soy el inspector Villegas, y estoy a cargo de la investigación. ¿Quiere acompañarme a la otra sala?   15

—Dios mío —articulé anonadado—. ¡Es inaudito!

Las palabras sonaron a huecas, a hipócritas. *(¡Ese dichoso*[29] *veneno dejaba huellas! ¿Pero cómo... cómo?)*

—¿Puedo... puedo verlo? —pregunté.

—Por el momento, no. Además, quiero que me conteste algunas preguntas.   20

—Como usted disponga...[30] —accedí azorado.

Lo seguí a la biblioteca vecina. Tras él se deslizaron suavemente dos acólitos. El inspector Villegas me indicó un sillón y se sentó en otro. Encendió frugalmente un cigarrillo y con evidente grosería no me ofreció ninguno.

—Usted es el sobrino... Claudio. —Pareció que repetía una lección aprendida   25
de memoria.

—Sí, señor.

—Pues bien: explíquenos qué hizo esta noche.

Yo también repetí una letanía.

—Cenamos los tres, juntos como siempre. Guillermo se retiró a su habita-   30
ción. Quedamos mi tío y yo charlando un rato; pasamos a la biblioteca. Después jugamos nuestra habitual partida de ajedrez; me despedí de mi tío y salí. En el vestíbulo me encontré con Guillermo que descendía por las escaleras rumbo a la calle. Cambiamos unas palabras y me fui.

—Y ahora regresa...   35

—Sí...

—¿Y los criados?

—Mi tío deseaba quedarse solo. Los despachó después de cenar. A veces le acometían estas y otras manías.

---

[29]*dichoso:* damned (literally, "happy")   [30]*Como usted disponga:* Just as you say

—Lo que usted dice concuerda en gran parte con la declaración del mayor-domo. Cuando éste regresó, hizo un recorrido por el edificio. Notó la puerta de la biblioteca entornada y luz adentro. Entró. Allí halló a su tío frente a un tablero de ajedrez, muerto. La partida interrumpida... De manera que jugaron la
5 partidita, ¿eh?

Algo dentro de mí comenzó a saltar violentamente. Una sensación de zozo-bra, de angustia, me recorría con la velocidad de un pebete. En cualquier momento estallaría la pólvora. *¡Los consabidos solitarios de mi tío!*[31]

—Sí, señor... —admití.
10 No podía desdecirme. Eso también se lo había dicho a Guillermo. Y proba-blemente Guillermo al inspector Villegas. Porque mi hermano debía de estar en alguna parte. El sistema de la policía: aislarnos, dejarnos solos, inertes, inde-fensos, para pillarnos.

—Tengo entendido que ustedes llevaban un registro de las jugadas. Para
15 establecer los detalles en su orden, ¿quiere mostrarme su libretita de apuntes, señor Álvarez?

Me hundía en el cieno.

—¿Apuntes?

—Sí, hombre —el policía era implacable—, deseo verla, como es de ima-
20 ginar. Debo verificarlo todo, amigo; lo dicho y lo hecho por usted.[32] *Si jugaron como siempre...*

Comencé a tartamudear.

—Es que... —Y después, de un tirón:[33] —¡Claro que jugamos como siempre! Las lágrimas comenzaron a quemarme los ojos. Miedo. Un miedo espantoso.
25 Como debió sentirlo tío Néstor cuando aquella «sensación de angustia... de muerte próxima..., enfriamiento profundo, generalizado...» Algo me taladraba el cráneo. Me empujaban. El silencio era absoluto, pétreo. Los otros también estaban callados. Dos ojos, seis ojos, ocho ojos, mil ojos. ¡Oh, qué angustia! Me tenían... me tenían... Jugaban con mi desesperación... Se divertían con mi
30 culpa...

De pronto, el inspector gruñó:

—¿Y?

Una sola letra ¡pero tanto!

—¿Y? —repitió—. Usted fue el último que lo vio con vida. Y, además,
35 muerto. El señor Álvarez no hizo anotación alguna esta vez, señor mío.[34]

No sé por qué me puse de pie. Tenso. Elevé mis brazos, los estiré. Me estrujé las manos, clavándome las uñas, y al final chillé con voz que no era la mía:

---

[31]*solitarios de mi tío:* games my uncle played alone   [32]*lo... usted:* what you said and what you did   [33]*de un tirón:* all at once   [34]*señor mío:* my good man

—¡Basta! Si lo saben, ¿para qué lo preguntan? ¡Yo lo maté! ¡Yo lo maté! ¿Y qué hay?[35] ¡Lo odiaba con toda mi alma! ¡Estaba cansado de su despotismo! ¡Lo maté! ¡Lo maté!

El inspector no lo tomó tan a la tremenda.[36]

—¡Cielos! —dijo—. Se produjo más pronto de lo que yo esperaba. Ya que se 5 le soltó la lengua,[37] ¿dónde está el revólver?

El inspector Villegas no se inmutó. Insistió imperturbable.

—¡Vamos, no se haga el tonto[38] ahora! ¡El revólver! ¿O ha olvidado que lo liquidó de un tiro? ¡Un tiro en la mitad de la frente, compañero! ¡Qué puntería!

EXERCISES

A. Questions and Opinions

1. ¿Qué crimen había cometido el narrador, Claudio Álvarez?
2. ¿Qué guardaban Claudio y su tío en sus libretas?
3. ¿Por qué odiaba a su tío el hermano de Claudio?
4. ¿Qué ultimátum le había lanzado Matilde a Guillermo?
5. ¿Cree Ud. que Claudio insultó a su hermano, diciendo «Después de todo, no te animarías, ¿verdad?»?
6. ¿Qué hizo Claudio con el frasquito de veneno?
7. ¿En dónde entró Claudio para calmar los nervios?
8. ¿Quiénes esperaban a Claudio cuando regresó a casa?
9. ¿Dijo la verdad Claudio en todo lo que declaró al inspector?
10. ¿Cómo murió el tío Néstor?
•11. ¿Por qué se confesó Claudio Álvarez?
•12. ¿Cree Ud. que pueda haber «un crimen perfecto»? ¿Por qué?

B. Verb Practice

Use each of the following verbal phrases in an original sentence in Spanish, either based on the story or of your own design. Be prepared to explain the meaning of your sentences.

1. **quedar** + *past participle*
2. **acostumbrarse a**
3. **hacerse** + *adjective*

---

[35]*¿Y qué hay?* And what of it?   [36]*no... tremenda:* did not seem too surprised   [37]*Ya... lengua:* Since your tongue's loosened up   [38]*no... tonto:* don't play dumb

4. **dedicarse a** + *infinitive*
5. **tener inconveniente en** + *infinitive*
6. **tomársela con**
7. **resolver**
8. **resultar**
9. **pensar en**
10. **encontrarse con**

C. Vocabulary Practice

Complete the sentences below, matching the expressions on the right with the English words on the left. Be sure to use the correct form of each verb. Then use each expression in an original Spanish sentence and indicate in English what your sentence means.

1. *I understand* que a su tío le gustaba jugar al ajedrez casi todos los días.

   a pesar de

2. Ahora odia el ajedrez *with all his heart and soul.*

   estar dispuesto a

3. Creo que mi tío habrá tomado el veneno *in one swallow.*

   en paz

4. Estaba preocupado *in spite of* que el veneno no dejaba huellas.

   cerrar el paso

5. Siempre *I was inclined toward* el pesimismo.

   de un trago

6. Cuando el sobrino quería entrar en la sala, el policía le *blocked the way.*

   a cargo de

7. Quería que su tío no le molestara y que lo dejara *alone.*

   tener entendido

8. ¿Quién está *in charge of* la investigación?

   como es de imaginar

9. *As you can imagine,* el sobrino estaba terriblemente asustado.

   con vida

10. Nunca lo volvieron a ver *alive.*

   con toda mi (su, el, etc.) alma

D. Communication Practice

1. Say you think a lot about your future.
2. State that yesterday everyone left you alone.
3. Express the idea that Claudio would never become accustomed to being poor.
4. Say that Jorge's brother is always picking on you.
5. Indicate that you wouldn't mind helping with the party.

E. Completion Exercise

Complete the following sentence fragments with your own ideas. Be sure to use the appropriate mood and tense with verbs you introduce.

1. Teníamos entendido que...
2. Resulta que el asesino...
3. Durante años su tío se dedicó a...
4. Yo no estoy dispuesto a que...
5. Quedó arreglado que...

EL ÁNGEL CAÍDO

AMADO NERVO

AMADO NERVO (1870–1919) was born in Mexico and began
his public career as a journalist. Later he became a diplomat
representing Mexico in Spain, Argentina, and Uruguay. Before
the turn of the century, he was associated with the Modernist
movement in literature and early established a reputation as a
modernista poet. Though Nervo is remembered today mainly
for his poetry, he wrote many stories, and his novel *El bachiller,*
published when he was twenty-six, was a considerable, though
somewhat scandalous, success.

In the story «El ángel caído» the vision and delicate expression of the poet are evident. There is humor, too, together with
a profound religious feeling, which is fundamental to all of
Nervo's best poetry. The style is lucid, and there is a gentleness
and simplicity of spirit about it that is perfectly suited to the
telling of this humble miracle of innocence.

A PRELIMINARY LOOK AT KEY EXPRESSIONS

Be sure to study these expressions before you read the story.

1. (38:11) **en fin** *anyway*
2. (38:12) **acercarse a** *to approach, get near, go up to*
3. (38:13) **ayudar a** + *infinitive to help (someone)* + *verb* The person helped is either a direct or indirect object: **El chico le (lo) ayudó a levantarse.** *The boy helped him get up.*
4. (38:15) **ponerse en (de) pie** *to stand up, get on, to one's feet*
5. (38:23) **empezar a** + *infinitive to start, begin* + *infinitive*
6. (39: 1) **tutear** *to speak to someone in the familiar* **tú** *form:* —¿**Lo tuteas?** —**No, siempre le hablo de usted.** *"Do you call him* **tú***?" "No, I always call him* **usted***."*
7. (39: 3) **¿Qué es esto de...?** *What are these . . . you're talking about?*
8. (39:21) **unos cuantos** *some, a few* **Varios** or **algunos** means *some, several* when the speaker has in mind exactly which ones he or she is talking about.
9. (39:23) **fijarse (en)** *to notice, observe*
10. (39:26) **alejarse (de)** *to leave, go away (from)*
11. (39:27) **éste** *the latter, he, this one* The demonstrative pronouns **éste, ésta,** etc. are used to refer to the last-named of two possible antecedents: **Grande fue la piedad de la madre del niño cuando éste le mostró a su alirroto compañero.** *Great was the pity of the child's mother when he showed her* (rather than *she showed him,* which would be **ésta** . . .) *his broken-winged companion.*
12. (40: 7) **hacer falta** *to be necessary, needed* **Hacer falta** is virtually synonymous with **necesitar** except that the person who needs something is the indirect object: **Eso es lo que le hace falta.** *That (shoes) is what he needs* (literally, *"makes a lack to him"*).
13. (40:13) **no poder** *(in preterit)* + *infinitive to fail, be unable to* + *infinitive* This always indicates that an unsuccessful attempt was made: **No pudo contenerse.** *She was unable (failed) to restrain herself* (so she spoke out). **No poder** in the imperfect simply indicates the lack of ability, whether an attempt was ever made or not: **El ángel sabía que no podía volar con el ala rota.** *The angel knew he couldn't fly with a broken wing (so he didn't try).*
14. (40:28) **hacer daño** *to damage, hurt, harm*
15. (41:14) **ponerse** + *adjective to become, get* + *adjective* This expression is used with conditions subject to change, such as **triste, enfermo, satisfecho, mejor,** etc.
16. (41:21) **llevarse** *to take, carry away (off)* **Tomar** is *to take* (into one's*

possession); **llevar** is *to take* or *carry* (from one place to another); and **llevarse** is *to take away* or *remove* (from one place).

17. (42:13) ¿**Qué tienes?** *What's wrong (the matter) with you?* The angel's response, with an entire clause, **Tengo que ya estoy bueno;** *I'm well now—that's what's wrong,* is informal and not very common.

18. (42:19) **haber de** + *infinitive to be supposed to, be to, have to* + *verb* This expression is often used to register a mild protest or some irritation, indicating that the speaker really doesn't know what to do, or disagrees with the person he or she is speaking with, or is even impatient with the latter: ¿**Cómo he de saberlo?** *How am I supposed to (should I) know that?* It is also used for scheduled events: **El avión ha de llegar a las 19.** *The plane is supposed to arrive at 7 P.M.*

19. (42:25) **de pronto** *suddenly*

20. (43:14) **a través de** *through, across* This phrase is used either with space: **A través de sus alas se veía el sol.** *Through his wings you could see the sun,* or time: **A través de los siglos** *Down through (across) the centuries.*

EL ÁNGEL CAÍDO

Cuento de Navidad, dedicado a
mi sobrina María de los Ángeles

Érase un ángel[1] que, por brincar más de la cuenta[2] sobre una nube crepuscular teñida de violetas, perdió pie y cayó lastimosamente a la tierra.

Su mala suerte quiso que, en vez de dar sobre[3] el fresco césped, diese contra bronca piedra,[4] de modo y manera que el cuitado se estropeó un ala, el ala derecha, por más señas.[5]

Allí quedó despatarrado, sangrando, y aunque daba voces de socorro,[6] como no es usual que en la tierra se comprenda el idioma de los ángeles, nadie acudía en su auxilio.

En esto[7] acertó a pasar[8] no lejos un niño que volvía de la escuela, y aquí empezó la buena suerte del caído,[9] porque como los niños sí suelen comprender[10] la lengua angélica (en el siglo XX mucho menos, pero en fin...) el chico se acercó al mísero, y sorprendido primero y compadecido después, le tendió la mano y le ayudó a levantarse.

Los ángeles no pesan, y la leve fuerza del niño bastó y sobró[11] para que aquél se pusiese en pie.

Su salvador le ofreció el brazo y se vio entonces el más raro espectáculo; un niño conduciendo a un ángel por los senderos de este mundo.

Cojeaba el ángel lastimosamente, ¡es claro![12] Le acontecía lo que acontece a los que nunca andan descalzos; el menor guijarro le pinchaba de un modo atroz. Su aspecto era lamentable. Con el ala rota dolorosamente plegada, manchado de sangre y lodo el plumaje resplandeciente, el ángel estaba para dar compasión.[13]

Cada paso le arrancaba un grito; los maravillosos pies de nieve empezaban a sangrar también.

—No puedo más[14]—dijo al niño.

Y éste, que tenía su miaja de sentido práctico, le respondió,

---

[1]*Érase un ángel:* Once upon a time there was an angel   [2]*más de la cuenta:* more than he should have   [3]*dar sobre:* landing on   [4]*diese contra bronca piedra:* fall on solid rock   [5]*por más señas:* to be specific   [6]*daba voces de socorro:* called for help   [7]*En esto:* Just then   [8]*acertó a pasar:* there chanced to pass by   [9]*del caído:* of the fallen one   [10]*los niños... comprender:* children usually do understand (The *sí* here serves to emphasize the verb.)   [11]*bastó y sobró:* was more than enough   [12]*¡es claro!* naturally!   [13]*estaba para dar compasión:* was a pitiful sight   [14]*No puedo más:* I can't go on anymore

—A ti (porque desde un principio se tutearon), a ti lo que te falta es un par de zapatos. Vamos a casa, diré a mamá que te los compre.

—¿Y qué es esto de zapatos? —preguntó el ángel.

—Pues mira —contestó el niño mostrándole los suyos—; algo que yo rompo
5 mucho y que me cuesta buenos regaños.[15]

—Y yo he de ponerme esto tan feo...

—Claro... ¡o no andas! Vamos a casa. Allí mamá te frotará con árnica[16] y te dará zapatos.

—Pero si[17] ya no me es posible andar... ¡cárgame!

10 —¿Podré contigo?[18]

—¡Ya lo creo!

Y el niño alzó en vilo[19] a su compañero, sentándolo en su hombro, como lo hubiera hecho un diminuto San Cristóbal.[20]

—¡Gracias! —suspiró el herido—; qué bien estoy así...[21] ¿Verdad que no
15 peso?

—¡Es que yo tengo fuerzas! —respondió el niño con cierto orgullo y no queriendo confesar que su celeste bulto era más ligero que uno de plumas.

En esto se acercaban al lugar,[22] y les aseguro a ustedes que no era menos extraño ahora que antes el espectáculo de un niño que llevaba en brazos a un
20 ángel, al revés de lo que nos muestran las estampas.[23]

Cuando llegaron a la casa, sólo unos cuantos chicuelos curiosos los seguían. Los hombres, muy ocupados en sus negocios, las mujeres que comadreaban en las plazuelas y al borde de las fuentes, no se habían fijado en que pasaban un niño y un ángel. Sólo un poeta que divagaba por aquellos contornos, asom-
25 brado, clavó en ellos los ojos y sonriendo beatamente los siguió durante buen espacio de tiempo con la mirada... Después se alejó pensativo...

Grande fue la piedad de la madre del niño cuando éste le mostró a su alirroto compañero.

—¡Pobrecillo! —exclamó la buena señora—; le dolerá mucho el ala,[24] ¿eh?

30 El ángel, al sentir que le hurgaban la herida, dejó oír un lamento armonioso.[25] Como nunca había conocido el dolor, era más sensible a él que los mortales, forjados para la pena.[26]

---

[15]*que... regaños:* that gets me good scoldings   [16]*árnica:* a solution for massaging sprains and bruises   [17]*si:* should not be translated   [18]*¿Podré contigo?* Will I be able to carry you?   [19]*en vilo:* up in the air   [20]*como... San Cristóbal:* as a little St. Christopher might have done (St. Christopher was the patron saint of travelers.)   [21]*qué bien estoy así:* this is very comfortable   [22]*al lugar:* the village   [23]*estampas:* (religious) illustrations   [24]*le dolerá... ala:* your wing must really hurt (Note again the use of the future to suggest conjecture.)   [25]*dejó... armonioso:* let out a harmonious wail   [26]*era... pena:* he was more sensitive to it than mortals, who are built for pain

Pronto la caritativa dama le vendó el ala, a decir verdad con trabajo,[27] porque era tan grande que no bastaban los trapos, y más aliviado, y lejos ya de las piedras del camino, el ángel pudo ponerse en pie y enderezar su esbelta estatura.

Era maravilloso de belleza.[28] Su piel translúcida parecía iluminada por suave luz interior y sus ojos, de un hondo azul de incomparable diafanidad, miraban   5
de manera que cada mirada producía un éxtasis.

—Los zapatos, mamá, eso es lo que le hace falta. Mientras no tenga zapatos, ni María ni yo (María era su hermana) podremos jugar con él —dijo el niño.

Y esto era lo que le interesaba sobre todo: jugar con el ángel.

A María, que acababa de llegar también de la escuela, y que no se hartaba de   10
contemplar al visitante, lo que le interesaba más eran las plumas; aquellas plumas gigantescas, nunca vistas,[29] de ave del Paraíso, de quetzal[30] heráldico... de quimera, que cubrían las alas del ángel. Tanto que no pudo contenerse, y acercándose al celeste herido, le cuchicheó estas palabras:

—Di, ¿te dolería que te arrancase yo una pluma?[31] La deseo para mi   15
sombrero...

—Niña —exclamó la madre, indignada, aunque no comprendía del todo aquel lenguaje.

Pero el ángel, con la más bella de sus sonrisas, le respondió extendiendo el ala sana.   20

—¿Cuál te gusta?

—Esta tornasolada...

—¡Pues tómala!

Y se la arrancó resuelto, con movimiento lleno de gracia, extendiéndola a su nueva amiga, quien se puso a contemplarla embelesada.   25

No hubo manera de que ningún zapato le viniese al ángel.[32] Tenía el pie muy chico, y alargado en una forma deliciosamente aristocrática, incapaz de adaptarse a las botas americanas (únicas que había en el pueblo), las cuales le hacían un daño tremendo, de suerte que cojeaba peor que descalzo.

La niña fue quien[33] sugirió, al fin, la buena idea: 30

—Que le traigan —dijo— unas sandalias.[34] Yo he visto a San Rafael[35] con ellas, en las estampas en que lo pintan de viaje,[36] con el joven Tobías,[37] y no parecen molestarle en lo más mínimo.[38]

El ángel dijo que, en efecto, algunos de sus compañeros las usaban para viajar por la tierra; pero que eran de un material finísimo, más rico que el oro, y   35

---

[27]*a decir... trabajo:* to be truthful, with some difficulty   [28]*Era maravilloso de belleza:* He was marvelously beautiful.   [29]*nunca vistas:* never before seen   [30]*quetzal:* tropical climbing bird, with soft iridescent green and red feathers, found in southern Mexico and Guatemala   [31]*Di... pluma?* Say, would it hurt you if I pulled a feather out?   [32]*No... ángel:* There was no way of getting a shoe on the angel.   [33]*quien:* the one who   [34]*Que... sandalias:* Someone get him some sandals.   [35]*San Rafael:* one of the Archangels   [36]*lo pintan de viaje:* they show him traveling   [37]*Tobías:* a Biblical Jew celebrated for his piety, who was taken to the land of the Medes by the Archangel Raphael.   [38]*en lo más mínimo:* in the least

estaban cuajadas de piedras preciosas. San Crispín, el bueno de San Crispín,[39] las fabricaba.

—Pues aquí —observó la niña— tendrás que contentarte con unas menos lujosas, y déjate de santos[40] si las encuentras.

* * *

5   Por fin, el ángel, calzado con sus sandalias y bastante restablecido de su mal, pudo ir y venir por toda la casa.

Era adorable escena verle jugar con los niños. Parecía un gran pájaro azul, con algo de mujer y mucho de paloma, y hasta en lo zurdo de su andar[41] había gracia y señorío.

10   Podía ya mover el ala enferma, y abría y cerraba las dos con movimientos suaves y con un gran rumor de seda, abanicando a sus amigos.

Cantaba de un modo admirable, y refería a sus dos oyentes historias más bellas que todas las inventadas por los hijos de los hombres.

No se enfadaba jamás. Sonreía casi siempre, y de cuando en cuando se ponía 15 triste.

Y su faz, que era muy bella cuando sonreía, era incomparablemente más bella cuando se ponía pensativa y melancólica, porque adquiría una expresión nueva que jamás tuvieron los rostros de los ángeles y que tuvo siempre la faz del Nazareno,[42] a quien, según la tradición nunca se le vio reír y sí se le vio muchas 20 veces llorar.[43]

Esta expresión de tristeza augusta fue, quizá, lo único que se llevó el ángel de su paso por la tierra...

* * *

¿Cuántos días transcurrieron así? Los niños no hubieran podido contarlos; la sociedad de los ángeles, la familiaridad con el Ensueño, tienen el don de ele-25 varnos a planos superiores, donde nos sustraemos a las leyes del tiempo.

El ángel, enteramente bueno ya, podía volar, y en sus juegos maravillaba a los niños, lanzándose al espacio con una majestad suprema; cortaba para ellos la fruta de los más altos árboles, y, a veces, los cogía a los dos en sus brazos y volaba de esta suerte.[44]

30   Tales vuelos, que constituían el deleite mayor para los chicos, alarmaban profundamente a la madre.

---

[39]*el bueno de San Crispín:* good old St. Crispin (St. Crispin is the patron saint of shoemakers.)   [40]*y déjate de santos:* and don't worry about what the saints do   [41]*en... andar:* in the clumsy way he walked   [42]*el Nazareno:* Jesus Christ   [43]*nunca... llorar:* was never seen to laugh, but *was* seen to weep many times (Note again the use of *sí* for emphasis.)   [44]*de esta suerte:* in this manner

—No vayáis a dejarlos caer por inadvertencia,[45] señor Ángel —le gritaba la buena mujer—. Os confieso que no me gustan juegos tan peligrosos...

Pero el ángel reía y reían los niños, y la madre acababa por reír también, al ver la agilidad y la fuerza con que aquél los cogía en sus brazos, y la dulzura infinita con que los depositaba sobre el césped del jardín... ¡Se hubiera dicho que hacía su aprendizaje de Ángel Custodio![46]

—Sois muy fuerte, señor Ángel —decía la madre, llena de pasmo.

Y el ángel, con cierta inocente suficiencia infantil,[47] respondía:

—Tan fuerte, que podría zafar de su órbita a una estrella.

* * *

Una tarde, los niños encontraron al ángel sentado en un poyo de piedra, cerca del muro del huerto, en actitud de tristeza más honda que cuando estaba enfermo.

—¿Qué tienes?[48] —le preguntaron al unísono.

—Tengo —respondió— que ya estoy bueno;[49] que no hay ya pretexto para que permanezca con vosotros...;[50] ¡que me llaman de allá arriba, y que es fuerza que me vaya![51]

—¿Que te vayas? ¡Eso, nunca! —replicó la niña.

—¡Eso, nunca! —repitió el niño.

—¿Y qué he de hacer si me llaman...?

—Pues no ir...

—¡Imposible!

Hubo una larga pausa llena de angustia.

Los niños y el ángel lloraban.

De pronto, la chica, más fértil en expedientes, como mujer, dijo:

—Hay un medio de que no nos separemos...[52]

—¿Cuál? —preguntó el ángel, ansioso.

—Que nos lleves contigo.

—¡Muy bien! —afirmó el niño palmoteando.

Y con divina confusión, los tres se pusieron a bailar como unos locos.

Pasados, empero, estos transportes,[53] la niña se quedó pensativa, y murmuró:

---

[45]*No... inadvertencia:* Don't get careless and drop them (The mother, to show extreme respect, addresses the angel in the second-person plural, which has now passed from conversational usage in Spanish America.)   [46]*¡Se... Custodio!* One would have said that he was serving his apprenticeship to become a Guardian Angel.   [47]*con... infantil:* with that certain innocent assuredness of a child   [48]*¿Qué tienes?* What's wrong?   [49]*Tengo... bueno:* I'm well now—that's what's wrong   [50]*vosotros:* Note that the angel also uses the plural *vosotros.* This non-Spanish-American usage lends an odd flavor to his speech.   [51]*es fuerza que me vaya:* I have to leave   [52]*Hay... separemos:* There's one way that we won't have to be separated.   [53]*Pasados, empero, estos transportes:* Nevertheless, when these raptures were over

—Pero ¿y nuestra madre?

—¡Eso es![54] —corroboró el ángel—; ¿y vuestra madre?

—Nuestra madre —sugirió el niño— no sabrá nada... Nos iremos sin decírselo..., y cuando esté triste, vendremos a consolarla.

5 —Mejor sería llevarla con nosotros —dijo la niña.

—¡Me parece bien! —afirmó el ángel—. Yo volveré por ella.

—¡Magnífico!

—¿Estáis, pues, resueltos?

—Resueltos estamos.

* * *

10 Caía la tarde fantásticamente, entre niágaras de oro.

El ángel cogió a los niños en sus brazos, y de un solo ímpetu se lanzó con ellos al azul luminoso.

La madre en esto llegaba al jardín, y toda trémula los vio alejarse.

El ángel, a pesar de la distancia, parecía crecer. Era tan diáfano, que a través 15 de sus alas se veía el sol.

La madre, ante el milagroso espectáculo, no pudo ni gritar. Se quedó alelada, viendo volar hacia las llamas del ocaso aquel grupo indecible, y cuando, más tarde, el ángel volvió al jardín por ella, la buena mujer estaba aún en éxtasis.

EXERCISES

A. Questions and Opinions

1. ¿Por qué cayó el ángel a la tierra?
2. ¿Quién ayudó al ángel a levantarse?
3. ¿Qué le faltaba al ángel para que caminara sin sufrir?
4. ¿Cómo llevó el niño al ángel hasta su casa?
5. ¿Qué sugirió María para el ángel en vez de zapatos?
6. ¿Qué parecía el ángel mientras jugaba con los niños?
7. ¿Cómo divertía el ángel a los niños?
8. ¿Por qué estaba el ángel en una actitud de tristeza un día?
9. ¿Qué medio sugirió la chica al ángel para no separarse?
10. ¿Hasta dónde llevó el ángel a la madre y a sus hijos?
●11. ¿Se siente Ud. feliz con el final de este cuento? ¿Por qué?
●12. Si existen los ángeles, ¿serán como nosotros?

---

[54]*¡Eso es!* That's right!

B. Verb Practice

Use each of the following verbal phrases in an original sentence in Spanish, either based on the story or of your own design. Be prepared to explain the meaning of your sentences.

1. **acercarse a**
2. **ayudar a** + *infinitive*
3. **empezar a** + *infinitive*
4. **tutear**
5. **fijarse (en)**
6. **hacer falta**
7. **no poder** *(in preterit)* + *infinitive*
8. **ponerse** + *adjective*
9. **llevarse**
10. **haber de** + *infinitive*

C. Vocabulary Practice

Complete the sentences below, matching the expressions on the right with the English words on the left. Be sure to use the correct form of each verb. Then use each expression in an original Spanish sentence and indicate in English what your sentence means.

1. El chico ayudó al ángel a *get on his feet.*   **en fin**
2. Ha habido muchas historias de ángeles caídos *down through* los siglos.   **ponerse en (de) pie**
3. ¿Por qué no vuelas? *What's wrong?*   **¿Qué es esto de...?**
4. *Anyway,* el ángel no tuvo más remedio que pasar un tiempo con los hombres. **unos cuantos**
5. El ángel miró con dulzura al chico y a la mamá y *she* quedó extática.   **alejarse (de)**
6. *What are these* alas rotas y pies sangrientos *you're talking about?*   **éste(–a)**
7. El ángel perdió pie en una nube y *suddenly* se encontró en la tierra.   **hacer daño**
8. Es mejor que *we move back* un poco.   **¿Qué tienes?**
9. Creo que todas las piedras y rocas en el camino *are going to hurt him.*   **de pronto**
10. El ángel se quedó pensativo *a few* momentos.   **a través de**

D. Communication Practice

1. Suggest to a friend that you both use the **tú** form with each other.
2. Say that the only thing we need now is time to do the work.

3. Express the idea that everyone had returned home when it began to rain.
4. Indicate that you had never noticed that Diego spoke Spanish with a Mexican accent.
5. State that you would like to help your friend finish the job if you had a free hour.

E. Review Exercise

Following is a list of verbs found in this story. You can probably guess their meanings — if they are not immediately clear — since the "core" of each is a noun, pronoun, or adverb with which you are likely already familiar. See if you can spot the familiar element in these verbs and give its meaning; then give the meaning of the verb itself. This is another way of increasing your "recognition" vocabulary.

sangrar	**acercarse**	**maravillar**
acertar	**alejarse**	**preguntar**
tutear	**usar**	**palmotear**

UN PACTO CON EL DIABLO

JUAN JOSÉ ARREOLA

JUAN JOSÉ ARREOLA (1918–   ) is a Mexican who has produced two volumes of excellent short stories that have earned him the reputation as one of his country's most accomplished authors. *Varia invención* (1949) and *Confabulario* (1952) are made up of elaborately wrought tales in which graceful, though sometimes biting humor, gentle satire, and a carefully sustained play of intellectual ideas predominate.

   In «Un pacto con el diablo» Arreola draws the story's circumstances from a celebrated narrative by the American author Stephen Vincent Benét (1898–1943) entitled "The Devil and Daniel Webster." He transfers the story's setting from New England to a city in his native Mexico and introduces a film version of the tale as the means of getting his narrator to consider the idea of making a deal with the strange fellow he meets in the darkened movie theater. While the story does not involve the stirring battle of wits that we encounter in the Benét original, the narrator's simple faith seems more than sufficient when put to the test.

A PRELIMINARY LOOK AT KEY EXPRESSIONS

Be sure to study these expressions before you read the story.

1. (50: 7) **gustar** *to be pleasing to*   Although *like* is the normal English way of saying this, **gustar** works differently in Spanish: the thing liked is the *subject* and the person pleased is the *indirect object*. Thus, if someone expresses a like for more than one thing, the verb in Spanish is in the plural: **Le gustan las películas sentimentales.** *He likes sentimental movies* (literally, *"Sentimental movies are pleasing to him"*).
2. (50:14) **argumento** *plot (of a book, movie,* etc.)   *Argument* is **discusión, disputa,** or **debate.**
3. (50:29) **no poder menos de** + *infinitive   not to be able to help but* + *verb:* **No pude menos de preguntar...** *I couldn't help but ask* or *I couldn't help asking.*
4. (50:31) **encontrarse** + *adjective   to be, find oneself* + *adjective*
5. (50: 4) **ignorar** *not to know*   This simply means **no saber.** *To ignore* is **no hacer caso de** or **a.**
6. (51: 6) **en cambio** *on the other hand*
7. (51:20) **salirle mal a uno** *to turn out badly for someone:* **El negocio le salió mal.** *The business deal didn't work out for him.*
8. (51:24) **cumplir** *to keep one's word, show up on time,* etc.   **Cumplir** can also be used with an object: **cumplir el contrato** *to honor the contract,* **cumplir su palabra** *to keep one's word.*
9. (51:29) **de parte de** *on the side of, favoring*
10. (51:34) **sentarle mal a uno** *to disagree with one, not to suit one*   This means both *not to look good on:* **A su mujer le sentaban mal las alhajas.** *The jewels didn't look right on his wife* and also *not to agree with one:* **Me sientan mal las ostras.** *Oysters don't agree with me* (literally, *"sit badly on me"*).
11. (52: 6) **cualquier cosa** *anything (whatever, at all)   Some thing (one thing in particular)* is **alguna cosa.**
12. (52: 6) **faltarle a uno** *to be missing, lacking*   Just as with **gustar** and **bastar,** the thing missing or lacking is the subject in Spanish, and the person missing it is the indirect object: **No quiero que nada le falte a Paulina.** *I don't want Paulina to be lacking (wanting for) anything.*
13. (52:25) **decidirse a** + *infinitive   to decide, make up one's mind* + *infinitive.*
14. (52:26) **empeñarse en** + *infinitive   to insist on* + *present participle:* **Se empeñó en ir a la película.** *He insisted on going to the movie.*   This verb is also used with the subjunctive when one person insists that someone else do something: **Paulina se empeñó en que yo viniera.** *Paulina insisted that I come.*
15. (52:31) **cuidarse de** + *infinitive   to take care, be careful to* + *verb:* **La gente ya no se cuida de vestirse.** *People aren't careful about the way they dress anymore.*

16. (54: 8) **de nuevo** *again*   Synonyms are **nuevamente, otra vez,** and **volver a** + *infinitive.*
17. (54:15) **sin embargo** *nevertheless, however*
18. (54:20) **echar de menos...** *to miss* . . . in the sense of regret over someone's or something's absence: **Echo de menos a mis antiguos compañeros de clase.** *I miss my old classmates.*
19. (54:28) **en medio de** *in the middle of*
20. (54:31) **cada vez más...** *more and more* . . . . : **cada vez más de prisa** *faster and faster;* **cada vez más grande** *bigger and bigger.*

UN PACTO
CON EL DIABLO

Aunque me di prisa y llegué al cine corriendo, la película había ya comenzado. En el salón oscuro me puse a buscar un sitio. Vine a quedar junto a un hombre de singular aspecto. Le dije:

—Perdone usted, ¿no podría contarme brevemente lo que ha ocurrido en la pantalla?

—Sí. Daniel Webster, a quien ve usted allí, ha hecho un pacto con el diablo.

—Gracias. Ahora me gustaría conocer las condiciones de ese pacto, ¿podría explicármelas?

—Con mucho gusto. El diablo se compromete a proporcionar la riqueza a Daniel Webster durante siete años. Naturalmente, a cambio de su alma.

—¿Siete no más?

—El contrato puede renovarse. No hace mucho,[1] Daniel Webster lo firmó con un poco de sangre.

Yo podía completar con estos datos el argumento de la película. Eran suficientes, pero quise saber algo más. El complaciente desconocido parecía hombre de criterio.[2] En tanto que[3] Daniel Webster embolsaba una buena cantidad de monedas de oro, pregunté:

—En su concepto, ¿quién de los dos se ha comprometido más?

—El diablo.

—¿Cómo es eso? —repliqué sorprendido.

—El alma de Daniel Webster, créame usted, no valía gran cosa en el momento en que la cedió.

—Entonces el diablo...

—Va a salir muy perjudicado en el negocio, porque Daniel se manifiesta deseoso de dinero, mírelo usted.

Efectivamente, Webster gastaba el dinero a puñados. Su alma de campesino se desquiciaba. Con ojos de reproche, mi vecino añadió:

—Ya llegarás al séptimo año, ya.[4]

Tuve un estremecimiento. Daniel Webster me inspiraba simpatía.[5] No pude menos de preguntar:

—Usted, perdóneme, ¿no se ha encontrado pobre alguna vez?

---

[1]*No hace mucho:* Not long ago *(tiempo* is understood after *mucho)*   [2]*hombre de criterio:* a discerning man   [3]*En tanto que:* While   [4]*Ya... ya:* Just wait until the seventh year.   [5]*simpatía:* liking, friendly feeling, as expressed in *simpático*

El perfil de mi vecino, esfumado por la oscuridad, sonrió débilmente. Apartó los ojos de la pantalla donde ya Daniel Webster comenzaba a sentir remordimientos, y dijo, sin mirarme:

—Ignoro en qué consiste la pobreza, ¿sabe usted?

5 —Siendo así...[6]

—En cambio, sé muy bien lo que puede hacerse en siete años de riqueza.

Hice un esfuerzo para comprender lo que serían esos años, y vi la imagen de Paulina, sonriente, con un traje nuevo, y rodeada de cosas hermosas. Esta imagen dio origen a otros pensamientos:

10 —Usted me dijo hace poco[7] que el alma de Daniel Webster no valía nada, ¿cómo, pues, el diablo le ha dado tanto?

—El alma de ese pobre muchacho puede mejorar, los remordimientos, pueden hacerlo crecer —contestó filosóficamente mi vecino, agregando luego con malicia—: Entonces el diablo no habrá perdido su tiempo.

15 —¿Y si Daniel se arrepiente?...

Mi interlocutor pareció disgustado[8] por la piedad que yo manifestaba. Hizo un movimiento como para hablar, pero solamente salió de su boca un pequeño sonido gutural. Yo insistí:

—Porque Daniel Webster podría arrepentirse, y entonces...

20 —No sería la primera vez en que al diablo le salieran mal estas cosas. Algunos hombres se le han ido ya de las manos[9] a pesar del contrato.

—Realmente es muy poco honrado.

—¿Qué dice usted?

—Si el diablo cumple, con mayor razón[10] debe el hombre cumplir.

25 —Por ejemplo...

—Aquí está Daniel Webster. Adora a su mujer. Mire usted la casa que le ha comprado. Por amor ha dado su alma, y debe cumplir.

A mi compañero le desconcertaron mucho estas razones.

—Perdóneme, hace un instante, usted estaba de parte de Daniel.

30 —Y sigo de su parte. Pero debe cumplir.

—Usted, ¿cumpliría?

No pude responder. En la pantalla, Daniel Webster se hallaba sombrío. La opulencia no bastaba para hacerle olvidar su vida sencilla de campesino. Su casa era grande y lujosa, pero extrañamente triste. A su mujer le sentaban mal las 35 alhajas.[11] ¡Parecía tan cambiada!

Los años transcurrían veloces y las monedas saltaban rápidas de las manos de Daniel, como antaño la semilla. Pero tras él crecían en lugar de plantas, tristezas, remordimientos.

---

[6]*Siendo así:* In that case   [7]*hace poco:* not long ago (again *tiempo* is understood)   [8]*disgustado:* displeased   [9]*se... manos:* have already escaped his clutches   [10]*con mayor razón:* all the more reason   [11]*A su... alhajas:* The jewels didn't look right on his wife

Hice un esfuerzo y dije:

—Daniel debe cumplir. Yo también cumpliría. Nada existe peor que la pobreza. Se ha sacrificado por su mujer, lo demás no importa.

—Dice usted bien. Usted comprende porque también tiene mujer, ¿no es cierto?

—Daría cualquier cosa porque[12] nada le faltase a Paulina.

—¿Su alma?

Hablábamos en voz baja. Sin embargo, las personas que nos rodeaban parecían molestas. Varias veces nos habían pedido que calláramos. Mi amigo, que parecía vivamente interesado en la conversación, me dijo:

—¿Quiere usted que salgamos a uno de los pasillos? Podremos ver más tarde la película.

No pude rehusar, y salimos. Miré por última vez a la pantalla: Daniel Webster confesaba llorando a su mujer el pacto que había hecho con el diablo.

Yo seguía pensando en Paulina, en la desesperante estrechez con que vivíamos, en la pobreza que ella soportaba dulcemente, y que me hacía sufrir mucho más. Decididamente, no comprendía yo a Daniel Webster, que lloraba con los bolsillos repletos.

—Usted, ¿es pobre?

Habíamos atravesado el salón, y entrábamos en un angosto pasillo, oscuro, y con un leve olor de humedad. Al trasponer la cortina gastada, mi acompañante volvió a preguntarme:

—Usted, ¿es muy pobre?

—En este día —le contesté—, las entradas al cine cuestan más baratas que de ordinario, y, sin embargo, si supiera usted qué lucha para decidirme a gastar ese dinero. Paulina se ha empeñado en que viniera: hablando con ella se me ha pasado la hora del programa.[13]

—Entonces, un hombre que resuelve sus problemas tal como lo hizo Daniel, ¿qué concepto le merece?[14]

—Es cosa de pensarlo.[15] Mis asuntos marchan muy mal. Las personas ya no se cuidan de vestirse. Van de cualquier modo. Reparan sus trajes, los limpian, los arreglan una y otra vez. Paulina misma sabe entenderse[16] muy bien. Hace combinaciones, y añadidos, se improvisa trajes; lo cierto es que desde hace mucho tiempo, no tiene un vestido nuevo.

—Le prometo hacerme su cliente. En esta semana le encargaré un par de trajes.

—Gracias. Tenía razón Paulina al pedirme que viniera al cine. Cuando lo sepa va a ponerse contenta.

---

[12]*porque = para que:* so that [13]*se me... programa:* I got here late for the start of the show [14]*¿qué concepto le merece?* What is your considered opinion of him? [15]*Es... pensarlo:* It's something to think about. [16]*entenderse:* get along

—Podría hacer algo más por usted; por ejemplo, me gustaría proponerle un negocio, hacerle una compra...

—Perdón, no tenemos ya nada por vender; lo último, unos aretes de Paulina...

5 —Piense usted bien, hay algo que quizá olvida...

Hice como que[17] meditaba un poco. Hubo una pausa que mi benefactor interrumpió con voz extraña:

—Reflexione usted, mire, allí tiene usted a Daniel Webster, poco antes de que usted llegara, no tenía nada para vender, y, sin embargo...

10 Noté, de pronto, que el rostro de aquel hombre se hacía más agudo. La luz roja de un letrero puesto en la pared, daba en sus ojos un fulgor extraño, como fuego. Él advirtió mi turbación, y dijo con voz clara y distinta:

—A estas alturas,[18] señor mío, resulta por demás una presentación.[19] Estoy por completo a sus órdenes.

15 Hice instintivamente la señal de la cruz con mi mano derecha, pero sin sacarla del bolsillo. Esto pareció quitar al signo su virtud, porque el diablo, componiendo el nudo de su corbata, dijo con toda calma:

—Aquí, en el bolsillo, llevo un documento que...

Yo estaba perplejo. Volví a ver a Paulina de pie en el umbral de nuestra casa, 20 con su traje gracioso y desteñido, en la actitud en que se hallaba cuando me vine: el rostro inclinado y sonriente, las manos ocultas en los pequeños bolsillos de su delantal.

Pensé que nuestra fortuna estaba en mis manos. Esta noche apenas si teníamos algo para comer. Mañana habría manjares sobre la mesa. Y también 25 vestidos y joyas, y una casa grande y hermosa. ¿El alma?

Mientras me hallaba sumido en tales pensamientos, el diablo había sacado un pliego crujiente, y en una de sus manos brillaba una aguja. «Daría cualquier cosa porque nada te faltara.» Esto lo había yo dicho muchas veces a mi mujer. Cualquier cosa. ¿El alma? Ahora estaba frente a mí el que podía hacer efectivas 30 mis palabras. Pero yo seguía meditando. Dudaba. Sentía una especie de vértigo. Bruscamente, me decidí:

—Trato hecho.[20] Sólo pongo una condición.

El diablo, que ya trataba de pinchar mi brazo con su aguja, pareció desconcertado:

35 —¿Qué condición?

—Me gustaría ver el final de la película —contesté.

—¡Pero, qué le importa a usted lo que ocurra a ese imbécil de Daniel Webster! Además, eso es un cuento. Déjelo usted y firme, el documento está en regla,[21] sólo hace falta su firma,[22] aquí, sobre esta pequeña raya.

---

[17]*Hice como que:* I pretended that   [18]*A estas alturas:* At this point   [19]*resulta... presentación:* an introduction is not at all necessary   [20]*Trato hecho:* It's a deal.   [21]*en regla:* in order   [22]*sólo... firma:* the only thing necessary is your signature

La voz del diablo era insinuante, ladina, como un sonido de monedas de oro. Añadió:

—Si usted gusta, puedo hacerle ahora mismo un anticipo.

Parecía un comerciante astuto. Yo repuse con energía:

—Necesito ver el final de la película. Después firmaré. 5

—¿Me da usted su palabra?

—Sí.

Entramos de nuevo en el salón. Yo no veía en absoluto,[23] pero mi guía supo hallar fácilmente dos asientos.

En la pantalla, es decir, en la vida de Daniel Webster, se había operado un 10 cambio sorprendente, debido a no sé qué misteriosas circunstancias.

Una casa campesina, destartalada y pobre. La mujer de Webster estaba junto al fuego, preparando la comida. Era el crepúsculo y Daniel volvía del campo con la azada al hombro. Sudoroso, fatigado, con su burdo traje lleno de polvo, parecía, sin embargo, dichoso. 15

Apoyado en la azada, permaneció junto a la puerta. Su mujer se le acercó, sonriendo. Los dos contemplaron el día que se acababa dulcemente, prometiendo la paz y el descanso de la noche. Daniel miró con ternura a su esposa, y recorriendo luego la limpia pobreza de la casa, preguntó:

—Pero, ¿no echas tú de menos nuestra pasada riqueza? ¿Es que no te hacen 20 falta todas las cosas que teníamos?

—Es que tu alma vale más que todo eso, Daniel...

El rostro del campesino se fue iluminando, su sonrisa parecía extenderse, llenar toda la casa, salir al paisaje. Una música surgió de esa sonrisa, y parecía disolver poco a poco las imágenes. Entonces, de la casa dichosa y pobre de 25 Daniel Webster brotaron tres letras blancas[24] que fueron creciendo, creciendo, hasta llenar toda la pantalla.

Sin saber cómo, me hallé, de pronto en medio del tumulto que salía de la sala, empujando, atropellando, abriéndome paso[25] con violencia. Alguien me cogió por un brazo y trató de sujetarme. Con gran energía me solté, y pronto salí a la 30 calle. Era de noche. Comencé a caminar de prisa, cada vez más de prisa, hasta que acabé por echar a correr. No volví la cabeza ni una sola vez, y no me detuve hasta estar en la puerta de mi casa. Entré lo más tranquilamente que pude, y cerré la puerta con cuidado.

Paulina me esperaba. Echándome los brazos al cuello, dijo: 35

—Pareces agitado.

—No, nada, es que...

—¿No te ha gustado la película?

—Sí, pero...

---

[23]*Yo... absoluto:* I couldn't see a thing   [24]*tres letras blancas:* the word *FIN*, of course   [25]*abriéndome paso:* pushing my way through

Yo me hallaba turbado. Me llevé las manos a los ojos. Paulina se quedó mirándome, y luego, sin poderse contener, comenzó a reír, a reír alegremente de mí, que deslumbrado y confuso me había quedado sin saber qué decir.[26] En medio de su risa, me dijo con festivo reproche:

5 —¿Es posible que te hayas dormido?

Estas palabras me tranquilizaron. Me señalaron un rumbo. Como avergonzado, contesté:

—Es verdad, me he dormido.

Y luego, en son de disculpa, añadí:

10 —Tuve un sueño, y voy a contártelo.

Cuando acabé mi relato, Paulina me dijo que era la mejor película que yo podía haberle contado. Parecía contenta y se reía mucho.

Sin embargo, cuando yo me acostaba, pude ver cómo ella, sigilosamente, trazaba con un poco de ceniza la señal de la cruz sobre el umbral de nuestra casa.

EXERCISES

A. Questions and Opinions

1. ¿Quién le contó al narrador lo ocurrido en la película antes de su llegada?
2. ¿Dónde obtuvo Daniel Webster la buena cantidad de dinero que tenía?
3. ¿Cómo sabemos que el narrador era un hombre pobre?
4. Si tuviera mucho dinero el narrador, ¿qué haría con él?
5. ¿Cómo le salía a Daniel Webster su pacto con el diablo?
6. Aunque hablaba de otras cosas, ¿qué quería el diablo comprar al narrador?
7. ¿Por qué no firmó el narrador el contrato en seguida?
8. Aparentemente, ¿qué decidió hacer Daniel Webster al final de los siete años del pacto?
9. ¿Por qué salió de prisa del cine el narrador después de terminarse la película?
10. ¿Cuál fue la reacción de Paulina ante la historia que su esposo le contó?
●11. ¿Qué opinión tiene Ud. de la manera en que el narrador trató al diablo?
●12. ¿Qué podría tener de malo el hacer un pacto con el diablo?

---

[26]*que... decir:* Since I had become bewildered and confused, not knowing what to say

B. Verb Practice

Use each of the following verbal phrases in an original sentence in Spanish, either based on the story or of your own design. Be prepared to explain the meaning of your sentences.

1. **gustar**
2. **no poder menos de** + *infinitive*
3. **encontrarse** + *adjective*
4. **ignorar**
5. **cumplir**
6. **faltarle a uno**
7. **decidirse a** + *infinitive*
8. **empeñarse en** + *infinitive*
9. **cuidarse de** + *infinitive*
10. **echar de menos**

C. Vocabulary Practice

Complete the sentences below, matching the expressions on the right with the English words on the left. Be sure to use the correct form of each verb. Then use each expression in an original Spanish sentence and indicate in English what your sentence means.

1. Una vida de rico *wouldn't suit me.*
2. La conversación con el hombre desconocido me tenía *more and more* preocupado.
3. Me pidió *again* que firmara el contrato.
4. Yo nunca estaba *on the side of* el Diablo.
5. *On the other hand,* yo no estaba de acuerdo con Daniel Webster tampoco.
6. ¿Quieres contarme *the plot* de la película?
7. Las letras FIN aparecieron *in the middle of* la pantalla.
8. Yo daría *anything* menos mi alma.
9. *Nevertheless,* el desconocido empezaba a convencerme.
10. Me alegro de no haber firmado porque *it wouldn't work out for me.*

argumento
en cambio

salirle mal a uno
cualquier cosa
sentarle mal a uno

de parte de
de nuevo

sin embargo
en medio de

cada vez más...

D. Communication Practice

1. Say you don't know why Pablo insisted on being so difficult.
2. Indicate that no one would like to make a pact with the devil.
3. Ask your friends when they are going to decide to have that party.
4. State that you have always kept your word.
5. Ask your classmates if they are going to miss you next year.

E. Completion Exercise

Complete the following sentence fragments with your own ideas. Be sure to use the appropriate mood and tense with verbs you introduce.

1. A Paulina no le gusta que...
2. En ese momento no pude menos de...
3. La chica se encontraba triste cuando...
4. El pacto le ha salido mal al diablo porque...
5. A nosotros nos faltaban...

JUAN DARIÉN

HORACIO QUIROGA

HORACIO QUIROGA (1878–1937), an Uruguayan by birth,
spent much of his life in the Argentine province of Misiones.
Throughout his career as a writer, this tropical region along the
Paraná River offered him a colorful background for dozens of
the memorable stories upon which is based his reputation as
one of Spanish America's finest short story writers. His life was
marked by tragedy and poor health, and this was reflected in a
good part of his work. In addition to the influence of Edgar
Allan Poe and the French Parnassians, which Quiroga acknowl-
edged in his somber stories, one notes a similar literary debt to
Rudyard Kipling. Kipling's *Jungle Books* and *Just So Stories,*
written for a young audience, undoubtedly inspired many of
Quiroga's brighter tales, such as those in his widely known
Cuentos de la selva (1918).

«Juan Darién» is taken from the mixed collection of stories
entitled *El desierto* (1924). Although here we once more have
the jungle setting so characteristic of the charming tales men-
tioned above, it is apparent that this story is pervaded by a bitter
tone of disillusionment and revenge—a quality that dramati-
cally reveals the darker side of Quiroga's nature.

A PRELIMINARY LOOK AT KEY EXPRESSIONS

Be sure to study these expressions before you read the story.

1. (62: 2) **asistir a** *to attend*   This is another example of a deceptive cognate. *To assist* is **ayudar,** and **atender** is *to take care of, look after.*
2. (62:29) **dormirse** *to fall asleep*
3. (63:23) **a menos que** *unless*   This conjunction always takes the subjunctive in Spanish: **A menos que una madre de entre los hombres lo acuse...** *Unless a mother of men accuses him. . .*
4. (63:30) **por todas partes** *everywhere*
5. (63:38) **bastar** *to be enough*   The person for whom the subject is enough is the indirect object in Spanish: **Le bastaba el amor de su hijo.** *Her child's love was enough for her.*
6. (64: 6) **burlarse de** *to make fun of*   This is synonymous with **hacer burla de,** which occurred in the first story.
7. (64: 7) **a menudo** *often*   This is synonymous with **con frecuencia** or **frecuentemente** but even more common in conversation.
8. (64: 9) **cumplir... años** *to be (turn) . . . years old*   This expression is used, of course, to indicate one's birthday, which is **el cumpleaños.**
9. (65: 9) **tocarle a uno** *to be one's turn*   The person whose turn it is is the indirect object in Spanish: **Ahora le toca a Juan Darién.** *Now it's Juan Darien's turn.* **Tocar** with a direct object also means *to touch* and *to play (a musical instrument).*
10. (65:15) **demorar (en** + *infinitive)   to delay (in* + *present participle)*
11. (65:17) **por ejemplo** *for example*
12. (65:33) **moverse** *to move*   This verb expresses the activity of moving around; **mudarse** is *to move* in the sense of *to change one's residence.*
13. (66: 3) **reírse (de)** *to laugh (at)*
14. (66: 9) **tarde o temprano** *sooner or later*   Notice that the words are "reversed" in Spanish (or perhaps in English).
15. (66:11) **puesto que** *since*   This expression means *because. Since* in the time sense is **desde que.**
16. (66:14) **hay que** + *infinitive   one must, it is necessary to* + *verb*   This expression is used when anyone and everyone in general is involved: **Con los hombres hay que proceder con cuidado.** *With men "you" have to (one must, it is necessary to) proceed with caution.*
17. (66:21) **ni siquiera** *not even*
18. (68:16) **de este modo** *in this way*
19. (69: 6) **ir** + *present participle   to be* + *present participle slowly (gradually)*   **Ir** is one of several verbs that can be used to combine with the present participle in the progressive tense. Each one provides a different shade of meaning: **estar** *to be,* **seguir** *to continue, keep on,* and

andar *to go around* + *present participle*. In the story **Las luces se iban apagando** means that *The lights were going out little by little.*

20. (70:18) **volverse** *to turn around*   **Volver** has many meanings, as we have seen. In addition to *to turn around,* **volverse** means *to become:* **Se volvió sordo.** *He became (went) deaf;* and *to turn back:* **Iba hacia la selva, pero luego se volvió.** *He was headed for the jungle, but then he turned (came) back.*

JUAN DARIÉN

Aquí se cuenta la historia de un tigre que se crió y educó entre los hombres, y que se llamaba Juan Darién. Asistió cuatro años a la escuela vestido de pantalón y camisa, y dio sus lecciones corrientemente,[1] aunque era un tigre de las selvas; pero esto se debe a que su figura era de hombre, conforme se narra[2] en las siguientes líneas.

Una vez, a principios de otoño, la viruela visitó un pueblo de un país lejano y mató a muchas personas. Los hermanos perdieron a sus hermanitas, y las criaturas que comenzaban a caminar quedaron sin padre ni madre. Las madres perdieron a su vez a sus hijos, y una pobre mujer joven y viuda llevó ella misma a enterrar a su hijito, lo único que tenía en este mundo. Cuando volvió a su casa, se quedó sentada pensando en su chiquito. Y murmuraba:

—Dios debía haber tenido más compasión de mí, y me ha llevado a mi hijo. En el cielo podrá haber ángeles,[3] pero mi hijo no los conoce. Y a quien él conoce bien es a mí,[4] ¡pobre hijo mío!

Y miraba a lo lejos, pues estaba sentada en el fondo de su casa, frente a un portoncito donde se veía la selva.

Ahora bien; en la selva había muchos animales feroces que rugían al caer la noche y al amanecer. Y la pobre mujer, que continuaba sentada, alcanzó a ver en la obscuridad una cosa chiquita y vacilante que entraba por la puerta, como un gatito que apenas tuviera fuerzas para caminar. La mujer se agachó y levantó en las manos un tigrecito de pocos días, pues aún tenía los ojos cerrados. Y cuando el mísero cachorro sintió el contacto de las manos, runruneó de contento,[5] porque ya no estaba solo. La madre tuvo largo rato suspendido en el aire aquel pequeño enemigo de los hombres, a aquella fiera indefensa que tan fácil le hubiera sido exterminar. Pero quedó pensativa ante el desvalido cachorro que venía quién sabe de dónde, y cuya madre con seguridad había muerto. Sin pensar bien en lo que hacía llevó al cachorrito a su seno y lo rodeó con sus grandes manos. Y el tigrecito, al sentir el calor del pecho, buscó postura cómoda, runruneó tranquilo y se durmió con la garganta adherida al seno maternal.

La mujer, pensativa siempre, entró en la casa. Y en el resto de la noche, al oír los gemidos de hambre del cachorrito, y al ver cómo buscaba su seno con los ojos

---

[1] *dio sus lecciones corrientemente:* he recited his lessons in the usual way (In Spanish, students "give" lessons and examinations and teachers "take" them, just the opposite of English usage.) [2] *conforme se narra:* just as is told [3] *podrá haber ángeles:* maybe there are angels [4] *Y... mí:* And I'm the one he knows well [5] *de contento:* with happiness

cerrados, sintió en su corazón herido que, ante la suprema ley del Universo, una vida equivale a otra vida...

Y dio de mamar[6] al tigrecito.

El cachorro estaba salvado, y la madre había hallado un inmenso consuelo.
5 Tan grande su consuelo, que vio con terror el momento en que aquél le sería arrebatado, porque si se llegaba a saber[7] en el pueblo que ella amamantaba a un ser salvaje, matarían con seguridad a la pequeña fiera. ¿Qué hacer? El cachorro, suave y cariñoso—pues jugaba con ella sobre su pecho—, era ahora su propio hijo.

10 En estas circunstancias, un hombre que una noche de lluvia pasaba corriendo ante la casa de la mujer oyó un gemido áspero—el ronco gemido de las fieras que, aun recién nacidas, sobresaltan al ser humano—. El hombre se detuvo bruscamente, y mientras buscaba a tientas el revólver, golpeó la puerta. La madre, que había oído los pasos, corrió loca de angustia a ocultar al tigrecito en
15 el jardín. Pero su buena suerte quiso que al abrir la puerta del fondo se hallara ante una mansa, vieja y sabia serpiente que le cerraba el paso. La desgraciada mujer iba a gritar de terror, cuando la serpiente habló así:

—Nada temas, mujer —le dijo—. Tu corazón de madre te ha permitido salvar una vida del Universo, donde todas las vidas tienen el mismo valor. Pero
20 los hombres no te comprenderán, y querrán matar a tu nuevo hijo. Nada temas, ve tranquila. Desde este momento tu hijo tiene forma humana; nunca le reconocerán. Forma su corazón, enséñale a ser bueno como tú, y él no sabrá jamás que no es hombre. A menos... a menos que una madre de entre los hombres lo acuse; a menos que una madre no le exija que devuelva con su sangre lo que
25 tú has dado por él, tu hijo será siempre digno de ti. Ve tranquila, madre, y apresúrate, que el hombre va a echar la puerta abajo.

Y la madre creyó a la serpiente, porque en todas las religiones de los hombres la serpiente conoce el misterio de las vidas que pueblan los mundos. Fue, pues, corriendo a abrir la puerta, y el hombre, furioso, entró con el revólver en la
30 mano y buscó por todas partes sin hallar nada. Cuando salió, la mujer abrió, temblando, el rebozo bajo el cual ocultaba al tigrecito sobre su seno, y en su lugar vio a un niño que dormía tranquilo. Traspasada de dicha, lloró largo rato en silencio sobre su salvaje hijo hecho hombre; lágrimas de gratitud que doce años más tarde ese mismo hijo debía pagar con sangre sobre su tumba.
35 Pasó el tiempo. El nuevo niño necesitaba un nombre: se le puso Juan Darién. Necesitaba alimentos, ropa, calzado: se le dotó de todo, para lo cual la madre trabajaba día y noche. Ella era aún muy joven, y podría haberse vuelto a casar,[8] si hubiera querido; pero le bastaba el amor entrañable de su hijo, amor que ella devolvía con todo su corazón.

---

[6]*dio de mamar:* she nursed   [7]*si... saber:* if people found out   [8]*podría... casar:* she could have gotten married again

Juan Darién era, efectivamente, digno de ser querido: noble, bueno y generoso como nadie. Por su madre, en particular, tenía una veneración profunda. No mentía jamás. ¿Acaso por ser un ser salvaje en el fondo de su naturaleza? Es posible; pues no se sabe aún qué influencia puede tener en un animal recién nacido la pureza de una alma bebida con la leche en el seno de una santa mujer. 5

Tal era Juan Darién. E iba a la escuela con los chicos de su edad, los que se burlaban a menudo de él, a causa de su pelo áspero y su timidez. Juan Darién no era muy inteligente; pero compensaba esto con su gran amor al estudio.

Así las cosas, cuando la criatura iba a cumplir diez años, su madre murió. Juan Darién sufrió lo que no es decible, hasta que el tiempo apaciguó su pena. 10 Pero fue en adelante un muchacho triste, que sólo deseaba instruirse.

Algo debemos confesar ahora: a Juan Darién no se le amaba en el pueblo. La gente de los pueblos encerrados en la selva no gustan de los muchachos demasiado generosos y que estudian con toda el alma. Era, además, el primer alumno de la escuela. Y este conjunto precipitó el desenlace con un acontecimiento que 15 dio razón a la profecía de la serpiente.[9]

Apróntabase el pueblo a celebrar una gran fiesta, y de la ciudad distante habían mandado fuegos artificiales. En la escuela se dio un repaso general a los chicos, pues un inspector debía venir a observar las clases. Cuando el inspector llegó, el maestro hizo dar la lección al primero de todos: a Juan Darién. Juan 20 Darién era el alumno más aventajado; pero con la emoción del caso, tartamudeó y la lengua se le trabó con un sonido extraño.

El inspector observó al alumno un largo rato, y habló en seguida en voz baja con el maestro.

—¿Quién es ese muchacho? —le preguntó—. ¿De dónde ha salido? 25

—Se llama Juan Darién —respondió el maestro—, y lo crió una mujer que ya ha muerto; pero nadie sabe de dónde ha venido.

—Es extraño, muy extraño... —murmuró el inspector, observando el pelo áspero y el reflejo verdoso que tenían los ojos de Juan Darién cuando estaba en la sombra. 30

El inspector sabía que en el mundo hay cosas mucho más extrañas que las que nadie[10] puede inventar, y sabía al mismo tiempo que con preguntas a Juan Darién nunca podría averiguar si el alumno había sido antes lo que él temía: esto es, un animal salvaje. Pero así como hay hombres que en estados especiales recuerdan cosas que les han pasado a sus abuelos, así era también posible que, 35 bajo una sugestión hipnótica, Juan Darién recordara su vida de bestia salvaje.

Por lo cual el inspector subió a la tarima y habló así:

—Bien, niño. Deseo ahora que uno de ustedes nos describa la selva. Ustedes se han criado casi en ella y la conocen bien. ¿Cómo es la selva? ¿Qué pasa en

---

[9]*dio... serpiente:* confirmed the serpent's prophecy   [10]*nadie:* anyone

ella? Esto es lo que quiero saber. Vamos a ver, tú —añadió, dirigiéndose a un alumno cualquiera[11]—. Sube a la tarima y cuéntanos lo que hayas visto.

El chico subió, y aunque estaba asustado, habló un rato. Dijo que en el bosque hay árboles gigantes, enredaderas y florecillas. Cuando concluyó, pasó
5 otro chico a la tarima, y después otro. Y aunque todos conocían bien la selva, todos respondieron lo mismo, porque los chicos y muchos hombres no cuentan lo que ven, sino lo que han leído sobre lo mismo que acaban de ver. Y al fin el inspector dijo:

—Ahora le toca al alumno Juan Darién.
10 Juan Darién dijo más o menos lo que los otros. Pero el inspector, poniéndole la mano sobre el hombro, exclamó:

—No, no. Quiero que tú recuerdes bien lo que has visto. Cierra los ojos. Juan Darién cerró los ojos.

—Bien —prosiguió el inspector—. Dime lo que ves en la selva.
15 Juan Darién, siempre con los ojos cerrados, demoró un instante en contestar.

—Pronto vas a ver. Figurémonos que son las tres de la mañana, poco antes del amanecer. Hemos concluido de comer, por ejemplo... Estamos en la selva, en la obscuridad... Delante de nosotros hay un arroyo... ¿Qué ves?

Juan Darién pasó otro momento en silencio. Y en la clase y en el bosque
20 próximo había también un gran silencio. De pronto Juan Darién se estremeció, y con voz lenta, como si soñara, dijo:

—Veo las piedras que pasan y las ramas que se doblan... Y el suelo... Y veo las hojas secas que se quedan aplastadas sobre las piedras...

—¡Un momento! —le interrumpió el inspector—. Las piedras y las hojas que
25 pasan, ¿a qué altura las ves?

El inspector preguntaba esto porque si Juan Darién estaba «viendo» efectivamente lo que él hacía en la selva cuando era animal salvaje e iba a beber después de haber comido, vería también que las piedras que encuentra un tigre o una pantera que se acercan muy agachados al río pasan a la altura de los ojos. Y
30 repitió:

—¿A qué altura ves las piedras?

Y Juan Darién, siempre con los ojos cerrados, respondió:

—Pasan sobre el suelo... Rozan las orejas... Y las hojas sueltas se mueven con el aliento... Y siento la humedad del barro en...
35 La voz de Juan Darién se cortó.

—¿En dónde? —preguntó con voz firme el inspector—. ¿Dónde sientes la humedad del agua?

—¡En los bigotes! —dijo con voz ronca Juan Darién, abriendo los ojos espantado.

---

[11]*un alumno cualquiera:* the first student he saw

Comenzaba el crepúsculo, y por la ventana se veía cerca la selva ya lóbrega. Los alumnos no comprendieron lo terrible de aquella evocación; pero tampoco se rieron de esos extraordinarios bigotes de Juan Darién, que no tenía bigote alguno. Y no se rieron, porque el rostro de la criatura estaba pálido y ansioso.

La clase había concluido. El inspector no era un mal hombre; pero, como todos los hombres que viven muy cerca de la selva, odiaba ciegamente a los tigres; por lo cual dijo en voz baja al maestro:

—Es preciso matar a Juan Darién. Es una fiera del bosque, posiblemente un tigre. Debemos matarlo, porque, si no, él, tarde o temprano, nos matará a todos. Hasta ahora su maldad de fiera no ha despertado; pero explotará un día u otro, y entonces nos devorará a todos, puesto que le permitimos vivir con nosotros. Debemos pues, matarlo. La dificultad está en que no podemos hacerlo mientras tenga forma humana, porque no podremos probar ante todos que es un tigre. Parece un hombre, y con los hombres hay que proceder con cuidado. Yo sé que en la ciudad hay un domador de fieras. Llamémoslo, y él hallará modo de que Juan Darién vuelva a su cuerpo de tigre. Y aunque no pueda convertirlo en tigre, las gentes nos creerán y podremos echarlo a la selva. Llamemos en seguida al domador, antes que Juan Darién se escape.

Pero Juan Darién pensaba en todo menos en escaparse,[12] porque no se daba cuenta de nada. ¿Cómo podía creer que él no era hombre, cuando jamás había sentido otra cosa que amor a todos, y ni siquiera tenía odio a los animales dañinos?

Mas las voces fueron corriendo de boca en boca,[13] y Juan Darién comenzó a sufrir sus efectos. No le respondían una palabra, se apartaban vivamente a su paso, y lo seguían desde lejos de noche.

—¿Qué tendré? ¿Por qué son así conmigo? —se preguntaba Juan Darién.

Y ya no solamente huían de él, sino que los muchachos le gritaban:

—¡Fuera de aquí! ¡Vuélvete donde has venido! ¡Fuera!

Los grandes también, las personas mayores, no estaban menos enfurecidas que los muchachos. Quién sabe qué llega a pasar[14] si la misma tarde de la fiesta no hubiera llegado por fin el ansiado domador de fieras. Juan Darién estaba en su casa preparándose la pobre sopa que tomaba, cuando oyó la gritería de las gentes que avanzaban precipitadas hacia su casa. Apenas tuvo tiempo de salir a ver qué era. Se apoderaron de él, arrastrándolo hasta la casa del domador.

—¡Aquí está! —gritaban, sacudiéndolo—. ¡Es éste! ¡Es un tigre! ¡No queremos saber nada con[15] tigres! ¡Quítele su figura de hombre y lo mataremos!

Y los muchachos, sus condiscípulos a quienes más quería, y las mismas personas viejas, gritaban:

—¡Es un tigre! ¡Juan Darién nos va a devorar! ¡Muera Juan Darién![16]

---

[12]*pensaba... escaparse:* was thinking about anything but escaping   [13]*Mas... boca:* But the news began to spread   [14]*qué llega a pasar:* what would have happened   [15]*saber nada con:* to have anything to do with   [16]*¡Muera Juan Darién!* Death to Juan Darién!

Juan Darién protestaba y lloraba porque los golpes llovían sobre él, y era una criatura de doce años. Pero en ese momento la gente se apartó, y el domador, con grandes botas de charol, levita roja y un látigo en la mano, surgió ante Juan Darién. El domador lo miró fijamente, y apretó con fuerza el puño del látigo.

5 —¡Ah! —exclamó—. ¡Te reconozco bien! ¡A todos puedes engañar, menos a mí! ¡Te estoy viendo, hijo de tigres! ¡Bajo tu camisa estoy viendo las rayas del tigre! ¡Fuera la camisa, y traigan los perros cazadores! ¡Veremos ahora si los perros te reconocen como hombre o como tigre!

En un segundo arrancaron toda la ropa a Juan Darién y lo arrojaron dentro 10 de la jaula para fieras.

—¡Suelten los perros, pronto! —gritó el domador—. ¡Y encomiéndate a los dioses de tu selva, Juan Darién!

Y cuatro feroces perros cazadores de tigres fueron lanzados dentro de la jaula.

El domador hizo esto porque los perros reconocen siempre el olor del tigre; y 15 en cuanto olfatearan a Juan Darién sin ropa, lo harían pedazos, pues podrían ver con sus ojos de perros cazadores las rayas de tigre ocultas bajo la piel de hombre.

Pero los perros no vieron otra cosa en Juan Darién que al muchacho bueno que quería hasta a los mismos animales dañinos. Y movían apacibles la cola al olerlo.

20 —¡Devóralo! ¡Es un tigre! ¡Toca! ¡Toca![17] —gritaban a los perros. Y los perros ladraban y saltaban enloquecidos por la jaula, sin saber a qué atacar.

La prueba no había dado resultado.

—¡Muy bien! —exclamó entonces el domador—. Éstos son perros bastardos, de casta de tigre. No lo reconocen. Pero yo te reconozco, Juan Darién, y ahora 25 nos vamos a ver nosotros.[18]

Y así diciendo entró él en la jaula y levantó el látigo.

—¡Tigre! —gritó—. ¡Estás ante un hombre, y tú eres un tigre! ¡Allí estoy viendo, bajo tu piel robada de hombre, las rayas de tigre! ¡Muestra las rayas!

Y cruzó el cuerpo de Juan Darién de un feroz latigazo. La pobre criatura 30 desnuda lanzó un alarido de dolor, mientras las gentes, enfurecidas, repetían:

—¡Muestra las rayas de tigre!

Durante un rato prosiguió el atroz suplicio; y no deseo que los niños que me oyen vean martirizar de este modo a ser alguno.[19]

—¡Por favor! ¡Me muero! —clamaba Juan Darién.

35 —¡Muestra las rayas! —le respondían.

—¡No, no! ¡Yo soy hombre! ¡Ay, mamá! —sollozaba el infeliz.

—¡Muestra las rayas! —le respondían.

Por fin el suplicio concluyó. En el fondo de la jaula, arrinconado, aniquilado en un rincón, sólo quedaba su cuerpo sangriento de niño, que había sido Juan

---

[17]*¡Toca! ¡Toca!* Sic'im!   [18]*nos... nosotros:* you and I are going to have it out   [19]*no... alguno:* I don't want the children who are listening to me to see any creature tortured this way.

Darién. Vivía aún, y aún podía caminar cuando se le sacó de allí; pero lleno de tales sufrimientos como nadie los sentirá nunca.

Lo sacaron de la jaula, y empujándolo por el medio de la calle, lo echaban del pueblo. Iba cayéndose a cada momento, y detrás de él los muchachos, las mujeres y los hombres maduros, empujándolo.

—¡Fuera de aquí, Juan Darién! ¡Vuélvete a la selva, hijo de tigre y corazón de tigre! ¡Fuera, Juan Darién!

Y los que estaban lejos y no podían pegarle, le tiraban piedras.

Juan Darién cayó del todo,[20] por fin, tendiendo en busca de apoyo sus pobres manos de niño. Y su cruel destino quiso que una mujer, que estaba parada a la puerta de su casa sosteniendo en los brazos a una inocente criatura, interpretara mal ese ademán de súplica.

—¡Me ha querido robar mi hijo! —gritó la mujer—. ¡Ha tendido las manos para matarlo! ¡Es un tigre! ¡Matémosle en seguida, antes que él mate a nuestros hijos!

Así dijo la mujer. Y de este modo se cumplía la profecía de la serpiente: Juan Darién moriría cuando una madre de los hombres le exigiera la vida y el corazón de hombre que otra madre le había dado con su pecho.[21]

No era necesaria otra acusación para decidir a las gentes enfurecidas. Y veinte brazos con piedras en la mano se levantaban ya para aplastar a Juan Darién cuando el domador ordenó desde atrás con voz ronca:

—¡Marquémoslo con rayas de fuego! ¡Quemémoslo en los fuegos artificiales!

Ya comenzaba a obscurecer, y cuando llegaron a la plaza era noche cerrada. En la plaza habían levantado un castillo de fuegos de artificio, con ruedas, coronas y luces de bengala. Ataron en lo alto del centro a Juan Darién, y prendieron la mecha desde un extremo. El hilo de fuego corrió velozmente subiendo y bajando, y encendió el castillo entero. Y entre las estrellas fijas y las ruedas gigantes de todos colores, se vio allá arriba a Juan Darién sacrificado.

—¡Es tu último día de hombre, Juan Darién! —clamaban todos—. ¡Muestra las rayas!

—¡Perdón, perdón! —gritaba la criatura, retorciéndose entre las chispas y las nubes de humo. Las ruedas amarillas, rojas y verdes giraban vertiginosamente, unas a la derecha y otras a la izquierda. Los chorros de fuego tangente trazaban grandes circunferencias; y en el medio, quemado por los regueros de chispas que le cruzaban el cuerpo, se retorcía Juan Darién.

—¡Muestra las rayas! —rugían aún de abajo.

—¡No, perdón! ¡Yo soy hombre! —tuvo aún tiempo de clamar la infeliz criatura. Y tras un nuevo surco de fuego, se pudo ver que su cuerpo se sacudía convulsivamente; que sus gemidos adquirían un timbre profundo y ronco, y que su cuerpo cambiaba poco a poco de forma. Y la muchedumbre, con un grito

---

[20]*cayó del todo:* fell down flat   [21]*había... pecho:* had offered him at her breast

salvaje de triunfo, pudo ver surgir por fin, bajo la piel del hombre, las rayas negras, paralelas y fatales del tigre.

La atroz obra de crueldad se había cumplido; habían conseguido lo que querían. En vez de la criatura inocente de toda culpa, allá arriba no había sino
5 un cuerpo de tigre que agonizaba rugiendo.

Las luces de bengala se iban también apagando. Un último chorro de chispas con que moría una rueda alcanzó la soga atada a las muñecas (no: a las patas del tigre, pues Juan Darién había concluido), y el cuerpo cayó pesadamente al suelo. Las gentes lo arrastraron hasta la linde del bosque, abandonándolo allí para que
10 los chacales devoraran su cadáver y su corazón de fiera.

Pero el tigre no había muerto. Con la frescura nocturna volvió en sí, y arrastrándose presa de horribles tormentos se internó en la selva. Durante un mes entero no abandonó su guarida en lo más tupido del bosque, esperando con sombría paciencia de fiera que sus heridas curaran. Todas cicatrizaron por fin,
15 menos una, una profunda quemadura en el costado, que no cerraba, y que el tigre vendó con grandes hojas.

Porque había conservado de su forma recién perdida tres cosas: el recuerdo vivo del pasado, la habilidad de sus manos, que manejaba como un hombre, y el lenguaje. Pero en el resto, absolutamente en todo, era una fiera, que no se
20 distinguía en lo más mínimo de los otros tigres.

Cuando se sintió por fin curado, pasó la voz[22] a los demás tigres de la selva para que esa misma noche se reunieran delante del gran cañaveral que lindaba con los cultivos. Y al entrar la noche se encaminó silenciosamente al pueblo. Trepó a un árbol de los alrededores y esperó largo tiempo inmóvil. Vio pasar
25 bajo él sin inquietarse a mirar siquiera, pobres mujeres y labradores fatigados, de aspecto miserable; hasta que al fin vio avanzar por el camino a un hombre de grandes botas y levita roja.

El tigre no movió una sola ramita al recogerse para saltar. Saltó sobre el domador; de una manotada lo derribó desmayado, y cogiéndolo entre los
30 dientes por la cintura, lo llevó sin hacerle daño hasta el juncal.

Allí, al pie de las inmensas cañas que se alzaban invisibles, estaban los tigres de la selva moviéndose en la obscuridad, y sus ojos brillaban como luces que van de un lado para otro. El hombre proseguía desmayado. El tigre dijo entonces:

—Hermanos: Yo viví doce años entre los hombres, como un hombre mismo.
35 Y yo soy un tigre. Tal vez pueda con mi proceder borrar más tarde esta mancha. Hermanos: Esta noche rompo el último lazo que me liga al pasado.

Y después de hablar así, recogió en la boca al hombre, que proseguía desmayado, y trepó con él a lo más alto del cañaveral, donde lo dejó atado entre dos bambúes. Luego prendió fuego a las hojas secas del suelo, y pronto una llama-
40 rada crujiente ascendió.

[22]*pasó la voz:* he spread the word

Los tigres retrocedían espantados ante el fuego. Pero el tigre les dijo: «¡Paz, hermanos!» Y aquéllos se apaciguaron, sentándose de vientre[23] con las patas cruzadas a mirar.

El juncal ardía como un inmenso castillo de artificio. Las cañas estallaban como bombas, y sus gases se cruzaban en agudas flechas de color. Las llamaradas ascendían en bruscas y sordas bocanadas, dejando bajo ellas lívidos huecos; y en la cúspide, donde aún no llegaba el fuego, las cañas se balanceaban crispadas por el calor.

Pero el hombre, tocado por las llamas, había vuelto en sí. Vio allá abajo a los tigres con los ojos cárdenos alzados a él, y lo comprendió todo.

—¡Perdón, perdónenme! —aulló retorciéndose—. ¡Pido perdón por todo!

Nadie contestó. El hombre se sintió entonces abandonado de Dios, y gritó con toda su alma:

—¡Perdón, Juan Darién!

Al oír esto, Juan Darién, alzó la cabeza y dijo fríamente:

—Aquí no hay nadie que se llame Juan Darién. No conozco a Juan Darién. Éste es un nombre de hombre y aquí somos todos tigres.

Y volviéndose a sus compañeros, como si no comprendiera, preguntó:

—¿Alguno de ustedes se llama Juan Darién?

Pero ya las llamas habían abrasado el castillo hasta el cielo. Y entre las agudas luces de bengala que entrecruzaban la pared ardiente, se pudo ver allá arriba un cuerpo negro que se quemaba humeando.

—Ya estoy pronto, hermanos —dijo el tigre—. Pero aún me queda algo por hacer.

Y se encaminó de nuevo al pueblo, seguido por los tigres sin que él lo notara. Se detuvo ante un pobre y triste jardín, saltó la pared, y pasando al costado de muchas cruces y lápidas, fue a detenerse ante un pedazo de tierra sin ningún adorno, donde estaba enterrada la mujer a quien había llamado madre ocho años. Se arrodilló —se arrodilló como un hombre—, y durante un rato no se oyó nada.

—¡Madre! —murmuró por fin el tigre con profunda ternura—. Tú sola supiste, entre todos los hombres, los sagrados derechos a la vida de todos los seres del Universo. Tú sola comprendiste que el hombre y el tigre se diferencian únicamente por el corazón. Y tú me enseñaste a amar, a comprender, a perdonar. ¡Madre! Estoy seguro de que me oyes. Soy tu hijo siempre, a pesar de lo que pase en adelante, pero de ti sólo. ¡Adiós, madre mía!

Y viendo al incorporarse los ojos cárdenos de sus hermanos que lo observaban tras la tapia, se unió otra vez a ellos.

El viento cálido les trajo en ese momento, desde el fondo de la noche, el estampido de un tiro.

[23]*sentándose de vientre:* lying on their stomachs

—Es en la selva —dijo el tigre—. Son los hombres. Están cazando, matando, degollando.

Volviéndose entonces hacia el pueblo que iluminaba el reflejo de la selva encendida, exclamó:

5 —¡Raza sin redención! ¡Ahora me toca a mí!

Y retornando a la tumba en que acababa de orar, arrancóse de un manotón[24] la venda de la herida y escribió en la cruz con su propia sangre, en grandes caracteres, debajo del nombre de su madre:

Y

JUAN DARIÉN

10

—Ya estamos en paz —dijo. Y enviando con sus hermanos un rugido de desafío al pueblo aterrado, concluyó:

—Ahora, a la selva. ¡Y tigre para siempre!

EXERCISES

A. Questions and Opinions

1. ¿Quién era Juan Darién?
2. ¿Qué representaba el cachorro para la madre que lo crió?
3. ¿Por qué quería entrar un hombre a la casa de la mujer?
4. ¿Qué mandó la vieja serpiente que la madre hiciera con el tigrecito?
5. ¿Qué condición puso la serpiente en su profecía?
6. ¿Por qué no tuvo la madre interés en volver a casarse?
7. ¿Cómo era Juan Darién?
8. ¿Por qué no se le amaba a Juan en el pueblo?
9. ¿Qué sospechaba el inspector?
10. ¿Qué esperaba descubrir con la sugestión hipnótica?
11. ¿En qué se diferenciaba la descripción de la selva que hizo Juan de las de los otros alumnos?
12. ¿Por qué era necesario matar a Juan Darién?
13. ¿Por qué hizo llamar el inspector al domador de fieras?
14. ¿Qué esperaba el domador que los perros hicieran con Juan?
15. ¿Cómo se cumplió la profecía de la serpiente?
16. ¿Qué le hicieron a Juan para que mostrara sus rayas?

---

[24]*de un manotón:* with one swipe of his paw (hand)

17. ¿Cómo se escapó Juan después de ser quemado en medio de los fuegos artificiales?
18. ¿Cómo se vengó Juan del domador?
19. ¿Qué cosa era lo que únicamente la madre de Juan había comprendido?
20. ¿Con quiénes se marchó Juan al final del cuento?
•21. ¿Es cierto que nosotros los seres humanos podemos ser más crueles que los animales?
•22. ¿Cree Ud. que un acto de venganza puede ser justificado? Explique su respuesta.

B. Verb Practice

Use each of the following verbal phrases in an original sentence in Spanish, either based on the story or of your own design. Be prepared to explain the meaning of your sentences.

1. **asistir a**
2. **dormirse**
3. **bastar**
4. **cumplir... años**
5. **tocarle a uno**
6. **demorar (en** + *infinitive)*
7. **moverse**
8. **hay que** + *infinitive*
9. **ir** + *present participle*
10. **volverse**

C. Vocabulary Practice

Complete the sentences below, matching the expressions on the right with the English words on the left. Be sure to use the correct form of each verb. Then use each expression in an original Spanish sentence and indicate in English what your sentence means.

1. Juan Darién *often* deseaba volver a la selva como tigre.   **a menos que**
2. *In this way,* el domador de fieras podría revelar el secreto de Juan Darién.   **por todas partes**
3. Seguiría así como tigre *unless* una madre lo acusara.   **burlarse de**
4. Buscaron a Juan Darién *everywhere.*   **a menudo**
5. Los animales, *for example,* los perros cazadores de tigres, lo reconocerían.   **por ejemplo**
6. *Since* Horacio Quiroga vivió un tiempo en la selva, muchos cuentos suyos tratan de los animales salvajes.   **reírse (de)**

7. Juan Darién tendría que confesar su identidad *sooner or later*. **de este modo**

8. Los demás chicos *didn't laugh at* Juan Darién. **puesto que**

9. También tenían miedo de *make fun of him*. **ni siquiera**

10. Ellos *didn't even* querían jugar con él. **tarde o temprano**

D. Communication Practice

1. Say that in two weeks you will be twenty-one years old.
2. Ask whose turn it is to prepare dinner.
3. Indicate that it's necessary to wash the dishes before going to bed.
4. Tell a friend that $10 would be enough.
5. Say that last night you fell asleep before eight o'clock.

E. Review Exercise

The following *reflexive* verbs that appear in this story have *non-reflexive* counterparts; for example, **apartarse** *to move aside* and **apartar** *to put aside*. Give the meaning of each member of the pair and use them in Spanish sentences. For example, ¡**Apártense todos!** *Everybody step back!* **Hay que apartar todos los malos.** *You have to put aside (separate) all the bad ones.*

llamarse	casarse	volverse
dormirse	criarse	levantarse
detenerse	dirigirse	apagarse
hallarse	acercarse	sentirse

NOSOTRAS

María Elena Llana

MARÍA ELENA LLANA was born in Cuba in 1936. While still in her twenties, she published *La reja,* a volume of short stories from which the present narrative is taken. She is one of a large group of authors who, writing either in political exile or from the perspective of present-day Cuban life, have brought Cuban literature into a position of prominence it has never enjoyed before.

In recent years, Spanish-American women have assumed a more important and active role in the area of cultural activities. Increasing attention is being given today to the contributions of women to the literature of the Spanish-American nations, and these writers have now begun to fill in—sensitively and eloquently—the previously substantial gaps in the depiction of life and customs in our hemisphere.

«Nosotras» is an unusual story, a lucidly narrated and unsettling adventure that takes place in an impressionable dimension of the mind. It all starts out so innocently, with a wisp of a recollection from a dream. But the narrator has soon passed from the state of sleeping and dreaming into a more troubled waking state, one of growing incredulity and self-doubt. The story's ending—deliberately inconclusive—is but one more disconcerting feature of this narrative.

A PRELIMINARY LOOK AT KEY EXPRESSIONS

Be sure to study these expressions before you read the story.

1. (78: 1) **alegrarse** *to be happy, glad*
2. (78: 3) **justamente** *just, exactly, right*
3. (78: 5) **en vez de** *instead of*
4. (78: 9) **lavarse los dientes** *to brush* or *clean one's teeth* As usual with verbs having to do with personal bodily and grooming habits, the part of the body or article of clothing involved is preceded by the definite article rather than the possessive, and the verb in question is accompanied by a reflexive pronoun: **Ella se lavó los dientes.** *She brushed her (own) teeth.* If someone else performs the action on the first party, the latter is expressed by the indirect object: **El dentista le lavó los dientes.** *The dentist cleaned her teeth.*
5. (78:10) **mediodía** *noon* The definite article is added when the expression contains *at:* **al mediodía.**
6. (78:15) **descolgar** *to lift, pick up (the phone)* Literally, **descolgar** is *to unhook, take down.* The opposite is **colgar** (literally, *to hang)* to hang up (the phone).
7. (78:22) **bueno** *well, so* An introductory phrase to indicate that the speaker wants to change the subject, end the conversation, take some action, etc. To indicate approval, *good* is **bien, está bien, de acuerdo,** and other such phrases.
8. (78:23) **preguntar por** *to ask for; to inquire about* This expression is used both to request to talk to someone and to inquire about one's health. *To ask for,* in the sense of *request,* is **pedir.**
9. (79: 5) **arriesgarse (a)** *to take a chance* Notice that the verb retains the **ie** in all forms: **Tú te arriesgas, Nosotros nos arriesgamos,** etc.
10. (79:11) **recostarse** *to lie down, lean back, stretch out* This verb is used for a more temporary casual action; **acostarse** normally means *to lie down (to sleep)* or *to go to bed.*
11. (79:17) **sino** *but* (in the sense of *but rather* or *but also)* This word is used when what follows contradicts or replaces a previous negative element: **no el espejo sino el teléfono** *not the mirror but (rather) the telephone.* **No sólo...** always elicits the use of **sino** or **sino que** if a conjugated verb follows: **No sólo la llamó sino que le habló largo rato.** *She not only called her but talked to her for a long while.*
12. (79:21) **no poder más** *not to be able to go on, stand it* The phrase almost always stands alone rather than forming part of a longer sentence: **No puedo más.** *I'm all in; I've had it.*
13. (79:23) **mientras** *while*
14. (80: 4) **desde luego** *of course, naturally*

15. (80: 8) **molestar** *to bother, annoy* The person bothered is the indirect object: **Eso no le molestó nada.** *That didn't bother her at all.*
16. (80:10) **acabar por** + *infinitive   to end (by)* + *present participle:* **Acabé por llamarla.** *I ended up (by) calling her.*
17. (81: 7) **sea como sea** *be that as it may*
18. (81:23) **a riesgo de** *at the risk of*
19. (81:28) **a punto de** *on the point of*
20. (82:18) **tranquilizarse** *to calm down*   Like so many verbs that indicate a change in physical or emotional state, this one is usually reflexive. However, it can be used with a direct object when a second party is involved: **El pensamiento mismo me tranquiliza.** *The very thought makes me feel calm.*

NOSOTRAS

Soñé que venían de la Compañía a cambiar el número del teléfono. «Me alegro mucho —dije—, porque se pasan el día llamando a un número parecido y porque otros, cualquiera sabe quién o quiénes,[1] llaman justamente los sábados a las tres de la madrugada...» Bueno, a ellos no les interesó mucho mi alegría. Lo cambiaron y eso fue todo. Y yo, en vez de mirar al redondelito del centro del aparato, ahí donde se escribe el número, les pregunté: «¿Qué número es?» Y me respondieron: «El 20-58».

Brumas. Algo incoherente. Brumas. Despierto y doy los pasos de siempre:[2] desayuno, me lavo los dientes, tiendo la cama... Empieza un día como otro. Sin saber por qué, nunca se sabe exactamente por qué, al mediodía un número surge en mi cerebro, aletargado por la blandura de la hora.[3] «El 20...» Ligero gesto de extrañeza. ¿El 20...? Brumas. Algo incoherente. Brumas. ¡El 20-58! Sonrisa. ¡Es verdad, el 20-58! E inmediatamente, el gesto fatal: coger el teléfono y canalizar[4] una infantil curiosidad... Rac-rac-rac-rac. Y un timbrazo opaco y lejano inicia la conversación. Alguien descuelga y, pese a los vericuetos del hilo[5] la voz llega extrañamente lisa, extrañamente familiar.

—Oigo.[6]

—¿Qué casa?

—¿A quién desea?

—¿Es el 20-58?

—Sí.

Esa voz, esa voz... Bueno, continuemos la tontería. Si se supone que ése es mi nuevo número, preguntaré por mí misma.

—Con... Fulana.[7]

—Es la que habla.

Claro, algo de estupor. Estas cosas nunca pueden evitarse. Momento de vacilación. Algo incoherente pero ahora sin brumas. Insistencia desde el otro lado.

—Sí, soy yo, ¿quién es?

Total desconcierto. Mi misma imagen devuelta...[8] Bueno, hay que salir de esto. No se me ocurre nada más que la verdad y la digo no sin cierto temor.

---

[1]*cualquiera... quiénes:* I have no idea who   [2]*doy... siempre:* I follow my regular routine   [3]*aletargado... hora:* groggy from the midday heat   [4]*canalizar:* give in to   [5]*pese... hilo:* despite the long tortuous route of the telephone wire   [6]*Oigo:* Hello (literally, "I hear")   [7]*Fulana:* a fictitious name used in Spanish for any woman in general, like Jane Doe, so-and-so, such-and-such, what's-her-name, etc.   [8]*Mi misma imagen devuelta:* My own voice coming right back at me

—Soy yo, Fulana.

Pudo colgar, pudo decir cualquier cosa, pudo no decir nada, pudo hablar en copto,[9] pero lo que no debió decir nunca fue lo que dijo:

—Al fin me llamas.

5 Me arriesgo:

—Pero oye..., soy Fulana... de Tal.[10]

—Sí, ya lo sé. También yo soy Fulana de Tal.

Es demasiado. Un estremecimiento me recorre el espinazo... Ahora ya no sé qué decir. Esta vez, sin contenerme, en espera a que la otra cuelgue, cuelgo yo y

10 me quedo con la mano sobre el auricular, mirando el aparato como si fuera un animalejo que de un momento a otro pudiera echar a andar. Suspiro. Me recuesto en el sofá. ¿Una broma? ¿Habré hablado en sueños? ¿Se enteraría alguien de...?[11] ¡Pero si[12] es imposible!

Y ya todo gira como el rac-rac-rac-rac del 20-58. Puedo ir y venir por la casa,

15 arreglar este adornito, aderezar aquel marco, calentar el café, pero es como si estuviera vigilada. Como si los ojos que me siguen salieran del teléfono; no que estuvieran agazapados en él, sino que simplemente esperaran su momento. Había dicho «Al fin me llamas», y pudiera creerse que llevaba esperando mil años, por sólo hablar de los últimos tiempos. Voy y vengo; rehúyo cruzar muy

20 cerca del teléfono y después me río de mis aprensiones. «¡Como si tuviera garras que fueran a cogerme por la saya!» Hacia las seis de la tarde ya no puedo más. Descuelgo. Me falta un poco la respiración. Rac-rac-rac-rac. El corazón tamborilea mientras aguardo. Cuando al fin oigo su voz ya no sé qué me pasa.

—Oigo.

25 No puedo evitarlo, tartamudeo:

—¿El... 20... 58...?

—Sí.

—¿Quién habla?

La voz me salió valiente,[13] pero la respuesta tuvo el mismo efecto de un

30 cubito de hielo concienzudamente pasado a lo largo de la columna vertebral.

—Sí, soy yo. Ya sé que eres tú otra vez.

—¿Yo? ¿Quién?

—Yo misma.

Esto parece complicarse. Ahora me acometen deseos de discutir. Digo con

35 acento de poner las cosas en su lugar.[14]

—Tú misma, no. Yo misma.

---

[9]*copto:* Coptic, an extinct language of ancient Egypt, still used by Egyptian Christians in their liturgy. We might say "Greek" in such a situation.   [10]*Fulana... de Tal: de Tal* is often added to such imaginary names (see note 7)   [11]*¿Se enteraría alguien de...?* Could anyone have found out about. . .? Note again the use of the conditional to express conjecture in the past.   [12]*si:* should not be translated   [13]*La... valiente:* My voice came out sounding brave   [14]*con... lugar:* in a very businesslike tone

—Es igual.

—Pero aunque todo esto fuera algo juicioso, yo estoy primero.[15]

—¿Por qué? ¿No eres Fulana de Tal?

—Sí, desde luego.

—Pero es que yo soy Fulana de Tal.   5

—Aunque sea verdad, hay que aclarar que tú eres también Fulana de Tal.

—¿Y por qué? Yo soy Fulana de Tal. Tú eres Fulana de Tal *también.*

Ahora ya no me desconcierta, me molesta. Estoy enfureciéndome, pero de pronto... Sí, pudiera ser... Hay que investigar un poco más, eso es todo. Han sido coincidencias, pero las coincidencias acaban por fallar cuando se razona.[16] Mi   10
voz suena conciliadora, casi gentil, cuando digo:

—Es mejor ir despacio. Veamos:[17] las dos nos llamamos Fulana de Tal y eso es ya una casualidad.

—¿Tú crees?

Su tonito irónico, desafiante, me desarma. Continúo todo lo gentil que   15
puedo, dadas las circunstancias.

—Yo nací en el pueblo de...

—De X, exactamente. Yo nací allí; hija de Zutana y Esperancejo.[18]

Trago en seco,[19] pero no me dejo abatir. Le espeto como un fiscal:

—¡Segundo apellido!   20

—Tal, querida. Soy Tal y Tal.

Ahora ya empiezo a sentirme decididamente mal. ¿Quién puede saber todo eso? ¿De quién es la broma? ¿De quién el ardid? Ella toma la iniciativa:

—¿Qué te pasa? ¿Por qué ponerte así? ¿Ves que no miento? ¿Por qué habría de hacerlo?[20]   25

Quisiera contenerme. Si en definitiva es cierto lo que ocurre, no hay razón para que ella lo tome así, tranquilamente, y yo lo tome así, arrebatadamente. Pero me siento engañada. Siento que alguien se ha confabulado. No puedo evitarlo. Entonces, jugándome el todo por el todo,[21] pregunto:

—Si somos la misma, debemos serlo en todo, ¿no? ¿Cómo estoy vestida?   30

—Con mi bata..., es decir, voy a evitar el posesivo. Con la bata de casa azul. Por cierto que ya el descosido de la manga molesta.[22]

—Sí, molesta, pero...

Me detengo. ¿Por qué camino estoy tomando? ¿Es que voy a transigir? No, no. Ahora ella habla otra vez, es decir, no tengo constancia de que sea «ella».   35
Para ser más exacta, me escucho decir:

---

[15]*primero:* here an adverb, thus showing no agreement with the female subject after the verb *estoy*   [16]*las... razona:* coincidences don't hold up when you submit them to logic   [17]*Veamos:* See here   [18]*Zutana y Esperancejo:* These are both imaginary names like *Fulana.*   [19]*Trago en seco:* I gulp (literally, "I swallow dry")   [20]*¿Por qué... hacerlo?* Why would I want to do that?   [21]*jugándome... todo:* going all the way (literally, "Gambling everything for everything")   [22]*Por... molesta:* Of course, those stitches coming out on the sleeve are annoying.

—La aguja está en una esquina de la gaveta superior de la mesita de noche. La dejaste allí la última vez que la usaste, y yo, desde luego, la volví a colocar.[23] Cuando creíste que se había perdido, era que yo estaba zurciendo la sayuela rosada.

5   Ahora empiezo a flaquear. Ayer me sorprendió ver la sayuela cosida y deduje que lo había hecho la lavandera, lo que es muy extraño, pero no le vi otra explicación.[24] Sea como sea, algo se ha ablandado en mí. Casi estoy a punto de suplicar cuando digo:

—¿A qué conduce esto?

10   —No sé. Fuiste tú quien llamó, ¿recuerdas? ¿Por qué lo hiciste?

¿Qué puedo contestarle? ¿Decirle lo del sueño? De pronto me siento infeliz. Todas las fuerzas ceden ante esta repentina autoconmiseración... Ella me hace dar un salto:

—Por favor, me haces sentir mal. ¿Por qué este estado de ánimo?

15   Ya no puedo menos que[25] indignarme.

—¿Hasta cuándo va a durar esto?

—Hasta que tú quieras. Basta que cuelgues.[26] Nunca te he molestado, ¿no? ¿Por qué balbuceo? No lo sé:

—¿Y si... si cuelgo...?

20   —No volverás a saber de mí, como hasta ahora.[27] Todo esto lo empezaste tú.

Estoy dispuesta a colgar. Hay algo irritante en... en..., ¡bueno,[28] en ella! Pero ha sido tan comprensiva, tan paciente, ¿qué derecho tengo para enojarme? Sin embargo, aun a riesgo de parecer infantil, pregunto:

—¿Puedo saber cuál es tu dirección?

25   —Está en la Guía.

—¿A nombre de quién?

—Mío, desde luego.

Estoy a punto de caer en la trampa, pero reacciono:

—Si tu nombre es el mío, lo buscaré y encontraré mi propia dirección.

30   —Es lógico.

Ya vuelvo a desesperarme.

—Pero y entonces, ¿cómo puedes tener un teléfono distinto?

—La que lo tiene distinto eres tú.

¿Se estará[29] poniendo agresiva? Su tono ha sido ya algo molesto. Sonrío. Me 35 empiezo a adueñar de la situación. Quizá con un poco de sangre fría[30] llegue a desconcertarla. Quizá me lo diga todo. Quizá..., ¡pero ahora recuerdo que tengo que hacer una salida urgente! Voy a decírselo cuando ella me interrumpe:

---

[23]*la volví a colocar:* put it back again   [24]*no... explicación:* I saw no other explanation for it   [25]*no puedo menos que:* I can't help but   [26]*Basta que cuelgues:* All you have to do is hang up.   [27]*No... ahora:* You'll never find out any more about me than you know now.   [28]*¡bueno:* well! (interjection)   [29]*estará:* Note again the use of the future for probability in the present.   [30]*sangre fría:* sangfroid (Fr.), lit. "cold blood," meaning "calm," "composure," "coolness"

—Bueno, creo que por hoy es bastante. Tengo que hacer.[31] Cuando quieras, ya sabes dónde me tienes.[32]

—Sí, sí..., yo también tengo que...

¡Qué curioso! Cuando recuerdo que se hace tarde, ella parece recordar lo mismo. Bueno, no sé si despedirme o no. No quisiera ser grosera, pero tampoco 5 tengo por qué ser[33] amable. Ella, sin embargo, apresura las cosas. En el fondo[34] se lo agradezco.

—Hasta otra ocasión, ¿eh?

Y cuelga. Me quedo con el auricular en la mano. Lo miro. Me paso la otra mano por la frente. Otra vez lo inexplicable me cerca, como esas pesadillas en las 10 que no podemos despegar los pies del suelo. La urgencia del tiempo me decide. Cuelgo de una vez y voy a mi habitación, a vestirme. No sé exactamente qué traje ponerme, pero voy directamente hacia el claro, de algodón... Es como si alguien ya hubiese decidido por mí. La idea me desconcierta, pero entonces ya tengo presencia de ánimo para desecharla. «No, no —me digo—, mejor es no 15 pensar en eso. Si está, en el caso de que «esté», es allí, en el teléfono, esperando en el 20-58.» El razonamiento es desesperadamente pobre, pero lo hago por tranquilizarme y me tranquiliza, al menos mientras me visto. Sin embargo..., el germencito no ha muerto; la raicilla de la misma idea se agita buscando sol. Hasta que aflora: «¿Y si la llamo, sin teléfono? Bastará[35] decir su nombre, que es 20 el mío, y esperar a... ¿Contestará?» En esto he terminado de vestirme y voy al tocador. Cuando alzo los ojos estoy a punto de retroceder. Esos ojos, esos ojos, los míos, que acaban de reflejarse en el espejo, no parecen haberse alzado en este momento. Es como si ya hubieran estado mirándome. Me apoyo en la mesa del tocador. ¿Esa sensación de vahído? Sé que estoy a punto de gritar y no quiero, 25 sencillamente no quiero. Así que cojo la cartera y echo a correr hacia la puerta.

Ya en la escalera estoy casi en disposición de sonreír; como si me hubiera escapado de una trampa. Pienso que el aire de la calle me refrescará, que todo esto ha de pasar, como si la salida[36] de la casa pudiera significar un cambio en las cosas, y al regreso todo esté olvidado. 30

Empiezo a bajar la escalera. Aún el ¡pram! de la puerta al cerrarse resuena en el fondo de mis tímpanos, cuando me detengo. Sé que he hecho ese gesto de sorpresa, un gesto cortado que nos mantiene con la mirada fija al frente por un instante y que hace que los labios balbuceen algo...

—Las llaves..., no metí las llaves en la cartera. 35

Suspiro. Estoy casi derrotada. Hago memoria[37] y veo las llaves, claramente, encima del aparador. Allí las dejé anoche, cuando volví del cine. Allí estaban mientras hablé por teléfono..., ¡esa maldita conversación! Desde el sofá las veía

---

[31]*Tengo que hacer:* I've got things to do.   [32]*dónde me tienes:* where you can reach me   [33]*por qué ser:* any reason to be   [34]*En el fondo:* Secretly   [35]*Bastará:* It will be enough for me   [36]*la salida:* my going out   [37]*Hago memoria:* I try to remember

cada vez que mis ojos recorrían la pieza, mientras hablaba. Y la salida precipi-
tada, la estúpida huída de mi casa, me hizo olvidarlas... ¿Y ahora? De momento
siento la necesidad imperiosa de volver. No puedo irme sabiendo que al regreso
no podré entrar. Subo los dos o tres escalones que he bajado. Me paro a mirar
5 tontamente la puerta cerrada. Vacilo. De pronto se me ocurre y no me doy
tiempo a rechazar la idea. Toco el timbre y retrocedo expectante... No sé si la
sangre ha aumentado su velocidad dentro de cada vena, de cada arteria, de cada
humilde vasito capilar. No sé si, por el contrario, se ha detenido. Como tampoco
sé si es frío o calor lo que me invade, deseos de reír tranquila o de echar a correr
10 despavorida, cuando la puerta empieza a abrirse, lentamente, frente a mí.

EXERCISES

A. Questions and Opinions

1. ¿Qué cosa había soñado la narradora?
2. ¿Qué hizo la mujer para satisfacer su «infantil curiosidad»?
3. ¿Con quién se comunicó la mujer llamando el 20-58?
4. ¿Por quién se sentía vigilada la narradora?
5. ¿Por qué volvió a llamar a las seis de la tarde?
6. ¿Qué datos íntimos sabía la otra mujer acerca de la narradora?
7. ¿Por qué preguntó a la otra mujer cómo estaba vestida?
8. ¿Con qué pretexto finalmente terminó la narradora la conversación?
9. ¿Qué cosa rara notó la mujer en el espejo del tocador?
10. Cuando volvió la narradora a su casa por las llaves, ¿quién le abrió la puerta?
●11. ¿Cuál puede ser la explicación de lo que ocurre en este cuento?
●12. ¿A Ud. le ha pasado alguna vez algo parecido?

B. Verb Practice

Use each of the following verbal phrases in an original sentence in Spanish,
either based on the story or of your own design. Be prepared to explain the
meaning of your sentences.

1. **alegrarse**
2. **lavarse los dientes**
3. **descolgar**
4. **preguntar por**
5. **arriesgarse**
6. **recostarse**
7. **no poder más**

8. **molestar**
9. **acabar por** + *infinitive*
10. **tranquilizarse**

C. Vocabulary Practice

Complete the sentences below, matching the expressions on the right with the English words on the left. Be sure to use the correct form of each verb. Then use each expression in an original Spanish sentence and indicate in English what your sentence means.

1. *Instead of* llamarme a mí misma, vine a visitarme.   **justamente**
2. *Well,* ¿vas a seguir llamándome?   **en vez de**
3. *¡Of course!*   **mediodía**
4. Estaba *on the point of* caer en la trampa.   **bueno**
5. Pero, ¡llamarme todos los sábados *exactly* a las tres de la madrugada!   **sino**
6. *At the risk of* mostrar demasiada curiosidad, pregunté: —¿Quién eres?   **mientras**
7. ¡No fue ella *but* yo!   **desde luego**
8. ¿Te decidiste a llamar al *noon,* o a la medianoche?   **sea como sea**
9. *Be that as it may,* creo que es hora de llamar a la policía.   **a riesgo de**
10. Yo me quedo aquí *while* tú llamas.   **a punto de**

D. Communication Practice

1. Say you've already brushed your teeth.
2. State that you won't be able to go on any longer.
3. Indicate that someone called and asked for Elsa.
4. Express the idea that you'd like to lie down for a few minutes.
5. Indicate that you're glad that no one calls you at three o'clock in the morning.

E. Completion Exercise

Complete the following sentence fragments with your own ideas. Be sure to use the appropriate mood and tense with verbs you introduce.

1. El bebé se tranquilizó cuando su madre...
2. Es probable que acabarán por...
3. Cuando sonó el teléfono, estaba a punto de...
4. Lo que te molesta es que ellos...
5. Si te arriesgas así...

EL PAPEL
DE PLATA

Alfonso Ferrari
Amores

ALFONSO FERRARI AMORES (1903–   ) was born in
Buenos Aires, and there he has pursued his subsequent literary
career. He is a journalist by profession and a fiction writer
during "outside" hours. His short stories have appeared in the
leading Argentine newspapers and magazines, and his novel
Gaucho al timón (1948) received a literary prize. Also honored
by a similar award was his radio script «Mástiles quebrados». In
addition, he has had several stage dramas produced in the
Argentine capital. To round out his varied background, we
might add that Ferrari has written a number of tangos that have
enjoyed great popularity in his country and abroad.

Ferrari is widely known as a mystery story writer — an author of "whodunits." Under pseudonyms, as well as under his
own name, he has published over a dozen detective novels with
scenes laid outside Argentina. His detective short stories, which
he signs himself, are clever tales usually set against a typically
Argentine backdrop. His best work in the field of crime fiction
has been done in the shorter form, as you may well judge from
this ingenious story — «El papel de plata».

A PRELIMINARY LOOK AT KEY EXPRESSIONS

Be sure to study these expressions before you read the story.

1. (87: 3) **saludar** *to greet, say hello to*
2. (87: 6) **salir** *to go out*   Although **salir** sometimes means *to leave,* it more often means *to go out* or *come out,* or even *to go out on a date.*
3. (87: 6) **a pesar mío** *in spite of myself, against my wishes*   This expression can also be **a pesar tuyo, a pesar suyo,** etc.
4. (87:11) **en frente** *in front of, before one*
5. (87:19) **sacar en limpio** *to gather, conclude:*   **Espero que saques algo en limpio.** *I hope you gather something out of it.*
6. (87:19) **acomodarse** *to settle oneself, settle down:*   **Me acomodé lo mejor posible en mi silla.** *I settled down as best I could in my chair.* This verb also means *to get a "soft" job* or, *to marry into money* and occurs with this meaning on p. 88, l. 3.
7. (88: 3) **de repente** *suddenly*
8. (88: 3) **dar que hablar** *to give occasion for talk, comment:*   **Eso dio que hablar.** *That caused a lot of talk (gossip).*
9. (88:10) **ganarse el pan** *to earn a living* (literally, *to earn bread for oneself*)
10. (88:22) **por separado** *separately:*   **Hay que servir los dos tipos de hongos por separado.** *You have to serve both types of mushrooms separately.*
11. (88:24) **por si acaso** *just in case*
12. (88:25) **mostrarse** *to appear, look:*   **Se mostró muy interesado.** *He looked very interested.*
13. (88:25) **en seguida** *at once, right away*
14. (88:32) **convenir** *to be desirable, suitable, fitting, proper*   This is a deceptive cognate, which only rarely means *to be convenient.* It is often used with an indirect object: **Le conviene hacer eso.** *She really ought to do that.*
15. (88:37) **olvidarse de** *to forget*
16. (89: 3) **casarse con** *to marry, get married to*
17. (89: 6) **soler** + *infinitive   to be in the habit of, be accustomed to*   This verb is used only in the present and imperfect because of the nature of its repetitive meaning.
18. (89: 8) **comunicarse con** *to get in touch with*
19. (89:15) **tal como** *just as:*   **Hazlo tal como te dije.** *Do it just as I told you to.*
20. (89:21) **de paso** *in passing, while doing so, in the process:*   **Se comprobó, de paso, que yo no era el culpable.** *It was proved, in the process, that I was not the guilty one.*

EL PAPEL DE PLATA

Joaco Migueles, aquel borracho filósofo que fue uno de mis amigos más divertidos, vino de la calle trayendo en la mano un papel plateado, de los que se usan como envoltura de chocolatines y cigarrillos. Antes de saludarme fue hasta una caja y lo echó en ella. Explicó:

5   —Calafate para el techo. Mira. —Señaló una línea de hoyuelos en el piso de tierra—. Una gotera. Esta tarde salí a pesar mío —gruñó, rascándose la nuca. —El solazo me mata. Yo no hubiera querido salir, pero necesitaba vino, y no tuve más remedio que salir.[1] Sin embargo, ya ves, encontré el papel plateado, que es lo mejor que hay para tapar las goteras. Ahí tienes una lección optimista
10 que nos da el azar. No hay mal que por bien no venga,[2] como dice el refrán.

En esto se le volvió la sed y llenó de nuevo el vaso que tenía en frente. Los vasos en que echó Joaco el vino eran como floreros; poco faltaba para que alguno contuviese[3] tanto como la propia botella.

—Tú sabes que yo anduve por la Patagonia[4] cuando era mozo. Fue una
15 experiencia brava; y de no haberla sufrido,[5] sin embargo, no hubiera conocido la felicidad.

Me di cuenta en ese momento de que Joaco Migueles iba a contarme otra de sus memorables historias. A él no le gustaba sino charlar filosóficamente sobre lo que había sacado en limpio de sus experiencias en este mundo. Me acomodé lo
20 mejor posible en mi silla y me puse a escuchar el relato que sirvió para distraerme del mucho calor que hacía.

Acariciando su vaso, Joaco fijó vagamente su mirada en el techo, y me narró la historia que sigue y que he llevado al papel sin cambiar una letra.

—En un rincón de mi memoria donde nunca he barrido para no tener que
25 avergonzarme con lo que saldría a... (iba a decir a relucir, pero no es la miseria cosa que reluzca),[6] hay un tanque de cemento. Un depósito de agua que quedó convertido por mí en dormitorio. Fue en Río Negro,[7] justamente, en El Ñireco.[8] Tan despilchado andaba en aquel tiempo, que ni ganas de remendarme tenía, porque hubiera sido lo mismo que calafatear un barco hundido. En ese
30 entonces muchos otros muchachos hicieron plata[9] con los caminos, trabajando

---

[1]*no... salir:* I had no choice but to go out   [2]*No... venga:* "Every cloud has a silver lining." (Literally, "There is no ill that does not come to good.")   [3]*poco... contuviese:* one of them was almost big enough to hold   [4]*Patagonia:* region comprising the southern part of continental Chile and Argentina   [5]*de... sufrido:* if I hadn't gone through it   [6]*no... reluzca:* misery isn't something that glitters   [7]*Río Negro:* a province in southern Argentina, just north of Patagonia   [8]*El Ñireco:* small town in Río Negro province   [9]*plata:* money, "dough"

de sol a sol[10] en las cuadrillas de Vialidad.[11] Yo no tengo pasta para andar entablado,[12] tú sabes, como animal de tropilla. Seguí pobre, pero no por mucho tiempo. De repente, me acomodé. Eso dio que hablar a muchos. Todo el mundo opinó. Que esto, que lo otro, que lo de más allá.[13] Yo voy a referirme al caso, ya que también lo conozco, y después tú sacarás la conclusión que mejor te 5
parezca. Lo que dije del tanque al principio viene a que por él te explicarás fácilmente[14] que no podía yo negarme a disfrutar, cuando empezaron las nieves en Viedma,[15] de una cama en la trastienda de una herboristería, en la que me ofrecieron empleo como vendedor. Entre seguir en el tanque de cemento en El Ñireco y ganarme el pan en Viedma, ¿quién iba a titubear? Así, quedé como 10
único ocupante del boliche, y una tarde llegó allí a visitarme el viejo gringo[16] avaro, don Hellmuth. Charlamos de mil cosas, y en cierto momento le dije que si era verdad que la diabetes consiste en un exceso de glucosa, a mí me parecía que la ingestión de hongos venenosos, que matan por privar a la sangre de aquella substancia, podría ensayarse, en ciertas dosis, para curar a los diabé- 15
ticos. Era una simple cuestión de lógica. Entonces don Hellmuth me preguntó:

—¿Usted tiene hongos venenosos?

Por toda respuesta saqué[17] dos bolsitas del hueco del mostrador y se los mostré.

—Éstos son los buenos, y éstos son los malos. ¿No parecen idénticos? Don 20
Hellmuth asintió, maravillado.

—Calcule usted —continué—. Si uno los sirve por separado, en dos platos, nadie podría diferenciar los venenosos de los otros. Claro que sería conveniente disponer de un antídoto, por si acaso.

—¿Cuál? —preguntó don Hellmuth, que se mostró en seguida muy 25
interesado.

—La misma glucosa.[18] Una solución muy concentrada, claro. Puede beberse o inyectarse.

—Déme hongos de las dos clases —dijo él—. Y el contraveneno.

Mientras le cobraba los hongos y el frasco, le dije: 30

—Claro que si ha de estar al alcance de un enemigo que haya comido los hongos venenosos, convendría disfrazar el antídoto, para que no lo tome.

—¿Y cómo? —preguntó don Hellmuth.

Yo tomé de un cajón una etiqueta donde se veía una calavera en rojo, y debajo de ella la palabra «Veneno», y la pegué en el frasco. 35

—Ya está —le dije—. Ahora únicamente nosotros dos sabemos que esto no es lo que dice la etiqueta. Trate de no olvidarse de este detalle.

---

[10]*de sol a sol:* from sunup to sundown   [11]*Vialidad:* highway department   [12]*Yo... entablado:* I'm not cut out for being herded around   [13]*Que... allá:* This, that, and the other thing.   [14]*viene... fácilmente:* was said so that you can easily understand   [15]*Viedma:* Coastal city of Río Negro province   [16]*gringo:* In some Latin American countries *gringo* refers to an American, but in others, like Argentina, it refers to any foreigner.   [17]*Por toda respuesta saqué:* My only reply was to take out   [18]*La misma glucosa:* Glucose, as I said.

Casualmente[19] aquella misma noche vino a refugiarse en mi botica la mujer de don Hellmuth, una criollita joven y linda a quien el gringo acostumbraba moler a palos,[20] y eso después de haberse casado con ella, o tal vez de rabia por haberlo hecho; y me contó que después de haber comido juntos un guiso con
5 hongos, la había echado de su casa corriéndola con un látigo. Don Hellmuth, que era hombre tan rico como avaro, solía tener arrebatos, pero nunca como esa vez, y la muchacha lloraba como una Magdalena.[21] (¡Y tanto que escaseaban por allá las mujeres![22]) Yo hice girar la manivela del teléfono, me comuniqué con don Hellmuth y le grité, asustado:
10 —¡Oiga! ¡Equivoqué las etiquetas de los hongos! Los comestibles son los venenosos, y los...

Dicen que lo encontraron al otro día envenenado con cianuro de potasio. El forense analizó el contenido del frasco que había vaciado de un trago don Hellmuth, y declaró:
15 —Veneno, tal como lo indica la etiqueta. Sin duda, don Hellmuth se suicidó.

No faltaron después quienes me miraron de reojo porque me casé con la viuda. Claro que la criollita era un bombón. Fue mi papel de plata, como el que hoy encontré para remediarme. Pero, ¿asunto a qué murmuraban?[23] De envidiosos, no más.[24] En todo ven el dinero. ¿Por qué no se les ocurre pensar que un
20 hombre, por más pobre que sea, puede ser desinteresado? A don Hellmuth le hicieron la autopsia; con ese motivo[25] se comprobó, de paso, que los hongos eran inofensivos. ¡Que iba a vender yo hongos venenosos![26]

EXERCISES

A. Questions and Opinions

1. ¿Qué había encontrado Joaco Migueles para impermeabilizar el techo?
2. ¿A qué refrán se refirió Joaco?
3. ¿Sobre qué cosas le gustaba a Joaco charlar?
4. ¿Por qué no trabajaba Joaco en los caminos de Río Negro con los otros muchachos?
5. ¿Qué trabajo le ofrecieron a Joaco en Viedma?
6. ¿Quién llegó un día a la tienda a visitar a Joaco?
7. ¿Qué dijo Joaco acerca de los hongos venenosos?

---

[19]*Casualmente:* By chance   [20]*acostumbraba moler a palos*: used to beat regularly   [21]*Magdalena:* Mary Magdalene, the repentant sinner depicted in the Bible   [22]*¡Y... mujeres!* And women were so scarce there, too!   [23]*¿asunto a qué murmuraban?* was that anything for them to gossip about?   [24]*De envidiosos, no más:* They were jealous, that's all.   [25]*con ese motivo:* in this way   [26]*¡Que... venenosos!* What would I be doing selling poisonous mushrooms!

8. ¿Qué acabó por comprar don Hellmuth?
9. ¿Quién vino a refugiarse en la tienda aquella misma noche?
10. ¿Cómo murió don Hellmuth?
●11. ¿Considera Ud. que Joaco Migueles es un asesino? ¿Por qué?
●12. ¿Es justificable lo que hizo Migueles? ¿Por qué?

B. Verb Practice

Use each of the following verbal phrases in an original sentence in Spanish, either based on the story or of your own design. Be prepared to explain the meaning of your sentences.

1. **saludar**
2. **salir**
3. **acomodarse**
4. **ganarse el pan**
5. **mostrarse**
6. **convenir**
7. **olvidarse de**
8. **casarse con**
9. **soler** + *infinitive*
10. **comunicarse con**

C. Vocabulary Practice

Complete the sentences below, matching the expressions on the right with the English words on the left. Be sure to use the correct form of each verb. Then use each expression in an original Spanish sentence and indicate in English what your sentence means.

1. Joaco *had gotten a lot out of* sus viajes por Patagonia. — **a pesar mío**
2. Si tienes hongos buenos y hongos malos, te conviene servirlos *separately*. — **en frente**
3. Me enamoré de la esposa de don Hellmuth *in spite of myself*. — **sacar en limpio**
4. Lo hice *just as* me dijeron. — **de repente**
5. Examinó con cuidado los hongos que tenía *before him*. — **dar que hablar**
6. Y, *in the process,* la policía descubrió que no había hongos venenosos. — **por separado**
7. Y don Hellmuth *suddenly* notó algo raro en el guiso. — **por si acaso**
8. Mejor que tengas glucosa en la casa, *just in case.* — **en seguida**

9. La criollita venía a visitarme con frecuencia y eso **tal como**
   caused a lot of talk.
10. Yo traté de comunicarme con don Hellmuth *right* **de paso**
    away.

D. Communication Practice

1. Say that you usually get up before 7:30.
2. Ask Carlos who Ana is marrying.
3. Indicate that it would be suitable to eat after the theater.
4. Tell Martín not to forget to call the restaurant.
5. Say you'll get in touch with Alice tomorrow afternoon.

E. Review Exercise

The following words from the story are based on shorter words that you might already know. The shorter words are defined in case you are not familiar with them. See if you know the meaning of the longer words. Check the end vocabulary if necessary.

1. **plata** *silver,* **plateado** _____
2. **gota** *drop,* **gotera** _____
3. **flor** *flower,* **florero** _____
4. **cómodo** *comfortable,* **acomodarse** _____
5. **vergüenza** *shame,* **avergonzarse** _____
6. **dormir** *to sleep,* **dormitorio** _____
7. **vender** *to sell,* **vendedor** _____
8. **veneno** *poison,* **venenoso** _____
9. **mostrar** *to show,* **mostrador** _____
10. **comer** *to eat,* **comestible** _____

LAS ABEJAS DE BRONCE

MARCO DENEVI

MARCO DENEVI was born in 1922 in Sáenz Peña, a suburb of Buenos Aircs. He achieved literary fame with *Rosaura a las diez,* the first book he wrote, winning with it the first prize in a contest held by the Editorial Kraft in Buenos Aires in 1955. It has been reprinted many times, has been translated into several languages, and was made into a movie. In 1961, Denevi submitted a long story entitled «Ceremonia secreta» to the first literary competition sponsored by *Life en Español,* the Latin American edition of *Life* magazine. It won the first prize of $5,000. Since then, he has continued writing (and winning prizes) as a novelist, short-story writer, and playwright.

Much of Denevi's work reveals a fondness for whimsy, fantasy, and — always just below the surface — social satire. The latter is reflected in «Las abejas de bronce», a story that criticizes an aspect of modern life against which Denevi has always rebelled. As a resident of the second largest city in the world south of the equator, he feels compelled here to point out certain consequences of the technological progress characteristic of the great metropolises of our age.

Be sure to study these expressions before you read the story.

1. (95: 1) **aparte de** *apart, aside from*
2. (95: 3) **tratar a** *to treat, deal with:* **Nadie como él sabía tratar a las Abejas.** *No one knew how to deal with the Bees as he did.*
3. (95: 5) **por otro lado** *furthermore, moreover, on the other hand* This expression usually follows **por un lado** *on the one hand.*
4. (95: 5) **entenderse con** *to handle, get along with:* **El Zorro sabía entenderse con el Oso.** *The Fox knew how to handle the Bear.*
5. (95: 6) **llevarse bien** *to get along (well)* This is another reflexive verb that can be used with one subject or two subjects reciprocally: **El Zorro se lleva bien con el Oso.** *The Fox gets along with the Bear.* And **El Zorro y el Oso se llevan bien.** *The Fox and the Bear get along (well).*
6. (95: 7) **al aire libre** *outside*
7. (95:19) **darse prisa** *to hurry*
8. (95:22) **(no) dejar de** + *infinitive* In the affirmative this expression means *to stop* + *present participle:* **Dejó de reír.** *He stopped laughing.* But in the negative it means *not to fail* + *infinitive* or *to be sure* + *infinitive:* **No dejes de llamar(me) si me necesitas.** Be sure to call (me) if you need me.
9. (96: 5) **a coro** *in chorus, all together*
10. (96:14) **de acuerdo** *agreed, OK*
11. (96:21) **de una buena vez** *once and for all*
12. (97: 8) **aprender a** + *infinitive* *to learn* + *infinitive*
13. (98: 2) **atreverse a** + *infinitive* *to dare* + *infinitive*
14. (98:16) **sobre todo** *above all, especially*
15. (99:33) **tener éxito** *to be successful*
16. (99:35) **quejarse** *to complain*
17. (100: 3) **tardar** + *time* + **en** + *infinitive* *to take* + *time* + *infinitive:* **Tardaron diez días en volver.** *It took them ten days to get back.* Notice that this expression really has nothing to do with the idea of *lateness,* as the adverb **tarde** does.
18. (100:26) **optar por** *to pick, choose*
19. (101:13) **más tarde** *later*
20. (101:21) **ninguna parte** *nowhere* This expression is usually preceded by a preposition: **No va a ninguna parte.** *He's not going anywhere.* Or **No lo pude encontrar en ninguna parte.** *I couldn't find it anywhere.*

LAS ABEJAS
DE BRONCE

Desde el principio del tiempo el Zorro vivió de la venta de la miel. Era, aparte de una tradición de familia, una especie de vocación hereditaria. Nadie tenía la maña del Zorro para tratar a las Abejas (cuando las Abejas eran unos animalitos vivos y muy irritables) y hacerles rendir al máximo. Esto por un lado.[1]

5   Por otro lado el Zorro sabía entenderse con el Oso, gran consumidor de miel y, por lo mismo,[2] su mejor cliente. No resultaba fácil llevarse bien con el Oso. El Oso era un sujeto un poco brutal, un poco salvaje, al que la vida al aire libre, si le proporcionaba una excelente salud, lo volvía de una rudeza de manera[3] que no todo el mundo estaba dispuesto a tolerarle.

10   (Incluso el Zorro, a pesar de su larga práctica, tuvo que sufrir algunas experiencias desagradables en ese sentido.) Una vez, por ejemplo, a causa de no sé qué cuestión baladí, el Oso destruyó de un zarpazo la balanza para pesar la miel. El Zorro no se inmutó ni perdió su sonrisa. *(Lo enterrarán con la sonrisa puesta,*[4] decía de él, desdeñosamente, su tío el Tigre.) Pero le hizo notar al Oso

15   que, conforme a la ley, estaba obligado a indemnizar aquel perjuicio.

—Naturalmente —se rió el Oso— te indemnizaré. Espera que corro a indemnizarte.[5] No me alcanzan las piernas para correr a indemnizarte.[6]

Y lanzaba grandes carcajadas y se golpeaba un muslo con la mano.

—Sí —dijo el Zorro con su voz tranquila—, sí, le aconsejo que se dé prisa,
20   porque las Abejas se impacientan. Fíjese, señor.

Y haciendo un ademán teatral, un ademán estudiado, señaló las colmenas. El Oso se fijó e instantáneamente dejó de reír. Porque vio que millares de Abejas habían abandonado los panales y con el rostro rojo de cólera, el ceño fruncido y la boca crispada, lo miraban de hito en hito,[7] y parecían dispuestas a atacarlo.

25   —No aguardan sino mi señal[8] —agregó el Zorro, dulcemente—. Usted sabe, detestan las groserías.

El Oso, que a pesar de su fuerza era un fanfarrón, palideció de miedo.

---

[1]*Esto por un lado:* This on the one hand   [2]*por lo mismo:* by the same token   [3]*lo... manera:* gave him such a crude manner   [4]*con la sonrisa puesta:* with that smile on his face   [5]*Espera... indemnizarte:* You just wait. I'll break my neck running to pay you back for the damage *(sarcastically, of course).*   [6]*No... indemnizarte:* I can't hurry fast enough to pay you back for the damage.   [7]*de hito en hito:* from head to foot   [8]*No... señal:* They're just waiting for my signal

—Está bien, Zorro —balbuceaba—, repondré la balanza. Pero por favor, dígales[9] que no me miren así, ordéneles que vuelvan a sus colmenas.

—¿Oyen, queriditas? —dijo el Zorro melífluamente, dirigiéndose a las Abejas—. El señor Oso nos promete traernos otra balanza.

Las Abejas zumbaron a coro. El Zorro las escuchó con expresión respetuosa. 5
De tanto en tanto[10] asentía con la cabeza y murmuraba:

—Sí, sí, conforme. Ah, se comprende. ¿Quién lo duda? Se lo transmitiré. El Oso no cabía en su vasto pellejo.[11]

—¿Qué es lo que están hablando, Zorro? Me tienes[12] sobre ascuas.

El Zorro lo miró fijo. 10

—Dicen que la balanza deberá ser flamante.

—Claro está, flamante. Y ahora, que se vuelvan.

—Niquelada.

—De acuerdo, niquelada.

—Fabricación extranjera. 15

—¿También eso?

—Preferentemente suiza.

—Ah, no, es demasiado. Me extorsionan.

—Repítalo, señor Oso. Más alto. No lo han oído.

—Digo y sostengo que... Está bien, está bien. Trataré de complacerlas. 20
Pero ordénales de una buena vez que regresen a sus panales. Me ponen nervioso tantas caras de Abeja juntas, mirándome.

El Zorro hizo un ademán raro, como un ilusionista, y las Abejas, después de lanzar al Oso una última mirada amonestadora, desaparecieron dentro de las colmenas. El Oso se alejó, un tanto mohíno y con la vaga sensación de que lo 25
habían engañado. Pero al día siguiente reapareció trayendo entre sus brazos una balanza flamante, niquelada, con una chapita de bronce donde se leía: Made in Switzerland.

Lo dicho:[13] el Zorro sabía manejar a las Abejas y sabía manejar al Oso. Pero ¿a quién no sabía manejar ese zorro del Zorro?[14] 30

Hasta que un día se inventaron las Abejas artificiales.

Sí. Insectos de bronce, dirigidos electrónicamente, a control remoto (como decían los prospectos ilustrativos), podían hacer el mismo trabajo que las Abejas vivas. Pero con enormes ventajas. No se fatigaban, no se extraviaban, no quedaban atrapadas en las redes de las Arañas, no eran devoradas por los Pájaros; no 35
se alimentaban, a su vez, de miel, como las Abejas naturales (miel que en la

---

[9]*dígales:* Note how the Bear, now nervous and fearful, switches to the polite form of address, using *diga* instead of *di.*   [10]*De tanto en tanto:* Every so often   [11]*El Oso... pellejo:* The Bear was beside himself (literally, "He didn't fit in his enormous hide.")   [12]*tienes:* Now the Bear switches back to the familiar form of address.   [13]*Lo dicho:* As I have said   [14]*¿a... Zorro?* Who didn't that foxiest of all foxes know how to deal with?

contabilidad y en el alma del Zorro figuraba con grandes cifras rojas); no había, entre ellas, ni reinas, ni zánganos; todas iguales, todas obreras, todas dóciles, obedientes, fuertes, activas, de vida ilimitada, resultaban, en cualquier sentido que se considerase la cuestión, infinitamente superiores a las Abejas vivas.

5   El Zorro en seguida vio el negocio, y no dudó. Mató todos sus enjambres, demolió las colmenas de cera, con sus ahorros compró mil Abejas de bronce y su correspondiente colmenar también de bronce, mandó instalar el tablero de control, aprendió a manejarlo, y una mañana los animales presenciaron, atónitos, cómo las Abejas de bronce atravesaban por primera vez el espacio.

10   El Zorro no se había equivocado. Sin levantarse siquiera de su asiento, movía una palanquita, y una nube de Abejas salía rugiendo hacia el norte, movía otra palanquita, y otro grupo de Abejas disparaba hacia el sur, un nuevo movimiento de palanca, y un tercer enjambre se lanzaba en dirección al este, *et sic de ceteris*.[15] Los insectos de bronce volaban raudamente, a velocidades nunca 15 vistas, con una especie de zumbido amortiguado que era como el eco de otro zumbido; se precipitaban como una flecha sobre los cálices, sorbían rápidamente el néctar, volvían a levantar vuelo, regresaban a la colmena, se incrustaban cada una en su alvéolo, hacían unas rápidas contorsiones, unos ruiditos secos, tric, trac, cruc, y a los pocos instantes destilaban la miel, una miel pura, 20 limpia, dorada, incontaminada, aséptica; y ya estaban en condiciones de recomenzar. Ninguna distracción, ninguna fatiga, ningún capricho, ninguna cólera. Y así las veinticuatro horas del día. El Zorro no cabía en sí de contento.[16]

    La primera vez que el Oso probó la nueva miel puso los ojos en blanco,[17] hizo chasquear la lengua y, no atreviéndose a opinar, le preguntó a su mujer:

25   —Vaya,[18] ¿qué te parece?

    —No sé —dijo ella—. Le siento gusto a metal.[19]

    —Sí, yo también.

    Pero sus hijos protestaron a coro:

    —Papá, mamá, qué disparate. Si se ve a la legua que esta miel es muy 30 superior. Superior en todo sentido. ¿Cómo pueden preferir aquella otra, elaborada por unos bichos tan sucios? En cambio ésta es más limpia, más higiénica, más moderna y, en una palabra, más miel.

    El Oso y la Osa no encontraron razones con que rebatir a sus hijos y permanecieron callados. Pero cuando estuvieron solos insistieron:

35   —Qué quieres,[20] sigo prefiriendo la de antes. Tenía un sabor...

    —Sí, yo también. Hay que convenir, eso sí, en que la de ahora viene pasteurizada. Pero aquel sabor...

---

[15]*et sic de ceteris:* and the same for all the rest *(Latin)*   [16]*no... contento:* was beside himself with joy   [17]*puso... blanco:* he rolled his eyes   [18]*Vaya:* Well now   [19]*Le... metal:* I get a metallic taste from it.   [20]*Qué quieres:* Say what you want

—Ah, aquel sabor...

Tampoco se atrevieron a decirlo a nadie, porque, en el fondo, se sentían orgullosos de servirse en un establecimiento donde trabajaba esa octava maravilla de las Abejas de bronce.

—Cuando pienso que, bien mirado,[21] las Abejas de bronce fueron inventadas 5 exclusivamente para nosotros... —decía la mujer del Oso.

El Oso no añadía palabra y aparentaba indiferencia, pero por dentro estaba tan ufano como su mujer.

De modo que por nada del mundo hubieran dejado de comprar y comer la miel destilada por las Abejas artificiales. Y menos todavía cuando notaron que 10 los demás animales también acudían a la tienda del Zorro a adquirir miel, no porque les gustase la miel, sino a causa de las Abejas de bronce y para alardear de modernos.[22]

Y, con todo esto, las ganancias del Zorro crecían como un incendio en el bosque. Tuvo que tomar a su servicio un ayudante y eligió, después de meditarlo 15 mucho, al Cuervo, sobre todo porque le aseguró que aborrecía la miel. Las mil Abejas fueron pronto cinco mil; las cinco mil, diez mil. Se comenzó a hablar de las riquezas del Zorro como de una fortuna fabulosa. El Zorro se sonreía y se frotaba las manos.

Y entretanto los enjambres iban, venían, salían, entraban. Los animales 20 apenas podían seguir con la vista aquellas ráfagas de puntos dorados que cruzaban sobre sus cabezas. Las únicas que, en lugar de admirarse, pusieron el grito en el cielo, fueron las Arañas, esas analfabetas. Sucedía que las Abejas de bronce atravesaban las telarañas y las hacían pedazos.

—¿Qué es esto? ¿El fin del mundo? —chillaron las damnificadas la primera 25 vez que ocurrió la cosa.

Pero como alguien les explicó luego de qué se trataba,[23] amenazaron al Zorro con iniciarle pleito. ¡Qué estupidez! Como decía la mujer del Oso:

—Es la eterna lucha entre la luz y la sombra, entre el bien y el mal, entre la civilización y la barbarie. 30

También los Pájaros se llevaron una sorpresa.[24] Porque uno de ellos, en la primera oportunidad en que vio una abeja de bronce, abrió el pico y se la tragó. ¡Desdichado! La abeja metálica le desgarró las cuerdas vocales, se le embutió en el buche y allí le formó un tumor, de resultas del cual falleció al poco tiempo, en medio de los más crueles sufrimientos y sin el consuelo del canto, porque había 35 quedado mudo. Los demás Pájaros escarmentaron.

---

[21]*bien mirado:* if one really thinks about it   [22]*alardear de modernos:* brag about being modern   [23]*de qué se trataba:* what it was all about   [24]*se llevaron una sorpresa:* were surprised

Y cuando ya el Zorro paladeaba su prosperidad, comenzaron a aparecer los inconvenientes. Primero una nubecita, después otra nubecita, hasta que todo el cielo amenazó tormenta.

La serie de desastres quedó inaugurada con el episodio de las rosas artificiales.
5 Una tarde, al vaciar una colmena, el Zorro descubrió entre la miel rubia unos goterones grises, opacos, de un olor nauseabundo y sabor acre. Tuvo que tirar toda la miel restante, que había quedado contaminada. Pronto supo, y por la colérica boca de la víctima, el origen de aquellos goterones repugnantes. Había sucedido que las Abejas de bronce, desprovistas de instintos, confundieron un
10 ramo de rosas artificiales de propiedad de la Gansa con rosas naturales, y cayendo sobre ellas les sorbieron la cera pintada de que estaban hechas y las dejaron convertidas en un guiñapo. El Zorro no solamente debió de sufrir la pérdida de la miel, sino indemnizar a la Gansa por daños y perjuicios.

—Malditas Abejas —vociferaba mentalmente—. Las otras jamás habrían
15 caído en semejante error. Tenían un instinto infalible. Pero quién piensa en las otras. En fin, nada es perfecto en este mundo.

Otro día, una Abeja, al introducirse como una centella en la corola de una azucena, degolló a un Picaflor que se encontraba allí alimentándose. La sangre del Pájaro tiñó de rojo la azucena. Pero como la Abeja, insensible a olores y
20 sabores, no atendía sino sus impulsos eléctricos, libó néctar y sangre, todo junto. Y la miel apareció después con un tono rosa que alarmó al Zorro. Felizmente su empleado le quitó la preocupación de encima.[25]

—Si yo fuese usted, Patrón —le dijo con su vocecita ronca y su aire de solterona—, la vendería como miel especial para niños.
25 —¿Y si resultase venenosa?

—En tan desdichada hipótesis yo estaría muerto, Patrón.

—Ah, de modo que la ha probado. De modo que mis subalternos me roban la miel. ¿Y no me juró que la aborrecía?

—Uno se sacrifica, y vean cómo le pagan —murmuró el Cuervo, poniendo
30 cara[26] de dignidad ultrajada—. La aborrezco, la aborreceré toda mi vida. Pero quise probarla para ver si era venenosa. Corrí el riesgo por usted. Ahora, si cree que he procedido mal, despídame, Patrón.

¿Qué querían que hiciese el Zorro, sino seguir el consejo del Cuervo? Tuvo un gran éxito con la miel rosa especial para niños. La vendió íntegramente. Y nadie
35 se quejó. (El único que pudo quejarse fue el Cerdo, a causa de ciertas veleidades poéticas que asaltaron por esos días a sus hijos. Pero ningún Cerdo que esté en su sano juicio[27] es capaz de relacionar la extraña locura de hacer versos con un frasco de miel tinta en la sangre de un Picaflor.)

---

[25]*le... encima:* took the worry off his shoulders   [26]*poniendo cara:* taking on an expression   [27]*sano juicio:* right mind

El Zorro se sintió a salvo. Pobre Zorro, ignoraba que sus tribulaciones iban a igualar a sus Abejas.

Al cabo de unos días observó que los insectos tardaban cada vez más tiempo[28] en regresar a las colmenas.

Una noche, encerrados en la tienda, él y el Cuervo consideraron aquel nuevo 5 enigma.

—¿Por qué tardan tanto? —decía el Zorro— ¿A dónde diablos van? Ayer un enjambre demoró cinco horas en volver. La producción diaria, así, disminuye, y los gastos de electricidad aumentan. Además, esa miel rosa la tengo todavía atravesada[29] en la garganta. A cada momento me pregunto: ¿Qué aparecerá hoy? 10 ¿Miel verde? ¿Miel negra? ¿Miel azul? ¿Miel salada?

—Accidentes como el de las flores artificiales no se han repetido, Patrón. Y en cuanto a la miel rosa, no creo que tenga de qué quejarse.

—Lo admito. Pero ¿y este misterio de las demoras? ¿Qué explicación le encuentra? 15

—Ninguna. Salvo...

—¿Salvo qué?

El Cuervo cruzó gravemente las piernas, juntó las manos y miró hacia arriba.

—Patrón —dijo, después de reflexionar unos instantes—. Salir y vigilar a las Abejas no es fácil. Vuelan demasiado rápido. Nadie, o casi nadie, puede se- 20 guirlas. Pero yo conozco un Pájaro que, si se le unta la mano,[30] se ocuparía del caso. Y le doy mi palabra que no volvería sin haber averiguado la verdad.

—¿Y quién es ese Pájaro?

—Un servidor.[31]

El Zorro abrió la boca para cubrir de injurias al Cuervo, pero luego lo pensó 25 mejor y optó por aceptar. Pues cualquier recurso era preferible a quedarse con los brazos cruzados, contemplando la progresiva e implacable disminución de las ganancias.

El Cuervo regresó muy tarde, jadeando como si hubiese vuelto volando desde la China. (El Zorro, de pronto, sospechó que todo era una farsa y que quizá su 30 empleado conocía la verdad desde el primer día.) Su cara no hacía presagiar nada bueno.[32]

—Patrón —balbuceó—, no sé cómo decírselo. Pero las Abejas tardan, y tardarán cada vez más, porque no hay flores en la comarca y deben ir a libarlas al extranjero. 35

—¿Cómo que no hay flores[33] en la comarca? ¿Qué tontería es esa?

—Lo que oye, Patrón. Parece ser que las flores, después que las Abejas les han sorbido el néctar, se doblan, se debilitan y se mueren.

---

[28]*cada vez más tiempo:* longer and longer   [29]*atravesada:* stuck   [30]*si... mano:* if you grease his palm   [31]*Un servidor:* Yours truly   [32]*Su... bueno:* His face didn't indicate good news.   [33]*¿Cómo... flores:* What do you mean there aren't any flowers

—¡Se mueren! ¿Y por qué se mueren?

—No resisten la trompa de metal de las Abejas.

—¡Diablos!

—Y no termina ahí la cosa. La planta, después que las Abejas le asesinaron
5 las flores...

—¡Asesinaron! Le prohíbo que use esa palabra.

—Digamos mataron. La planta, después que las Abejas le mataron sus flores,
se niega a florecer nuevamente. Consecuencia: en toda la comarca no hay más
flores. ¿Qué me dice, Patrón?

10 El Zorro no decía nada. Nada. Estaba alelado.

Y lo peor es que el Cuervo no mentía. Las Abejas artificiales habían devas-
tado las flores del país. Entonces pasaron a los países vecinos, después a los más
próximos, luego a los menos próximos, más tarde a los remotos y lejanos, y así,
de país en país, dieron toda la vuelta al mundo y regresaron al punto de partida.

15 Ese día los Pájaros se sintieron invadidos de una extraña congoja, y no
supieron por qué. Algunos, inexplicablemente, se suicidaron. El Ruiseñor quedó
afónico y los colores del Petirrojo palidecieron. Se dice que ese día ocurrieron
extraños acontecimientos. Se dice que, por ejemplo, los ríos dejaron de correr y
las fuentes, de cantar. No sé. Lo único que sé es que, cuando las Abejas de
20 bronce, de país en país, dieron toda la vuelta al mundo, ya no hubo flores en el
campo, ni en las ciudades, ni en los bosques, ni en ninguna parte.

Las Abejas volvían de sus viajes, anidaban en sus alvéolos, se contorsionaban,
hacían tric, trac, cruc, pero el Zorro no recogía ni una miserable gota de miel.
Las Abejas regresaban tan vacías como habían salido.

25 El Zorro se desesperó. Sus negocios se desmoronaron. Aguantó un tiempo
gracias a sus reservas. Pero incluso estas reservas se agotaron. Debió despedir al
Cuervo, cerrar la tienda, perder la clientela.

El único que no se resignaba era el Oso.

—Zorro —vociferaba—, o me consigues miel o te levanto la tapa de los
30 sesos.[34]

—Espere. Pasado mañana recibiré una partida del extranjero —le prometía el
Zorro. Pero la partida del extranjero no llegaba nunca.

Hizo unas postreras tentativas. Envió enjambres en distintas direcciones.
Todo inútil. El tric, trac, cruc como una burla, pero nada de miel.

35 Finalmente, una noche el Zorro desconectó los cables, destruyó el tablero de
control, enterró en un pozo las Abejas de bronce, recogió sus dineros y a favor de
las sombras[35] huyó con rumbo desconocido.

Cuando iba a cruzar la frontera escuchó a sus espaldas unas risitas y unas
vocecitas de vieja que lo llamaban.

---

[34]*te... sesos:* I'll beat your brains out   [35]*a... sombras:* under cover of darkness

—¡Zorro! ¡Zorro!

Eran las Arañas, que a la luz de la luna tejían sus telas prehistóricas.

El Zorro les hizo una mueca obscena y se alejó a grandes pasos.

Desde entonces nadie volvió a verlo jamás.

EXERCISES

A. Questions and Opinions

1. ¿De qué había vivido el Zorro desde el principio del tiempo?
2. ¿Qué maña especial tenía el Zorro?
3. ¿Cómo era el mejor cliente del Zorro?
4. ¿Qué experiencia desagradable sufrió el Zorro a causa del Oso?
5. ¿Qué tuvo que traerles el Oso al Zorro y a las Abejas?
6. ¿Cuáles eran las ventajas de las Abejas de bronce?
7. ¿Qué hizo el Oso al probar por primera vez la nueva miel?
8. ¿Por qué acudían todos los animales a la tienda del Zorro a adquirir miel?
9. ¿Qué perjuicios sufrieron las Arañas?
10. ¿Qué le ocurrió a un Pájaro que se tragó una abeja de bronce?
11. ¿Por qué tuvo que tirar el Zorro toda la miel en una ocasión?
12. ¿Por qué exclamó el Zorro: —Malditas Abejas?
13. ¿Qué tiñó de rosa la miel?
14. ¿Qué nueva miel tuvo un gran éxito?
15. ¿Cuánto tiempo demoró un enjambre en volver a la colmena?
16. ¿Qué sospechó el Zorro cuando el Cuervo regresó?
17. ¿Por qué no había flores en toda la comarca?
18. ¿Cuál fue la amenaza del Oso?
19. ¿Qué les ocurrió a algunos Pájaros? ¿Al Ruiseñor? ¿Al Petirrojo?
20. Al final del cuento, ¿cómo resolvió el Zorro el asunto?
•21. ¿Le tiene Ud. lástima al Zorro? ¿Por qué?
•22. ¿A Ud. le gustaría comer miel producida mecánicamente? ¿Por qué?

B. Verb Practice

Use each of the following verbal phrases in an original sentence in Spanish, either based on the story or of your own design. Be prepared to explain the meaning of your sentences.

1. **tratar a**
2. **entenderse con**
3. **llevarse bien**

4. **darse prisa**
5. **(no) dejar de** + *infinitive*
6. **aprender a** + *infinitive*
7. **atreverse a** + *infinitive*
8. **tener éxito**
9. **quejarse**
10. **tardar** + *time* + **en** + *infinitive*

C. Vocabulary Practice

Complete the sentences below, matching the expressions on the right with the English words on the left. Be sure to use the correct form of each verb. Then use each expression in an original Spanish sentence and indicate in English what your sentence means.

1. Las Abejas no pudieron encontrar néctar en *anywhere.*   **aparte de**

2. *Aside from* miel contaminada, el Zorro no tenía problemas al principio.   **por otro lado**

3. El Zorro y el Oso preferían pasar su tiempo *outdoors.*   **a coro**

4. Creo que el Zorro *will go for* el plan del Cuervo.   **de acuerdo**

5. Las Abejas, *later,* llegaron a tierras más lejanas.   **de una buena vez**

6. El Zorro insistió en una balanza flamante, y el Oso respondió: —*You got it!*   **sobre todo**

7. Por un lado, el Zorro sabía manejar a las Abejas, y, *furthermore,* sabía entenderse con el Oso.   **optar por**

8. *Especially* cuando el Oso tenía ganas de comer miel.   **más tarde**

9. ¡Dime *once and for all* si esta miel está contaminada!   **ninguna parte**

10. El Cuervo y el Oso protestaron *in a single voice.*   **al aire libre**

D. Communication Practice

1. Say that you hope that Mariana is successful.
2. Indicate that you and Rolando always get along well.
3. Tell your friend to hurry up.
4. Say that it was so hot in Acapulco that everyone was complaining.
5. Indicate that you learned to speak Spanish in Buenos Aires.

E. Completion Exercise

Complete the following sentence fragments with your own ideas. Be sure to use the appropriate mood and tense with verbs you introduce.

1. Sin duda, ellos no tardarán mucho en...
2. Si yo fuera Ud., optaría por...
3. Ella nunca se atrevía a...
4. Marcela, no dejes de...
5. Amalia se llevaba bien con todos porque...

UN SUICIDA

MARCOS VICTORIA

MARCOS VICTORIA (1901–1975), physician, poet, and author, taught in both the School of Medicine and School of Arts and Letters of the National University of La Plata. He retired from teaching in 1960 and in 1965 was named Director of Cultural Affairs of the Argentine Department of State. Contributor to *La Nación* and *La Prensa* and member of the Buenos Aires Academy of Medicine, he wrote more than thirty books on scientific and literary subjects. In this respect he was representative of the traditional part-time Spanish American author for whom literature is a separate career, pursued during the hours left free after one's "professional" day is ended.

Marcos Victoria composed many admirable short stories and novelettes, some of these collected in *Un verde paraíso* (1960), *María Rosa en primavera* (1960), *Novela de la ciudad y del río* (1961), and *Las uvas doradas del más allá* (1962). From the last of these we have selected «Un suicida», which offers a chilling, Orwellian vision of what human existence might be like in Buenos Aires four hundred years after Argentina first moved to seek independence from Spain.

A PRELIMINARY LOOK AT KEY EXPRESSIONS

Be sure to study these expressions before you read the story.

1. (108: 1) **por ambos lados** *on both sides*
2. (108: 5) **hacía cinco minutos** *five minutes before* **Hacer** with time units renders English *before* when used in the imperfect and *ago* when used with the preterit: **Hace un mes trató de suicidarse.** *He tried to commit suicide a month ago.*
3. (108:17) **detenerse** *to stop, come to a halt*
4. (108:18) **seguir** + *present participle* *to keep on, continue* + *present participle*
5. (108:22) **por encima de** *over, above*
6. (108:25) **tratar de** + *infinitive* *to try* + *infinitive*
7. (108:28) **tener que ver (con)** *to have to do with, be relevant* Unlike English, in Spanish the element **con** + *noun* can be left out: **¿Yo qué tengo que ver?** *What do I have to do with that (what has just been said)?* Or **Eso no tiene nada que ver.** *That has nothing to do with anything* or *That's not relevant.*
8. (109:10) **tener derecho (a)** *to have a right (to)* The element following **a** can be a verb: **¿Acaso no tengo derecho a concluir mi vida?** *Isn't it possible that I have a right to end my own life?* Or a noun: **No tienes derecho a ese dinero.** *You have no right to that money.*
9. (109:11) **no servir para nada** *to be useless, good for nothing*
10. (110:21) **realizar** *to carry out, make* This is another deceptive cognate in Spanish: *to realize* in the sense of *be aware* is **darse cuenta (de).**
11. (110:24) **entrometerse** *to intrude, interfere, butt in* Thus, someone who does this to excess is an **entrometido.**
12. (110:32) **quedarle a uno** *to have left* This verb is like **gustar, faltar,** and **bastar** in that the subject in English is the indirect object in Spanish: **Me quedan dos días.** *I have two days left* (literally, *"Two days remain to me"*).
13. (111: 1) **depender de** *to depend on*
14. (111:12) **querer decir** *to mean* This expression means the same as **significar** but is more common in conversation.
15. (111:15) **cinta** *tape* This word has a wide variety of meanings: *computer* or *recording tape, adhesive tape, ribbon, headband,* and even *shoelace* in some countries.
16. (111:24) **a su disposición** *at your disposal, available, at hand*

17. (111:28) **disponer de** *to have available, have use of*
18. (112: 8) **rechazar** *to turn down, reject, refuse*
19. (112: 9) **perder tiempo** *to lose, waste time*
20. (112:13) **de acuerdo con** *in accordance with, according to* This expression is somewhat more formal and precise than the conversational **según**.

UN SUICIDA

El hombre se internó en la avenida que conducía hasta los malecones. Por ambos lados, la cortina de acero y cemento de los depósitos aduaneros. La luz lechosa de los tubos luminosos se elevaba de los cordones de las aceras y descendía de las altas columnas blancas. Una noche de agosto, neblinosa y extremadamente fría.[1] Temblando, apresuró el ritmo de sus pasos. Hacía cinco 5 minutos, había descendido a la entrada del puerto desde una de las torres del ferrocarril suspendido que circundaba a Buenos Aires con sus cables de acero, a cincuenta metros sobre el suelo. En el vagón de ferrocarril la temperatura era soportable. Lo mismo ocurría en el centro de la ciudad que había inaugurado la calefacción electrónica de sus calles y plazas hacía un año, en 2210, precisa- 10 mente al celebrar la Argentina el cuarto centenario de su nacimiento a la vida libre.[2] El puerto estaba desierto y el viento húmedo del río le quemaba los ojos. El hombre sentía heladas las orejas y la nariz. Un poco más y todo quedaría terminado. Al frente, vislumbró la lámina metálica del Plata,[3] perfectamente iluminada hasta cincuenta metros del malecón, precisamente a causa de casos 15 como el suyo. Doscientos metros más y estaba a salvo.

—Deténgase —oyó que le ordenaba desde arriba una voz dura e impersonal. Siguió caminando, aunque no dudó que la voz desconocida se dirigía a él.

—Si da un paso más, disparo —insistió la voz. Se detuvo en seco.[4]

—Alce las manos. Escuche. —No sólo alzó las manos sino los ojos. 20

Las aletas de un diminuto helicóptero se movían silenciosamente, cinco metros por encima de su cabeza.

—Lo hemos seguido desde que descendió del tren elevado. Vino a suicidarse.

—¿Cómo lo sabe?

—No trate de engañarnos. Usted pertenece al circuito A5[5] de la ciudad, 25 donde se produjo la epidemia de suicidios del año pasado. No queremos que se repita este año.

—¿Y yo qué tengo que ver?

—Su carta al comisario de A5, firmada con su matrícula,[6] fue leída hace diez minutos. Hemos llegado a tiempo. 30

---

[1]*una noche... fría:* Keep in mind that in the southern hemisphere the seasons are "reversed," so to speak. Thus in Buenos Aires the weather in August is often cold.   [2]*precisamente... libre:* Argentina began its war of independence from Spain on May 25, 1810.   [3]*El Plata:* one of the main rivers of Latin America. It is formed by the confluence of the Paraná and Uruguay rivers, and its estuary at Buenos Aires is over 200 kilometers wide.   [4]*Se detuvo en seco:* He stopped short.   [5]*circuito A5:* an imaginary division of the city in the twenty-third century   [6]*matrícula:* number (of his identification card)

El hombre se sintió vencido. Imposible luchar contra aquella organización perfecta.

—Identifíquese. A5-p3213.

—Tupac Pérez.[7]

5 —¿Estado civil?[8]

—Viudo.

—¿Profesión?

—Escritor.

—No hay más escritores. Profesión desconocida.

10 —Bueno; pensionista del Estado. ¿Acaso no tengo derecho a concluir mi vida? No sirvo para nada desde que se cerraron las últimas editoriales.

—Eso lo dirá en el Depósito Central de calle Esmeralda. ¡Baje los brazos, por favor! Voy a descender. Cuando esté sobre la calle, abra la portezuela y entre. Nada de vivezas,[9] ¿eh?

15 Cuando el helicóptero se posó en tierra, abrió la portezuela y, como lo sospechaba, encontró vacía la cabina. Luz azulada en su interior. Sobre el tablero reluciente, múltiples cuadrantes y lucecitas rojas y verdes. La voz resonó todavía, más suave:

—Ajústese el cinturón de seguridad. —El helicóptero se elevó rápidamente.

20 Un ruido monótono, como el de un reloj (seguramente el mecanismo de control remoto) se escuchaba a sus espaldas. Pero él continuaba abstraído en su propio problema. Se decía: «Nada que pueda ocurrirme ahora me interesa. Mañana o pasado,[10] esto tiene que terminar». Tan abstraído, que no observó el espectáculo soberbio de Buenos Aires nocturno, con su tránsito aéreo (centenares de heli-

25 cópteros individuales, y los destellos luminosos con que advertían su vecindad) y el otro tránsito terrestre de las avenidas y la iluminación de los rascacielos. Tan preocupado estaba que no vio las dos avenidas superpuestas (lo que antes se llamaba Avenida de Mayo[11]) y la hoja de trébol de sus conexiones con los tres pisos de Avenida Nueve de Julio,[12] rutilantes de luces. La niebla esfumaba los

30 contornos pero daba telón de fondo[13] a los letreros de propaganda[14] y a las noticias de última hora, que proyectaban sobre el cielo sus letras corredizas:

---

[7]*Tupac Pérez:* This name is significant in the story. Tupac Amaru was a Peruvian Inca who rebelled against the Spaniards and was executed in 1579. Another Incan descendant of the same name met a similar fate for the same reason in 1780. *Pérez,* on the other hand, is such a common Spanish family name that it is often used to represent a typical ordinary person, something like "Smith," "Jones," or "Doe" in English.   [8]*Estado civil:* Marital status, a line always found on identification cards, passports, etc.   [9]*Nada de vivezas:* No tricks   [10]*pasado: pasado mañana* day after tomorrow   *Pasado* here is masculine to agree with *el mañana* "tomorrow," as opposed to *la mañana* "the morning."   [11]*Avenida de Mayo:* a principal street of Buenos Aires   [12]*Avenida Nueve de Julio:* another main street of Buenos Aires, reputedly the widest in the world   [13]*daba telón de fondo:* served as a backdrop   [14]*propaganda:* This word usually means "advertising" or "promotion," although in certain contexts it can have the same negative meaning as its English cognate.

«Compre su lote por mensualidades en la Antártida Argentina, junto al Hotel de Turismo de Isla Desolación...[15] Es la inversión perfecta...» «Acaba de ser electo Presidente de la Confederación de Repúblicas Democráticas del Planeta el General Truman Rockefeller»... «Coma patay,[16] y sus hijos nacerán fuertes»... Si hubiera podido abrir la portezuela herméticamente cerrada y aspirar a plenos pulmones[17] el aire de la noche, a quinientos metros de altura, habría podido saborear el profundo silencio de aquella ciudad zigzagueante de luces, pero absolutamente desprovista de ruidos. La propulsión atómica había proporcionado aquella ventaja, decisiva para la salud mental: la metrópolis enorme y taciturna, silenciosa como una película muda.

El helicóptero descendía. Se posó sobre una terraza, iluminada por potentes reflectores. La voz mecánica ordenó:

—Descienda por la escalera que tiene a la vista hasta el primer ascensor. Apriete el botón del Piso XXII.

Tupac Pérez ejecutó las órdenes puntualmente. Quería terminar de una vez. Salió del ascensor y se encontró frente a una puerta de metal liso. Hacia un costado, la placa: «Tribunal Supremo de Suicidas». Empujó y entró. Se quitó los guantes. Alisó sus cabellos blancos. Se retocó la corbata. Una sala de audiencias,[18] vacía, con asientos tapizados de un material plástico de color gris. Se sentó. Al frente, el estrado vacío. Una voz cansada comenzó a hablar.

—Usted ha realizado dos tentativas anteriores.

—Correcto.

—Iba a realizar hoy la tercera.

—La última, si no se hubieran entrometido...

—¿Las anteriores?

—La primera, un balazo en el corazón...

—¿Y? —El despecho empañó la voz de Pérez.

—Desgraciadamente, nadie muere ya de balazos en el corazón... La segunda, me arrojé al Subterráneo...[19]

—... y detuvo durante media hora toda la red de ferrocarriles... Y quemó instalaciones por valor de millones de sarmientos...[20]

—El sistema de seguridad funcionó a las mil maravillas.[21] No me quedaba más que el agua del Río de la Plata.

—Tiene que comprender que esta situación no debe prolongarse indefinidamente.

---

[15]*Isla Desolación:* Desolation Island, an imaginary name for a likely tourist stop in Antarctica   [16]*patay* m.: name of an imaginary food   [17]*a plenos pulmones:* in deep breaths   [18]*sala de audiencias:* conference or meeting room   [19]*Subterráneo:* the subway, now called by everyone in Buenos Aires *el subte.* The most common word for "subway" in other Hispanic countries is *el metro.*   [20]*sarmientos:* The author suggests that by the year 2210 the Argentine monetary unit, now the *austral,* will be the *sarmiento,* honoring one of the early Argentine patriots, former president Domingo Faustino Sarmiento (1811–1888).   [21]*a las mil maravillas:* wonderfully (literally "like a thousand marvels")

—De ustedes depende...

—El Estado no puede permitir suicidios caros como el suyo.

—Ahogarme en el río no perjudicaba a nadie.

—Podía envenenar las aguas. Los peces podían transmitir agentes patógenos
5 albergados en sus narices. Su tentativa individual encarece el suicidio. Pone
usted frente a frente la libre empresa y la estatización[22] de los servicios públicos.
Hace muchos lustros[23] que nos hemos decidido por la segunda. Los suicidios
irremediables están reservados al Estado y se efectúan con el menor costo
posible. Ventajas de la producción en masa. Usted no puede ignorar que su
10 tentativa está violando principios básicos de economía social.

—Enhorabuena.[24]

—¿Quiere decir que está de acuerdo con nosotros?

—Terminemos de una vez.

Tupac Pérez ansiaba que concluyera aquel diálogo singular. Tenía la impre-
15 sión de estar discutiendo con una cinta magnética.

—¿No tiene nada que agregar?

—No.

—Cumplamos entonces las formalidades legales. ¿Las conoce?

—Tengo una vaga idea.

20 —Se le ofrecerán a título gratuito[25] los placeres que más atraen a los hombres.
Es una compensación por las privaciones de su vida. Si los rechaza, procede-
remos al trámite final.

—Comience cuando quiera.

—Ponemos a su disposición el B 608.

25 —¿Qué es eso?

—Un placer erótico tan intenso, embriagador y peligroso que ha pasado a ser
propiedad secreta del Estado. Nuestra sociedad se disolvería si cualquier hombre
pudiera disponer libremente de él. Escapó a las enumeraciones del Kamasutra.[26]
El Caballero Casanova[27] lo describió en un codicilo único, conservado en la
30 Biblioteca Nacional de París y rescatado de sus ruinas por nuestro Servicio de
Informaciones. El conde de Bussy, Brantôme y Stendhal,[28] que lo conocieron,
no se atrevieron a hacerlo público. Lo reservamos para casos excepcionales, para
premiar a los sabios y a los grandes poetas, aunque, por precaución, sólo
arriesgamos el ofrecimiento cuando ellos son suficientemente ancianos... Es una
35 recompensa superior al Premio Nobel. ¿Acepta el B 608, Tupac Pérez?

---

[22]*estatización:* nationalization   [23]*lustros:* five-year periods observed in the Roman Empire   [24]*Enhorabuena:* Well and good, all right then.   [25]*a título gratuito:* free of charge   [26]*el Kamasutra:* a
2000-year-old Sanskrit treatise on the art of love   [27]*Casanova:* Giovanni Giacomo Casanova
(1725–1798), celebrated Italian narrator of amorous adventures in his autobiographical *Memoirs*
(1826–1838).   [28]*El conde... Stendhal:* The Count de Bussy (Roger Robustin, 1618–1693), Brantôme (Pierre de Bourdeilles, 1540–1614), and Stendhal (Henri Beyle, 1783–1842), were French
chroniclers of the sexual mores of their respective periods.

—No me tienta. ¿Qué más me ofrece?

La voz sin matices siguió enumerando, en un vano intento de corrupción.

—Tenemos para usted viajes espaciales; recetas de cocina, salvadas de la destrucción de Dijon,[29] en la segunda mitad del siglo XX; la posesión temporal de óleos de Corot[30] y acuarelas de Paul Klee,[31] vinos chilenos de hace cien años...   5

—Prefiero beber el agua turbia de nuestro río...

—¿Rechaza todas nuestras proposiciones?

—Estamos perdiendo un tiempo precioso...

No hubo palabras durante unos minutos. Sólo se escuchó un ronroneo sutil y prolongado, como el de los tubos luminiscentes. Era el computador electrónico   10 que justipreciaba las respuestas de aquel suicida y calculaba sus posibilidades de vida, de acuerdo con las estadísticas de los últimos cien años. Al final, la voz decidió.

—El Estado le concede la solución que desea. Nada podemos hacer para impedirlo. Le quedan cinco segundos.   15

Tupac Pérez se puso de pie y avanzó sin vacilar, el paso firme, hacia las puertas anaranjadas de la «Cámara de Desintegración», que se abrieron para dejarlo pasar y se cerraron rápidamente detrás de él.

Los helicópteros siguieron trayendo hasta el alba nuevos suicidas desde el Círculo A5 hasta el Depósito Central de calle Esmeralda 66.   20

EXERCISES

A. Questions and Opinions

1. ¿Cómo ha llegado el hombre al puerto de Buenos Aires?
2. ¿Cómo está el área del puerto a esa hora?
3. ¿Hacia dónde se dirige el hombre?
4. ¿Qué lo detiene?
5. ¿Desde dónde le hablan?
6. ¿Por qué ya no sirve la profesión de Tupac Pérez?
7. Cuando baja el helicóptero, ¿a quién encuentra Tupac Pérez en la cabina?
8. ¿Adónde lo llevan?

---

[29]*Dijon:* a city in eastern France, an oblique reference to the reputation of French cuisine   [30]*Corot:* Jean Baptiste Corot (1796–1875) was an influential nineteenth-century French painter.   [31]*Paul Klee:* Klee (1879–1940) was a Swiss painter of the abstract and surrealist schools.

9. ¿Qué cosas le ofrecen a Tupac Pérez para que no se empeñe en suicidarse?
10. Al final, ¿qué solución le permiten al escritor?
●11. ¿Reconoce Ud. que el suicidio puede llegar a ser preferible a seguir viviendo?
●12. ¿Cree Ud. que en el futuro de nuestra civilización ocurrirán cosas parecidas a lo que se narra en este cuento?

B. Verb Practice

Use each of the following verbal phrases in an original sentence in Spanish, either based on the story or of your own design. Be prepared to explain the meaning of your sentences.

1. **hacía cinco minutos**
2. **detenerse**
3. **seguir** + *present participle*
4. **tratar de** + *infinitive*
5. **tener que ver (con)**
6. **no servir para nada**
7. **quedarle a uno**
8. **depender de**
9. **querer decir**
10. **perder tiempo**

C. Vocabulary Practice

Complete the sentences below, matching the expressions on the right with the English words on the left. Be sure to use the correct form of each verb. Then use each expression in an original Spanish sentence and indicate in English what your sentence means.

1. Esto está *in accordance with* todas las leyes y reglas del Estado.
2. El Estado tiene *available* medidas extraordinarias para saber lo que está pasando.
3. En esta sociedad nadie *has a right to* suicidarse.
4. Me ofrecieron un ascenso a cambio de información, pero (yo) *turned it down.*
5. Los oficiales del Estado *stick their noses* en los asuntos de todos los ciudadanos.
6. Había una cortina de acero *on both sides* de la avenida.
7. Señor, estoy *at your service* en cualquier momento.
8. Hay un helicóptero a 10 metros *above* su cabeza.
9. ¿Puedo usar esta *tape* de mi grabadora para mi computadora también?
10. El Estado *has carried out* medidas extraordinarias para impedir el suicidio.

por ambos lados

por encima de

entrometerse

realizar

tener derecho (a)

cinta

a su disposición

disponer de

rechazar

de acuerdo con

D. Communication Practice

1. Say that you stopped at the corner a moment to speak to Ernesto.
2. Insist that Francisco's money has nothing to do with your friendship.
3. State that one single kiss doesn't mean that they are in love.
4. Say that life without freedom isn't worth anything.
5. Tell Mario not to waste time watching television.

E. Review Exercise

The following words from the story are cognates with English words, but they are "deceptive" in the sense that their meanings will not be the obvious ones. If you don't know them, look them up in the end vocabulary.

suicida	editoriales	ignorar
vagón	seguridad	recetas
paso	propaganda	
comisario	tentativas	

EL MUERTO ERA UN VIVO

PEPE MARTÍNEZ DE LA VEGA

PEPE MARTÍNEZ DE LA VEGA (1908–1954) was one of
Mexico's most popular humorists, and for years he wrote for a
series of successful radio comedy shows. There is a certain
irreverent flavor to his work that his Mexican audience re-
sponded to enthusiastically. When he turned to writing short
stories and created Péter Pérez, it was inevitable that his detective would not belong to the traditional school of detection.
Sure enough, the Péter Pérez tales are one leg pull after another.
Consider his solution of a locked-room mystery that had posi-
tively baffled the Mexico City police. Called to the scene of the
crime, Péter confirmed that the dead man had indeed been
found in a locked room, with all the windows and doors locked
and secured. No secret passages, no trap doors . . . Clearly an
impossible crime. But not for Péter. "Elementary, my dear
chaps," he observed calmly. "I have the solution. You will note
that the sealed room in question has no ceiling."

The author's friend and compatriot, the distinguished Mexican literary critic and writer, María Elvira Bermúdez, has accurately described the character of these stories. She writes: "Péter
Pérez is wise and gracious and always solves the crime, but his
methods are broad caricatures of traditional detective fiction
techniques. With generous doses of popular humor, he effec-
tively expresses scorn for everything that represents precision,
fastidiousness, and routine," which the reader may observe in
the amusing adventure entitled «El muerto era un vivo».

A PRELIMINARY LOOK AT KEY EXPRESSIONS

Be sure to study these expressions before you read the story.

1. (118: 2) **en efecto** *in fact, as a matter of fact*
2. (118: 5) **frente a** *in front of*   This also means *across the street from.*
3. (118:12) **nuevamente** *again*
4. (118:13) **¡Socorro!** *Help!*   This is the most common way in Spanish to call for help when you are in trouble. Another way is **¡auxilio!**
5. (118:14) **llamarse** *to be called*   However, the most common English way of saying this is *My (his, her, etc.) name is* . . . Remember that the reflexive pronoun agrees with the subject: **—Tú, ¿cómo te llamas? —Me llamo José Sicorro.**
6. (119:10) **más allá** *beyond, farther,* an adverb of place   There is also an expression used as a noun: **el más allá,** meaning *the great beyond.*
7. (119:15) **lo ocurrido** *what had happened*   **lo** + *adjective* is a common way of "nominalizing" an adjective, i.e., referring to it in a general way without mentioning a specific antecedent. For example, **lo bueno** *the good part,* **lo nuevo** *the new thing(s),* **lo importante** *what was (is) important.*
8. (120: 8) **dirigirse a** *to turn to, go up to, go toward; to speak to, address*   This expression can be used with people or things: **Se dirigió a Péter Pérez,** or **Se dirigió al teléfono.**
9. (120:14) **darse cuenta (de)** *to know, realize*   What is realized is the object of the preposition **de: Al momento me di cuenta.** *Right away I knew;* **Al momento me di cuenta de que la señora es la homicida.** *Right away I realized that the woman is the murderess.*
10. (120:24) **callar** *to be quiet*   This verb is sometimes reflexive, particularly in commands: **¡Cállate!** *Shut up!*
11. (120:27) **disponerse a** + *infinitive* *to get ready to* + *verb*
12. (120:29) **meter la pata**   This expression has two related meanings: *to butt in* and *to stick one's foot in it, "goof."* **Pata** is normally used only for animal and furniture legs—except in such expressions as this one.
13. (121: 6) **es decir** *that is to say, I mean*
14. (121:31) **quedar en** *to agree to, settle on*   This expression is usually followed by an infinitive: **Quedaron en encontrarse a las nueve.** *They agreed to meet at nine o'clock.*
15. (121:31) **por casualidad** *by chance, coincidence*   This is an example of a false cognate: **casualidad, casual,** and **casualmente** all have the idea of a completely unplanned, chance occurrence. *Casual* in the sense of "nonchalant" is **despreocupado** or **sin importancia.**
16. (121:36) **conocer** *to know, get to know, meet*   **Conocer** in the preterit or the perfect tenses means *to know for the first time* or *meet:* **Conocí a**

mi socio en la escuela. *I met my partner (for the first time) in school.* But in other tenses it means *to know* or *be acquainted with:* **No lo conozco bien.** *I don't know him very well.*

17. (122:29) **por falta de** *through, because of the lack of*
18. (123:25) **equivocarse** *to be wrong, mistaken*   Notice how this verb can render the English adjective "wrong": **Se equivocó de puertas.** *He got the wrong door* (literally, "He made a mistake 'door-wise'").
19. (123:27) **lograr** + *infinitive   to manage, get* + *infinitive*   This is virtually synonymous with **conseguir** + *infinitive* or **alcanzar a** + *infinitive.*
20. (123:29) **valerse de** *to make use of*

EL MUERTO
ERA UN VIVO[1]

... Por la elegante colonia[2] residencial pedaleaba un ciclista. Su cachucha lo delataba como mensajero de telégrafo, y, en efecto, eso era: un mensajero de telégrafos.

Tras de cerciorarse del nombre de la calle por donde iba, el ciclista se detuvo frente al número 135 y se acercó al timbre eléctrico para hacer lo que los líderes 5 hacen con el obrero a la hora de cobrarle la cuota sindical: oprimirlo.[3]

Ya desesperaba el mensajero de entregar el telegrama, pues tenía diez minutos llamando,[4] cuando apareció una señora en la puerta de la lujosa mansión. La dama era joven y guapa. Recibió el mensaje, firmó, y rasgó el sobre.

—Es para mi esposo —fue su comentario al cerrar la puerta. 10

El mensajero montó en su bicicleta y apenas iba a reanudar la marcha, cuando la señora joven y guapa salió nuevamente y gritó:

—¡Socorro..., socorro!

El de telégrafos, que se llamaba José Sicorro[5] González, se quitó cortésmente la cachucha diciendo: 15

—Mande usted,[6] señora...

—¡Socorro, socorro...! —volvió a exclamar la dama.

—Aquí estoy, señora, diga usted...

—¡Auxilio..., auxilio...! —gritó otra vez la señora.

—Esa es otra cosa, señora, ¿qué le pasa? 20

—Han asesinado a mi esposo; llame a la policía.

El mensajero telefoneó a la jefatura y comunicó la dirección al sargento Juan Vélez que estaba de guardia.

---

[1]*«El muerto era un vivo»:* Setting the tone for his story, the author creates a play on words in the title: "The Dead Man Was a Live One." Besides meaning "alive," *vivo* means "shrewd," "clever," "quick-witted."   [2]*colonia:* district or neighborhood (in Mexico City)   [3]*oprimirlo:* a play on words since *oprimir* is both "to squeeze" or "press" physically and "to oppress" politically or socially. Just as union leaders "put pressure" on their workers to pay their regular dues, José Sicorro similarly "presses" the bell. Another reference to union activities will occur later in the story.   [4]*tenía diez minutos llamando:* he had been ringing for ten minutes   [5]*Sicorro:* a Spanish surname similar in sound to the word *socorro* "help," all of which explains the ensuing exchange between the two characters   [6]*Mande usted:* At your service

Un Espectáculo Horrible

El sargento de detectives Juan Vélez se hallaba en su despacho charlando con el genial detective de Peralvillo,[7] Péter Pérez.

Acompañado del gran Péter, el sargento partió para la elegante casa donde se había cometido el asesinato.

5 La esposa de la víctima era la única persona viviente que había en la bella mansión. El espectáculo que se ofreció a la vista de Péter y del sargento era horrible, tan horrible como el mercado de San Juan,[8] pongamos por caso.[9]

En el centro de la pieza, lujosamente amueblada, estaba tirado el cuerpo del que en vida fue Saturnino Flores. Un reguero de sangre iba desde un sillón hasta 10 diez pasos más allá, bajo una mesilla ornamental. El cadáver tenía un puñal clavado en la espalda. El muerto conservaba una rosa en la mano izquierda y un puñado de flores en la derecha. Uno de los dedos de esa mano estaba tinto en sangre. Saturnino, antes de morir, había dibujado un extraño círculo con su propia sangre en el piso encerado.

15 La esposa relató brevemente lo ocurrido. Ella estaba oyendo la radio cuando tocaron a la puerta de la calle. Salió a abrir y recibió un mensaje telegráfico para su esposo. Lo leyó, y, aunque no tenía importancia, prefirió comunicárselo al punto a su marido. Al entrar en la habitación descubrió el crimen, llamó al mensajero y avisó a la policía. Eso era todo.

20 Péter Pérez había observado la extraña actitud[10] del muerto. El sargento echó sólo una ojeada y principió a tomar datos.

—Su nombre, señora —dijo a la viuda.

—Rosa Flores.

—¿Cuál era la profesión de su esposo?

25 —Agente de negocios.

En esos momentos Péter Pérez, el genial detective de Peralvillo, interrumpió el interrogatorio para suplicar a la señora:

—¿Tiene usted la bondad de prestarme[11] la pluma fuente de su esposo? No traje la mía y necesito tomar unos apuntes.

30 —Mi esposo no tenía pluma fuente —dijo la viuda.

—Bueno, pues su lápiz —solicitó de nuevo Péter.

—No usaba lápiz.

—Mil gracias —respondió Péter, con esa exquisita finura que guardaba siempre para las señoras guapas.

---

[7]*Peralvillo:* district of Mexico City   [8]*el mercado de San Juan:* a noisy and animated marketplace in Mexico City   [9]*pongamos por caso:* for example   [10]*actitud:* position (the body was in)   [11]*¿Tiene... prestarme:* Will you please lend me . . . (literally, "Would you have the kindness to lend me . . .")

La Derrota de Péter Pérez

El sargento Vélez vio la oportunidad y decidió obrar al punto.

Tenía ocasión, el sargento, de derrotar, por primera vez en su vida, al gran Péter en su propia presencia.

Así fue como, melodramáticamente, exclamó:

—Queda usted arrestada, señora, por el asesinato de su esposo...   5

La viuda palideció y murmuró:

—¡Es una infamia...!

El sargento Vélez, con teatralidad, se dirigió al teléfono y llamó al redactor de un diario matutino, pues le gusta mucho la publicidad.

—Dentro de diez minutos —dijo a la dama— le explicaré a usted los motivos   10
que me obligan a dar este paso. Por lo pronto, considérese detenida...

Y diez minutos más tarde, frente al representante de la prensa capitalina, el sargento Vélez inició su explicación:

—Al momento me di cuenta —dijo— de que la señora es la homicida. No había nadie más en la casa, aparte de que el muerto tiene en la mano izquierda   15
una rosa y en la derecha un puñado de flores. ¿Por qué ese extraño capricho de un agonizante?[12] Sólo hay una deducción: quiso señalar a su victimario. La dama aquí presente se llama Rosa Flores. Para mí, el asunto está tan claro como si el muerto hubiera dejado una carta...

—El muerto —exclamó Péter— no pudo dejar ninguna carta, porque era   20
analfabeto...

Pero el sargento Vélez no hizo caso alguno y sonrió satisfecho, ante las miradas de aprobación de dos gendarmes *lambiscones.*[13]

Péter Pérez calló. Vélez miró a Péter compasivamente, pues consideró que lo había derrotado en toda la línea.[14]   25

El sargento puso a la infeliz viuda las esposas de hierro en las muñecas y el periodista se disponía a retirarse, cuando el gran Péter habló y dijo:

—Un momento; la señora no mató a su esposo.

—No meta usted la pata, amigo —le indicó Vélez.

—No meto la pata, sargento —respondió fríamente el genial detective—   30
porque no tengo patas; soy un ser racional que posee únicamente dos pies.[15]

—Entonces, ¿quién mató a don Saturnino? —inquirió el diarista.

—Aún no lo sé; pero, de lo que sí estoy seguro es de que no fue la señora —declaró Péter. Y agregó:

—¿Me permite usted interrogar a la dama, sargento?   35

---

[12]*agonizante:* dying man   [13]*lambiscones:* "boot-licking," fawning   [14]*en toda la línea:* all along the line   [15]*no tengo... pies:* Although *pata* is used in slang expressions, it is actually the word for animal foot, leg, or paw. *Pierna* is a human leg, and *pie* a human foot.

—Hágalo, pero pronto —concedió de mala gana Vélez— pues no puedo perder mi tiempo.

—Gracias. ¿A qué hora se retiró usted a oír la radio? —preguntó a la señora.

—A las seis de la tarde.

5 —¿Cuánto tiempo después llegó el telegrama?

—Llegó a las diez de la noche. Es decir, cuatro horas más tarde. Nosotros, por el horario comercial, comemos a las cinco y ya no cenamos... Mejor dicho[16] —y rompió a llorar— comíamos antes; ahora comeré yo sola...

—Cálmese, señora —la consoló Péter—. ¿Su esposo recibió alguna visita?

10 —Sí, lo vino a ver su socio, el señor Méndez.

—¿Cuál es el nombre completo del señor Méndez?

—Juan R. Méndez —respondió la dama—. Estuvo con él en el comedor. Mi esposo le ofreció una copa,[17] pero el señor Méndez prefirió tomar café. Le puse la cafetera eléctrica llena de agua, y suficiente ración para que se hiciera las tazas 15 que gustara.

—¿Dónde está esa cafetera? Pero, antes, llame usted al señor Méndez por teléfono; necesito hablar con él.

—No está en su casa. Ya no debe tardar.[18] Fue al teatro *Iris* a oír la conferencia de un líder —dijo la señora—. Esto le dijo a mi esposo en mi presencia. 20 Quedó en volver aquí. Esta es la cafetera.

—Está vacía —exclamó el gran detective de Peralvillo.

—En efecto...[19]

—¿Cuántas tazas se pueden hacer con la cantidad de agua que usted le puso? —preguntó Péter a la dama.

25 —Siete...

—Gracias.

Segundos después llegó Juan R. Méndez y se mostró impresionadísimo con la suerte corrida por su querido amigo y socio.

Péter casi no lo dejó ni enterarse bien cuando se le quedó viendo[20] y le 30 preguntó a la boca de jarro:[21]

—Por casualidad..., perdonando la indiscreción, ¿no es usted pariente del...?

—¿...del guitarrista Ramos? —concluyó Juan con cierto sonsonete.

Y Méndez agregó, molesto:

—No, señor. Esa pregunta me la han hecho desde que estaba yo en la escuela.

35 —Dispense. ¿Dónde conoció usted a su socio? —volvió a preguntar Péter.

—En la escuela, precisamente.

—¿Dónde estuvo usted entre las seis de la tarde y las diez de la noche de hoy?

---

[16]*Mejor dicho:* What I mean to say is . . .   [17]*una copa:* a drink   [18]*Ya no debe tardar:* He won't be long now.   [19]*En efecto:* So I see.   [20]*se le quedó viendo:* he stared at him   [21]*a... jarro:* point blank

—Salí de aquí como a las siete, y me dirigí al teatro *Iris,* a oír la conferencia de un conocido líder obrero. Tengo mil testigos de que estuve allí...

El médico legista que había llegado al lugar, le informó brevemente al sargento que la muerte del señor Flores ocurrió entre las ocho y las nueve de la noche.

Esa interrupción sirvió para que el sargento Vélez diera ya por concluido todo.[22] Se acercó a Péter y le preguntó:

—¿Acabó usted?

—Estoy listo —respondió el genio de Peralvillo.

La Victoria de Péter Pérez

Y como quien no quiere la cosa,[23] añadió:

—Este señor también está listo para acompañarlo a usted —y señaló a Ramos—. Deténgalo, sargento. Es el asesino de su socio.

Y, ante el atónito periodista, el maravilloso detective, orgullo de su barriada, explicó:

—De lo primero que me percaté fue de que el muerto era un vivo. Porque muy vivo se necesita ser para que un analfabeto como él gane tanto dinero...

—¿Analfabeto? ¿Quiere usted decir que no sabía leer, ni escribir? —preguntó con sorna Vélez.

—Exacto, amigo, exacto... Eso de que era agente de negocios es cuento.[24] Se trata, indudablemente, del coyote de algún funcionario de polendas.[25] Vea usted qué muebles, y qué casa, y qué mujer.

Péter echó una mirada a la viuda y se relamió los labios.

—Al grano,[26] al grano —urgió el sargento.

—El muerto, que, repito, era un vivo, al ser herido mortalmente por este hombre, buscó la manera de delatarlo. No sabía escribir, cosa que pude comprobar con la ausencia de pluma fuente y lápices en esta casa, además de que la esposa, cuando recibió el telegrama, lo abrió seguramente para leerlo a su esposo y no por falta de educación,[27] pues esta señora tiene clase. Eso demuestra que el marido no podía leerlo por ser analfabeto. Al ser herido, vuelvo a decir, buscó la forma para denunciar a su asesino, y recordó que una vez había oído decir que el cero a la izquierda no vale nada. Dejó a la inteligencia de la policía la interpretación de su enigma. Tomó una rosa con la mano izquierda y dibujó un cero con su sangre para indicarnos que Rosa no era la culpable, dado que[28] al colocar la mano izquierda sobre el cero indicó que no valía nada, por estar el cero *a la*

---

[22]*diera... todo:* considered the matter closed   [23]*como... cosa:* nonchalantly   [24]*cuento:* a fairy tale   [25]*coyote... polendas:* the "bagman" for some high-level government official on the take   [26]*Al grano:* Get to the point   [27]*no... educación:* not because she was ill-mannered   [28]*dado que:* since

izquierda. Después tomó flores en la derecha, para señalarnos que las flores sí eran una afirmación.

—Ella se apellida Flores —dijo triunfante Vélez.

—Sí, pero no quiso indicar flores a secas.[29] Observe usted que entre dedo y
5 dedo, formó grupos de flores. Entonces deduje yo: *el muerto quiso decir ramos, no flores.* El socio no se llama Juan R. Méndez, sino Juan Ramos Méndez. Seguramente se quitó el «Ramos» para despistar a la policía, pues siempre ha sido un pillo. El sólo se delató sobre su verdadero apellido, ya que dijo que en la escuela le preguntaban si era pariente del guitarrista Ramos. ¿Por qué se lo
10 preguntaban? Sencillamente porque se apellida Ramos.

—Aquí lo agarré en un fallo, don Péter —dijo Vélez—, porque usted dice que el muerto era analfabeto, y, sin embargo, conoció al señor Méndez en la escuela...

—Exacto: lo conoció en la escuela. Y, suprímase el «don», sargento, porque
15 soy demócrata —dijo Péter—. Ramos estudiaba en la escuela, pero Saturnino no; era *bolero.*[30] Esto lo descubrí examinando los dedos del muerto, con huellas imborrables de crema para zapatos y observando que, en su alcoba, hay todo lo necesario para darse grasa.[31] No lo hacía por ahorro, sino por costumbre... Saturnino, en sus mocedades, *boleaba* a los alumnos de la escuela. Ahí lo
20 conoció, Ramos Méndez, su hoy victimario. Para Saturnino, Juan fue siempre «Ramos» y no Méndez. Por eso lo delató como «Ramos» cuando se sintió agonizante.

—Tengo una coartada perfecta —dijo Juan—. Estuve en la conferencia del líder en el *Iris.* Usted no puede probar nada...
25 —Se equivoca, amigo; puedo probarle todo. Ud. —y Péter lo señaló con el índice— estuvo aquí antes de ir al teatro y se bebió siete tazas de café para no dormirse durante la soporífera charla del salvador de masas. Logró permanecer despierto, pero los demás asistentes[32] cayeron dormidos. Usted salió cuando todos roncaban. Cometió el crimen, valiéndose, para entrar, de una llave falsa,[33]
30 de la cual se había provisto con anterioridad y regresó al teatro, donde los agremiados permanecían roncando. A usted lo vieron cuando llegó al teatro por primera vez, pero no pudieron verlo salir, ni regresar. Es usted inteligente, pero más vivo[34] que usted era el muerto...

Juan R. Méndez confesó su delito ante el cúmulo de pruebas reunidas por
35 Péter.

La viuda, jubilosa al verse libre, se abalanzó sobre Péter y le dio un beso. Después, arrepentida de su impulso, preguntó con los ojos bajos.

—¿Cuánto le debo?

---

[29]*no quiso... secas:* he wanted to do more than just indicate flowers   [30]*bolero:* shoeshine boy (in Mexico)   [31]*darse grasa:* to polish shoes. *Grasa* is shoe polish in Mexico.   [32]*asistentes:* those in attendance   [33]*una llave falsa:* a passkey   [34]*vivo:* See Note 1.

—Nada, señora —respondió Péter ruborizado y con delicada galantería—. Para mí, un beso de mujer vale más que todos los tesoros del mundo...

Y se retiró con la modestia que sólo tienen los genios.

Y sin recibir el beso.[35]

EXERCISES

A. Questions and Opinions

1. ¿Por qué desesperaba el mensajero de entregar el telegrama?
2. ¿Cómo había muerto Saturnino Flores?
3. ¿Qué había dibujado la víctima en el piso con su propia sangre?
4. ¿Por qué no le prestó la viuda a Péter la pluma o el lápiz que él le pidió?
5. ¿A quién arrestó el sargento Vélez por el asesinato del señor Flores?
6. ¿Qué observación hizo Péter sobre el hombre muerto?
7. ¿Quién vino a ver al señor Flores en la tarde de ese día?
8. ¿A dónde había ido Juan R. Méndez después de ver al señor Flores?
9. ¿A quién acusó Péter del asesinato del señor Flores?
10. ¿Por qué se había bebido siete tazas de café el señor Méndez?
•11. ¿Qué le parece a Ud. la coartada del señor Méndez?
•12. ¿Le interesan a Ud. los cuentos policiales *serios*? ¿Por qué?

B. Verb Practice

Use each of the following verbal phrases in an original sentence in Spanish, either based on the story or of your own design. Be prepared to explain the meaning of your sentences.

1. **llamarse**
2. **dirigirse a**
3. **darse cuenta (de)**
4. **callar**
5. **disponerse a** + *infinitive*
6. **quedar en**
7. **conocer** (in preterit)
8. **equivocarse**
9. **lograr** + *infinitive*
10. **valerse de**

---

[35]*y... beso:* Peter obviously had expected another kiss, which he never got.

C. Vocabulary Practice

Complete the sentences below, matching the expressions on the right with the English words on the left. Be sure to use the correct form of each verb. Then use each expression in an original Spanish sentence and indicate in English what your sentence means.

1. Señora, tenga la bondad de contarme *what happened.*
2. Bebió mucho café, *I mean,* ¡siete tazas!
3. Y, *in fact,* el pobre no sabía leer ni escribir.
4. Yo estaba seguro de que Péter Pérez iba a *butt in* en la investigación.
5. El policía se detuvo *in front of* el apartamento, se acercó y oprimió el timbre.
6. Cuando la señora encontró el cadáver de su esposo, gritó, «*Help*»!
7. El policía le preguntó *once more,* —¿Me permite usted interrogar a la dama?
8. El tipo siempre se entromete *through lack of* sentido común.
9. Había un sillón en la sala y el cadáver quedaba *farther on.*
10. ¿*By chance* encontró usted crema para zapatos en sus dedos?

en efecto

frente a

nuevamente

¡socorro!

más allá

lo ocurrido

meter la pata

es decir

por casualidad

por falta de

D. Communication Practice

1. Say you didn't realize what you had done.
2. Indicate that you hope Rubén manages to sell his car.
3. Suggest that perhaps Carmen has made a mistake.
4. Say that Laura stuck her foot in it again.
5. State that the mother was trying to quiet down her children.

E. Completion Exercise

Complete the following sentence fragments with your own ideas. Be sure to use the appropriate mood and tense with verbs you introduce.

1. Así que quedaron en....
2. Cuando por vez primera conocí a David...
3. El detective se levantó y se dirigió a...
4. Si yo fuera Ud., me valdría de...
5. En ese momento Juanito se disponía a...

EL PAJARITO
DE LOS DOMINGOS

María de Montserrat

MARÍA DE MONTSERRAT (1915–   ) was born in Camagüey, Cuba, where business had taken her parents, but she has spent her life since the age of two in Montevideo, Uruguay. She attended the Women's University there, then married and raised three children. Her first book, *Tres relatos* (1944), was followed by other volumes of short stories, a medium in which she has excelled. Her novels, beginning with *Los habitantes* (1968), deal imaginatively and nostalgically with Uruguay's historical past. Since 1978 she has been a member of the Uruguayan National Academy of Letters.

«El pajarito de los domingos», taken from her collection, *El sonido blanco* (1979), is a brief but uncommonly disturbing short story. The reader easily follows the account of the narrator, an adolescent girl, and effortlessly adopts a point of view from which to judge the events she recounts. For this reason, the story's conclusion will likely provide a sudden shock. Apart from this emotional aspect, this tale also seems to invite a moral judgment of the people depicted.

A PRELIMINARY LOOK AT KEY EXPRESSIONS

Be sure to study these expressions before you read the story.

1. (130: 4) **esforzarse por** + *infinitive* *to make an effort, try* + *infinitive*
2. (130:10) **rodear (de)** *to surround (with)*
3. (130:13) **quedarse** *to stay, remain*
4. (130:18) **educación** *upbringing, breeding* This refers mainly to the training given in the home to children by parents. *Education* in the sense of "schooling," "instruction," etc. is more often **instrucción, enseñanza,** etc.
5. (130:22) **elegir** *to choose, pick* In many South American countries **coger** and to a lesser extent, its derivatives, **escoger** and **recoger,** are taboo words. Thus other words, such as **elegir** for **escoger,** are used.
6. (130:24) **tener** + *definite article* + *part of the body* + *adjective possessive adjective* + *part of the body* + *to be* + *adjective* Spanish uses **tener** to express conditions of parts of the body: **Tengo las manos frías** *My hands are cold.* **Tienen colorados los cachetes** *Their cheeks are pink,* etc.
7. (130:26) **cargar con** *to carry* (something heavy)
8. (131: 5) **rogar** *to beg, ask* (someone to do something) This is a stronger version of **pedir.**
9. (131: 6) **valer la pena** *to be worthwhile, worth it*
10. (131: 6) **recién** + *past participle* *new(ly)* + *past participle* This use of **recién** is particularly common with **nacido** *newborn* and **casado** *newlywed.* Also **recién llegado** is *newcomer.*
11. (131: 6) **chocar (contra)** *to bump, crash (into, against)*
12. (131: 8) **tal vez** *perhaps, maybe*
13. (131:21) **admitir** *to admit, let in* **Confesar** is used for *admit* in the sense of *confess* or *own up to.*
14. (131:21) **de vez en cuando** *from time to time, once in a while, now and then*
15. (131:24) **apoyado** *leaning* Spanish uses a past participle to express physical position, in contrast to the present participle of English: **acostado** *lying,* **sentado** *sitting,* **colgado** *hanging,* **arrimado** *leaning,* etc.
16. (131:32) **¿Qué le pasa?** *What's the matter with you (him, her, it)?*
17. (131:34) **impedir** *to prevent, keep from* This verb is used with an indirect object and often an infinitive: **Me impiden ir tras ella.** *They keep me from going after her.*
18. (132: 3) **suceder** *to happen, occur* This is a slightly more formal synonym of **pasar** and **ocurrir.**

19. (132: 5) **cada uno** *each one, every one*   **Cada** is invariable in form: **cada libro, cada mesa, cada dos días.**
20. (132: 6) **avergonzarse** *to be embarrassed, ashamed*   Spanish does not ordinarily distinguish between these two ideas as English does. Remember also that **embarazada** is *pregnant,* not *embarrassed,* which is **avergonzado(–a).**

EL PAJARITO
DE LOS DOMINGOS

Mi mejor amiga es Pepita, la hija de los carboneros.[1] Tuve que dar muchas explicaciones a mi familia por esta preferencia y probar que tal amistad no me convierte en una chica sucia y desprolija, que no pierdo mis buenos modales ni nada de lo superior que se esfuerzan por inculcarme.[2]

El lugar más limpio que conozco, y el más cómodo, es la trastienda donde 5 viven los carboneros. Antes hay que pasar por la negrura y el tizne. Pero creo que no debe ser sólo por el contraste que allá lo blanco es más blanco que en cualquier otro sitio.

Y cuando Pepita está enferma, admiro sus sábanas dóciles y crujientes, según como ella se revuelve parecen rodearla de países fragantes y soleados.[3] La cama 10 esmaltada no tiene ninguna saltadura y el mosquitero que se frunce en lo alto, dentro de una corona de bronce, está arreglado como un velo de novia.[4]

Yo me quedaría para siempre en esta casa, por los cromos de las paredes, por las ventanas y sus cortinas recogidas con moños de cinta desde donde se ve un patiecito[5] lleno de plantas. Aquí se está bien,[6] por frío que esté afuera y siempre 15 hay agua pronta para el té sobre el calorífico de cisco. Se habla poco,[7] las personas son amables y reposadas, no se les nota que les falte por completo la educación como aseguran en casa.[8]

¡Estamos tan contentas! Hoy es sábado y ya hicimos los deberes del lunes. Pepita me ayudó en una redacción y yo la ayudé en los ejercicios de aritmética. 20 Mañana iremos, como todos los domingos, a la feria grande[9] con mi tía Melita y a más de curiosear, de comer bizcochos y comprar calcomanías, elegiremos un lindo pajarito.

Una mañana fría pero hermosa; tenemos los cachetes colorados, los pies calientes, las manos algo paspadas. Mi tía Melita nos ha comprado bizcochos y 25 un bastón de caramelo a cada una. Nosotras cargamos con la cesta llena de

---

[1]*carboneros:* coal peddlers   [2]*lo superior... inculcarme:* feelings of superiority that they have tried to drum into me   [3]*según... soleados:* which, as she moves around in bed, make her seem to be travelling through fragrant and sunny lands   [4]*un velo de novia:* a bridal veil   [5]*patiecito:* little patio (In Hispanic homes a *patio* is really a small interior courtyard, usually open to the sky.)   [6]*se está bien:* you're comfortable   [7]*Se habla poco:* There's not too much talking   [8]*no... casa:* it's not at all apparent that they have no class or breeding, as they keep telling me at home   [9]*la feria grande:* the market

naranjas y ella se oculta de los piropeadores[10] con un gran ramo de dalias matizadas. Ahora vamos al puesto de los pájaros. El hombre nos conoce pero nunca es muy amable. Se pone hosco y pregunta: ¿Van a llevar lo mismo? Yo propongo que esta vez llevemos un cardenal. ¡Son tan vistosos! Sobre todo los de
5 penacho rojo. Se lo ruego. Pero mi tía Melita levanta los hombros como hace cuando no vale la pena contestar. Los mistos parecen recién cazados, chocan continuamente contra los alambres. Hay pájaros menos chúcaros y más bonitos. No digo comprar un canario,[11] sería pedir mucho, pero tal vez un gargantillo. ¿Por qué no un gargantillo? Mi tía levanta los hombros por segunda vez y ya no
10 me atrevo a proponer nada más. «Será como siempre —le susurro a Pepita— no tienen un poco de imaginación».[12] Aquí está. Un misto ruin y descolorido. Lo ponen dentro de una bolsa de papel que tiene un agujerito para la respiración. Se la cedo a Pepita; con su mano libre la lleva con muchísimo cuidado.

En la puerta nos despedimos para vernos más tarde. Pero ahora Pepita pide
15 algo. «¿No me dejaría ver la pajarera de los mistos, señora?» Mi tía Melita va a contestar con alguna palabra cortante, lo piensa mejor y dice: «¿Quieres verla? Pasa, pasa».

Pepita camina entre nosotras, admirada. Le gustan los sillones de mimbre, tan blancos y floridos, las palmas en sus soportes de mayólica, y más que nada el
20 vitral del techo por el que bajan todos los colores que existen. Estoy contenta. Creo que ya la admitirán de vez en cuando.[13] Llegamos al segundo patio. Le murmuro a mi amiga: «Ahora vas a conocer a toda la familia». Mi madre sale de la cocina secándose las manos, mi tío se levanta con su libro bajo el brazo, mi abuela sale de su cuarto apoyada en el bastón. Todos nos acercamos a la jaula.
25 Tía Melita arrebata a mi amiga la bolsa de papel. Ella se sobresalta y la mira asombrada, aún sin entender.

—¡Aquí tienes el pajarito de los domingos, mi goloso!

Con su habilidad de siempre, tía Melita abre la puerta de la jaula al mismo tiempo que rasga el papel. El misto entra. ¡Tan feíto él![14] Después de un loco
30 revoloteo le viene el chucho como a los otros.[15] El caburé[16] lo mira. Hincha su pechera blanca, levanta su cola rayada. ¡Es tan gracioso! Giro hacia Pepita y veo a una desconocida.[17] ¿Pero qué le pasa? Retrocede alocada. ¡Casi hace caer a mi abuela! Ahora corre atropelladamente. ¡Pepita! ¡Pepita! Quiero ir tras ella pero me lo impiden.

---

[10]*piropeadores:* admirers (In Hispanic countries it is common for males to admire women in public and make remarks as they pass by.)   [11]*No... canario:* I don't suggest that we buy a canary   [12]*no... imaginación:* they haven't the slightest bit of imagination   [13]*ya... cuando:* from now on they'll have her in every once in a while   [14]*¡Tan feíto él!* The diminutive *feíto* (from *feo*) is for emphasis: "He's so ugly!"   [15]*le... otros:* it begins to tremble just like all the others   [16]*caburé:* pygmy owl, a bird native to southern South America. Its feathers are highly prized.   [17]*veo a una desconocida:* I can scarcely recognize her (literally, "I see a stranger")

Se ha ido gritándonos algo horrible. ¡Dios mío! El primer día que entraba en esta casa y que le dejábamos ver todo, hasta el precioso caburé en su momento más interesante. «¿Qué te decíamos, eh? Ya sucedió. La carbonerita ha mostrado su hilacha».[18]

Ahora cada uno vuelve a lo que estaba haciendo antes. No puedo menos que   5
avergonzarme. A causa de Pepita se han perdido la mayor distracción del domingo. El caburé ya se ha zampado la cabecita del misto. Y lo demás no vale tanto la pena.[19]

EXERCISES

A. Questions and Opinions

1. ¿Por qué tuvo que dar la narradora explicaciones sobre su amistad con Pepita?
2. ¿Cómo es la casa de Pepita?
3. ¿Adónde suelen ir los domingos las dos chicas?
4. ¿Por qué se dirigen al puesto de los pájaros?
5. ¿Por qué prefiere la narradora comprar un cardenal?
6. Por fin, ¿qué tipo de pajarito compran?
7. ¿Por qué quiere Pepita entrar a la casa de la narradora?
8. ¿Cómo es la casa de la narradora?
9. ¿Qué hay en la jaula?
10. ¿Qué le pasa al último pajarito de los domingos?
●11. ¿Le sorprendió a Ud. el final de este cuento? ¿Por qué?
●12. ¿Qué opina Ud. de la narradora y de su familia? ¿Y de Pepita?

B. Verb Practice

Use each of the following verbal phrases in an original sentence in Spanish, either based on the story or of your own design. Be prepared to explain the meaning of your sentence.

1. **esforzarse por**
2. **quedarse**
3. **elegir**
4. **cargar con**
5. **rogar**
6. **chocar (contra)**
7. **admitir**
8. **impedir**

---

[18]*La carbonerita... hilacha:* The little coal peddler has shown her true colors.   [19]*Y... pena:* And the rest isn't really worth the trouble to watch.

9. **suceder**
10. **avergonzarse**

C. Vocabulary Practice

Complete the sentences below, matching the expressions on the right with the English words on the left. Be sure to use the correct form of each verb. Then use each expression in an original Spanish sentence and indicate what your sentence means.

1. *Every now and then* su tía nos llevaba con ella. — **rodear de**

2. Allí estaba Pepita, *surrounded with* pájaros. — **educación**

3. Nadie entiende *what's wrong with* la chica. — **tener** + *part of the body* + *adjective*

4. A la chica le falta *breeding.* — **valer la pena**

5. Pagamos más de diez dólares *each.* — **recién** + *past participle*

6. Me dijo que *it wasn't worthwhile* ver la jaula. — **tal vez**

7. *Leaning* en la jaula, Pepita contemplaba el pajarito. — **de vez en cuando**

8. *Perhaps* nadie lo sabrá jamás. — **apoyado**

9. *My hands were very warm.* — **¿qué le pasa?**

10. La sala estaba *newly* pintada. — **cada uno**

D. Communication Practice

1. Say that the girl would have chosen a cardinal.
2. Tell Carlos to forget it, that it's not worth it.
3. Indicate that Clara admitted to you that she had done it [do not use **admitir**].
4. Say Angela's mother kept you from seeing her.
5. State that such things happen all the time.

E. Review Exercise

The following verbs, which have appeared in previous stories, also figured in «El pajarito de los domingos». Review your mastery of them by composing questions in Spanish using each of these verbs; then answer the questions.

faltarle a uno	**tener que**	**atreverse a**
acercarse a	**ponerse**	**levantarse**

EL HOMBRE QUE ROBÓ A BORGES

RUBÉN LOZA AGUERREBERRE

RUBÉN LOZA AGUERREBERRE (1945–   ) was born in Minas, Uruguay, but for many years has been living in Montevideo, where he has worked as a journalist and literary critic for two important publications there, *El País* and *Mundocolor*. He has also attained distinction as a short-story writer. Most of his tales have been collected in *La espera* (1973), *La casa del atardecer* (1977), *El hombre que robó a Borges* (1977), and *Pasado en limpio* (1984).

Loza was a personal friend of the late Jorge Luis Borges, whose brief parable, «Los dos reyes y los dos laberintos», opens the present volume. It seems appropriate, therefore, that we should end with a story in which Borges himself figures as a character. This tale, as you will discover, has a curious structure, a feature that Loza doubtlessly has drawn from his readings of Borges's prose and poetry. Be prepared, then, to have the conventional boundaries between reality and fantasy — between life and literature — perhaps slightly blurred. Such, indeed, is the effect produced by many of Borges's own writings. Loza's story, an homage of sorts to Borges, makes Bernardo Arévalo's fate a most strange and unsettling one.

A PRELIMINARY LOOK AT KEY EXPRESSIONS

Be sure to study these expressions before you read the story.

1. (138: 7) **atravesar** *to cross*
2. (138:18) **acabar** + *present participle* *to end up (by)* + *present participle* This expression has the same meaning as **acabar por** + *infinitive.* Thus **Acababa llevándose el Quijote** is the same as **Acababa por llevarse el Quijote.**
3. (138:21) **cualquiera** *any one* This word ends in -a when used not directly before a noun: **cualquiera de los libros, Dame cualquiera.** The -a has nothing to do with gender. The word is shortened to **cualquier** immediately before a masculine or feminine singular noun: **cualquier libro, cualquier mesa.** Neither word has a plural.
4. (139: 1) **cansarse** *to get tired*
5. (139: 4) **rumbo a** *bound, headed for, in the direction of*
6. (139: 4) **tener... años** *to be . . . years old*
7. (139: 7) **junto a** *next to* Since this is a preposition, it is invariable in form: **Las máquinas estaban junto a la ventana.**
8. (139: 9) **ingresar** *to enter* This verb is used for joining a company or enrolling in a school. **Entrar** is *to walk, go, come in,* as into a room, for example.
9. (139:22) **mareado** *lightheaded* This word has a wide range of meanings: *seasick, nauseated, dizzy, lightheaded, dazzled, overwhelmed,* etc. Only context can reveal which is meant.
10. (139:25) **dar cuerda a** *to wind* (a timepiece)
11. (139:27) **desvelado** *wide awake, not sleepy* This adjective comes from **desvelar** *to keep awake* and **desvelarse** *not to be able to sleep.*
12. (139:32) **de un tirón** *straight through, without a break, without stopping, all at once*
13. (139:33) **madrugada** *early morning* This noun refers to the "wee hours" of the morning when people are normally sleeping—from midnight to six or so. After that it is **mañana.**
14. (139:33) **soñar con** *to dream of, about*
15. (139:35) **imaginarse** *to imagine* This verb rarely occurs in any but the reflexive form.
16. (140: 2) **poder más** *to win out, get the better (of one), be stronger* This expression also occurs on p. 140, l. 32.
17. (140:26) **irse** *to leave, go away* English-speakers often use **salir** incor-

rectly for **irse. Salir** is *to leave* in the sense of *go* or *come out:* **irse** is *to leave* in the sense of *to go away* or *depart.*

18. (140:28) **hacérsele tarde a uno** *to get late*   In Spanish the person who thinks it's late or needs to watch the time is the indirect object.

19. (141:14) **trago** *sip, swallow*   This noun has become synonymous with an alcoholic drink, as in **echar un trago** *to have a drink* (literally, "to toss a swallow").

20. (141:15) **tropezar (con)** *to trip, stumble*

EL HOMBRE QUE ROBÓ A BORGES

El destino dibuja curiosos malentendidos.[1] La verdadera historia de Bernardo Arévalo me fue revelada mucho antes de que él traspusiera el umbral de mi casa, cuando ya mis ojos no veían el trazado de sus facciones,[2] la tarde del 24 de diciembre.

Bernardo Arévalo, hombre pequeño de mejillas con tintes rosa siempre bien afeitadas, azules los ojos y muy pulcro en todos los detalles de su vestimenta, que completaba con un infaltable portafolios en la mano derecha, atravesaba la plaza a las ocho menos cuarto y de pie ante el mostrador bebía un café, pagaba con monedas justas,[3] hacía una pequeña reverencia en la puerta a quien allí estuviera,[4] y continuaba su camino. Cinco minutos antes de las ocho resonaban sus tacos en el largo corredor de la Biblioteca Municipal. Saludaba a su compañero de labor y se sentaba a leer los diarios, aguardando a que alguien (generalmente jubilados o estudiantes, algunos jóvenes también) requiriera sus servicios. En esos momentos era un hombre feliz; brindaba sin retaceos cuanto estaba al alcance de su memoria,[5] que era casi prodigiosa, con una sonrisa permanente en sus labios finos. Había leído muchos libros; su cabeza era un ordenado fichero de títulos y autores de las más variadas materias. También tenía arraigadas preferencias; si alguien le solicitaba orientación literaria, invariablemente acababa llevándose bajo el brazo el tomo I del *Quijote*,[6] el *Esquema del porvenir* de H.G. Wells,[7] *Los siete pilares de la sabiduría* de T.E. Lawrence,[8] en las viejas ediciones de Ercilla[9] o, de lo contrario, cualquiera de los libros de Borges, en especial sus *Ficciones*.[10] Y él volvía a la penumbra de aquella sala silenciosa y

---

[1]*El destino... malentendidos:* Fate produces some strange misunderstandings.   [2]*mis ojos... facciones:* The supposed narrator of this story is the great contemporary Argentine writer, Jorge Luis Borges (1899–1986), the actual author of the first story in the present collection. Borges had been partially blind for years before his death.   [3]*monedas justas:* exact change   [4]*a... estuviera:* to anyone who happened to be there   [5]*brindaba... memoria:* he offered freely everything within his memory   [6]*tomo I del Quijote:* Volume I of *Don Quijote* (1605), the novel written by the Spaniard Miguel de Cervantes (1547–1616)   [7]*Esquema... Wells: The Shape of Things to Come* (1933), a work written by British novelist and historian H.G. Wells (1866–1946)   [8]*Los siete... Lawrence: The Seven Pillars of Wisdom* (1926), written by British soldier and writer, Thomas E. Lawrence (Shaw) (1888–1935), better known as Lawrence of Arabia   [9]*Ercilla:* a Chilean publishing house   [10]*Ficciones:* a collection of short stories (1944), written by Borges. A common theme in these stories and others by Borges is the shifting nature of roles or identities between the main characters.

solitaria, y sus ojos se cansaban descifrando pequeñas letras sobre hojas amarillecidas.

Bernardo Arévalo vivía con su madre. Su padre salió una mañana de invierno rumbo a la sastrería y no volvió nunca. Tenía cinco años, Bernardo, cuando ello
5 sucedió. Su madre no derramó una sola lágrima. Vendió a quienes lo tenían arrendado un campito[11] que había heredado de su abuela y se dedicó a pedalear una grande, oscura y pesada máquina de coser, día y noche, junto a la ventana que daba al patio. Luego agregó la luz macilenta de una lamparita.

Pasaron años. Bernardo ingresó como mandadero en la Biblioteca Munici-
10 pal.[12] Todas las Nochebuenas llegaban a su casa los tíos, desde el campo, y poco después de la medianoche se iban. Entre sus manos grandes tomaban la cabeza del niño y la besaban sonoramente y sonreían con cierta nostalgia antes de alejarse, entre los estruendos de los cohetes y los fuegos artificiales. Cuando Bernardo cumplió 41 años murió Ema, su madre. Era, para decirlo de una vez,
15 un hombre solitario de vida clara;[13] quedó más solo aún. La muerte de Ema alteró su ritmo, que recuperó poco después, sintiéndose liberado de toda congoja, situación que por las noches le sumía en penosas introspecciones. Pero acababa invariablemente releyendo algunas páginas de sus libros de cabecera: *Los siete pilares de la sabiduría, El Aleph*[14] *y Ficciones.*

20 Lo peor eran los crepúsculos que se prolongaban más que en las pasadas primaveras. Bernardo salía de la Biblioteca con sol alto y las horas permanecían quietas. Una tardecita, al abrir la ventana que daba al patio, mareado por el dulce olor de los jazmines, vio o creyó ver a su madre, a Ema, cortando unas flores cerca del limonero.

25 ¿Qué hacer? Bernardo llegaba y, luego de[15] bañarse, daba cuerda al reloj de péndulo de la sala, con el secreto deseo de que el tiempo transcurriera.

Una larguísima madrugada de finales de noviembre, Bernardo Arévalo, desvelado, imaginó un plan para su cercana licencia. Solo, ahora, podía arriesgarse a pasar unos días fuera de la ciudad; quizá fuera del país; podría llegar hasta
30 Buenos Aires. ¿Por qué no? y ver a Borges, claro.

Se sentó en la cama y diagramó sus pasos, día a día y hora a hora. Durante semanas—desde aquella noche durmió sin sobresaltos, de un tirón, salvo una madrugada de domingo cuando soñó con unos tigres o pumas, que le perseguían—no dejó de pensar en ello; en cada momento libre releía la poesía
35 de Borges, que conocía menos, preparándose para su encuentro. Se imaginó a ambos, en la calle, posando para una fotografía, mientras la gente pasaba junto a ellos y los miraba.

---

[11]*Vendió... campito:* She sold a small piece of land to the people who were renting it from her   [12]*la Biblioteca Municipal:* The Municipal Library (of Uruguay, located in Montevideo). Borges was for many years the Director of the Argentine *Biblioteca Nacional,* an institution on the scale of our Library of Congress.   [13]*vida clara:* plain, simple life   [14]*El Aleph:* another collection of short stories (1949) written by Borges   [15]*luego de:* after

Tuvo algunos contratiempos con su licencia, que se postergó por algunos días. Pudo más la ansiedad[16] y el 21 de diciembre viajó a Buenos Aires. En el bolsillo interior del saco llevaba una tarjeta que un escritor de su ciudad visitante de la Biblioteca, le dirigía a Ulyses Petit de Murat,[17] para que éste le hiciera accesible el camino hasta Borges.

La tarde del 24 de diciembre fue recibido por Borges en persona. «Si es oriental[18] es bienvenido», le dijo el escritor, ofreciéndole una temblorosa mano. Bernardo Arévalo jamás se había sentido tan emocionado. «Ulyses me habló de usted esta mañana», agregó el escritor mientras retornaba a la sala, sin el bastón.[19] Se orientaba sin problemas; a Bernardo le costaba creer[20] que no viera nada.

Se sentaron. Conversaron unos diez minutos; Borges recordó algunas imágenes del Uruguay que estaban en su memoria: un arco iris en el paso Molino,[21] los zaguanes de Montevideo y el agua clara del río Arapey,[22] donde se bañaron una mañana de verano con Enrique Amorín.[23] El monólogo de Borges fue interrumpido por dos periodistas de la televisión que querían un mensaje navideño del escritor. Con su voz apagada e impersonal, el escritor dijo dos o tres cosas que Bernardo juzgó geniales, y accedió a asomarse al balcón para una filmación final con la extendida ciudad como telón.

Tardaban. Entre los libros, a la derecha de Bernardo, asomaban unas hojas pálidas que, como si robara dinero, tomó temblorosamente. Miró unos párrafos; reconoció la pequeña letra de Borges. Sintió escalofríos.

Cuando retornaron—antes que ellos, le llegó el aviso de sus voces,[24]— Bernardo Arévalo se guardó los papeles en el bolsillo. Temblaba como una hoja al viento cuando lo vio entrar. Los periodistas se despidieron; Bernardo también: «Yo me voy, maestro».[25] Buscando el brazo del sillón con la mano abierta, Borges le preguntó si no quería un té. Bernardo le tomó la mano y, reteniéndola en la suya, le dijo: «Maestro, yo bajo con los señores. Se me hace tarde y hoy vuelvo a Uruguay. Ha sido un privilegio conocerlo y estrechar la mano con la cual escribe».

«Uruguay...» repitió Borges; luego recitó unos versos de Emilio Oribe.[26] «Buen viaje» le dijo, ya en la puerta. Pudo mas la sonrisa que los ojos ciegos del viejo escritor, e iluminó su rostro.

---

[16]*Pudo... ansiedad:* His impatience got the better of him   [17]*Ulyses Petit de Murat* (1907–1985): an Argentine writer, who was for many years a close friend of Borges   [18]*oriental:* This is a colloquial term for *Uruguayan.* It comes from the name given to Uruguay during colonial days, **la Banda Oriental,** *the Eastern Strip.*   [19]*sin el bastón:* without his cane (Remember that Borges was blind.)   [20]*a... creer:* Bernardo had a hard time believing   [21]*paso Molino:* a suburb of Montevideo, capital of Uruguay   [22]*río Arapey:* one of the main rivers of Uruguay   [23]*Enrique Amorín:* Enrique Amorim (1900–1960) was an Uruguayan novelist and a relative by marriage of Borges. The spelling **Amorín** represents exactly how this name is pronounced in Spanish.   [24]*le... voces:* their voices announced to him that they were on their way back   [25]*maestro:* literally, *master,* a term of respect used by a disciple or student with his teacher   [26]*Emilio Oribe:* Oribe (1893–1975) was an Uruguayan doctor and poet.

En su casa, en su dormitorio, a la noche siguiente, Bernardo Arévalo leyó el manuscrito de Borges. Necesitó de[27] la soledad y de las sombras para hacerlo.

Al principio le costó descifrar la esmerada caligrafía, llena de palitos en las «p» y en las «f», del escritor casi ciego; descubría palabras sueltas, al margen de
5 su significado y su correlación.[28] Hizo una pausa para beberse unos tragos del whisky que había traído de Buenos Aires, antes de aplicarse a la lectura. Sentado en la cama, muy cerca de la alta portátil,[29] leyó las primeras frases: «El destino dibuja curiosos malentendidos. La verdadera historia de Bernardo Arévalo me fue revelada mucho antes de que él traspusiera el umbral de mi casa, cuando ya
10 mis ojos no veían el trazado de sus facciones...»

Con la frente bañada en sudor leyó las cuatro carillas. El cuento del ladrón soñado por Borges estaba inconcluso. Las últimas palabras del manuscrito eran éstas: «Borracho, salió al patio de su casa, bajo el cielo estrellado. Se sentía tranquilo y feliz: hacía años que no lo estaba. Bebió un trago, el último y arrojó
15 lejos la botella vacía. Tropezando, entre los canteros, recogió la cuerda de colgar la ropa y la fue anudando,[30] mientras sus ojos buscaban la gruesa rama alta del limonero»...

EXERCISES

A. Questions and Opinions

1. ¿Por qué no podía el narrador ver las facciones de Bernardo Arévalo?
2. ¿Dónde trabajaba Arévalo y qué hacía?
3. ¿Cómo era la vida familiar de él?
4. ¿Quién era el autor predilecto de Arévalo?
5. ¿Dónde pensaba pasar Arévalo su cercana licencia?
6. ¿Quiénes interrumpieron su conversación con Borges?
7. ¿Qué hizo Arévalo con las hojas manuscritas de Borges?
8. ¿Cuándo se puso Arévalo a leer el manuscrito?
9. ¿De qué se dio cuenta Arévalo cuando terminó la lectura de las hojas?
10. ¿Qué cosas buscó el Arévalo del manuscrito cuando salió al patio?
•11. ¿Cree Ud. que Bernardo Arévalo iba a suicidarse? ¿Por qué?
•12. ¿Qué interpretación le daría Ud. a este cuento?

---

[27]*Necesitó de:* He needed some   [28]*descubría... correlación* he was able to make out words here and there although he wasn't sure of their meaning or how they fit into the text   [29]*la alta portátil:* the tall floor lamp   [30]*la fue anudando:* slowly tied a knot in it

B. Verb Practice

Use each of the following verbal phrases in an original sentence in Spanish, either based on the story or of your own design. Be prepared to explain the meaning of your sentences.

1. **atravesar**
2. **acabar** + *present participle*
3. **cansarse**
4. **tener... años**
5. **ingresar**
6. **soñar con**
7. **imaginarse**
8. **irse**
9. **hacérsele tarde a uno**
10. **tropezar**

C. Vocabulary Practice

Complete the sentences below, matching the expressions on the right with the English words on the left. Be sure to use the correct form of each verb. Then use each expression in an original Spanish sentence and indicate in English what your sentence means.

1. Su devoción *got the best of him* y le escribió a Borges una larga carta de admiración.   **cualquiera**
2. El empleado no llegó a casa hasta *the small hours of the night.*   **rumbo a**
3. Vamos a tomar un *drink* juntos cuando terminemos.   **junto a**
4. No importa, dame *any one.*   **mareado**
5. Me sentí algo *dizzy,* y me recosté.   **dar cuerda a**
6. Yo siempre prefiero leer una novela policial *straight through.*   **desvelado**
7. Partieron ayer *bound for* Montevideo.   **de un tirón**
8. Él estuvo *wide awake* toda la noche, haciendo sus planes para la licencia.   **la madrugada**
9. Yo los vi conversando *next to* la entrada.   **poder más**
10. *I wound* el reloj y me fui a la cama.   **trago**

D. Communication Practice

1. Say you have always dreamed of being a writer.
2. Tell your friend that you had to leave because it was getting late.
3. Ask Sara how old Marta's sister is.
4. Say that you ended up buying the car.
5. Indicate that you get tired when there's nothing to do.

E. Completion Exercise

Complete the following sentence fragments with your own ideas. Be sure to use the appropriate mood and tense with verbs you introduce.

1. Imagínese nuestra sorpresa cuando...
2. Julia atravesó la plaza para...
3. Felipe va a ingresar en el seminario porque...
4. Nos iremos mañana si...
5. Pablo tropezaba constantemente con los muebles porque...

VOCABULARY

The following words have been omitted from this vocabulary: (a) easily recognizable cognates; (b) well-known proper nouns; (c) proper nouns, cultural, historical, and geographical items explained in footnotes; (d) idioms and constructions explained in footnotes; and (e) forms that an average student of intermediate Spanish would be expected to know.

The gender of masculine nouns ending in **-o** is not listed, nor of feminine nouns ending in **-a, -d, -z,** and **-ión**. Radical stem changes for verbs are indicated after the infinitive. When there is one change, it is for the present tense: **volver (ue).** When there are two, the first is for the present tense and the second for the preterit: **seguir (i, i).** Prepositional usage is given after verbs—without parentheses if the verb is commonly used with the preposition and a following element: **dirigirse a,** and with parentheses if the verb can be used alone: **casarse (con).** Idioms and multiword expressions are listed under their most important words.

Many of the above criteria were not applied in an absolute fashion. Whenever we were not sure that an average intermediate student would understand a particular term, we included it.

ABBREVIATIONS

adj.	adjective	*m.*	masculine
adv.	adverb	*Mex.*	Mexican
arch.	archaic	*n.*	noun
Arg.	Argentine	*opp.*	opposite
aug.	augmentative	*p.p.*	past participle
aux.	auxiliary	*pers.*	person
coll.	colloquial	*pl.*	plural
dim.	diminutive	*pr.*	present
e.g.	for example	*pr. p.*	present participle
expl.	expletive	*prep.*	preposition
f.	feminine	*pret.*	preterit
Fr.	French	*sent.*	sentence
imp.	imperative	*sing.*	singular
inf.	infinitive	*subj.*	subjunctive
intrans.	intransitive	*sup.*	superlative
Lat.	Latin	*trans.*	transitive
lit.	literally		

A

abajo down, under, below; **para —** downward; **río —** downstream; **de arriba —** up and down, from top to bottom, from head to foot

abalanzarse to rush

abanicar to fan

abatir to depress, knock down; to humble, humiliate, discourage; **—se** to be disheartened

abeja bee

abismo abyss

ablandar to soften

abochornarse to be embarrassed

abofetear to punch, slap

abolido annulled

abominar to hate

aborrecer to hate

abrasar to burn

abrazar to embrace

abrigar to keep warm

abrigo shelter, cover, blanket; coat

abrir to open; **— el paso** to clear the way

abrumado oppressed

absoluto: en — (not) at all

abstraído absorbed

aburrirse to be (get) bored

acabar to finish, end; **— de** + *inf.* to have just + *p.p.;* **—(in** *pret.*) **de** + *inf.* to finish + *gerund* (e.g., **Acabó de escribir.** He finished writing.); **— por** to finish (end) up by

acaecer to happen

acallar to silence, shush

acangrejado crab-shaped

acariciador *adj.* caressing

acariciar to cherish; to caress, pet, fondle

acaso maybe, perhaps; **por si —** just in case

acceder to agree, consent

acceso attack

acechar to spy on

aceite *m.* oil

acera sidewalk

acerca de about, with regard to

acercarse (a) to approach, go (come) up (to), go (come) closer (to)

acero steel

acertar (ie) a to happen to, chance to; to succeed in

acicalado neat, clean

acogedor friendly, hospitable

acolchado quilted

acólito assistant

acometer to attack, come on; to undertake, attempt

acomodar to place, arrange; **—se** to settle oneself, settle down; to get a "soft" job; to marry into money

acompañante companion

acompasado measured, rhythmic, slow

acongojado afflicted, grieved

aconitina aconitine (*a poison made from the roots of certain plants*)

aconsejar to advise

acontecer to happen, befall

acontecimiento event, happening

acordar (ue) to decide, agree; **—se (de)** to remember

acorrer to help, aid

acosado beset, harassed

acostar (ue) to put to bed; **—se** to lie down, go to bed

acostumbrar + *inf.* to be in the habit of + *pr. p.;* **—se a** to get used to

acre sour

acto continuo immediately afterward

actual present, present-day

acuarela watercolor

acudir to come, appear, run up; to come to the rescue; to hurry, rush

acuerdo agreement, accord; **de — a, con** in accordance with, according to; **de —** agreed, in agreement; **ponerse de —** to come to an agreement

acurrucado huddled

adecuado adequate

adelantar to advance; **—se (a)** to excel, outdo; to take the lead, get ahead (of)

adelante forward, onward, ahead; **de hoy en —** from today on; **en —** from then (now) on

ademán *m.* gesture, movement of the hand

adentro inward, inside

aderezado set (*places at a table*)

aderezar to straighten

adherido pressed, held against

adinerado well-to-do, wealthy

adivinar to guess, figure out, divine, prophesy

adjudicar to award

admirable excellent, admirable

admirado amazed, surprised

adornado decorated

adornito knick-knack

adosado stuck, fastened

aduanero *adj.* customs

adueñarse de to take possession of, take charge of, take over

adusto stern, sullen

advertir (ie, i) to notify; to warn, inform; to notice, observe

afamado noted, famous

afán *m.* eagerness

afanosamente laboriously, painstakingly

afecto fondness, affection, feeling

afeitar to shave

afilado sharp

afirmar to assert; to rest, secure

afligir to afflict, sadden

aflorar to crop out, appear on the surface

afónico mute

afrentado insulted, ashamed

afrontar to face, put up with

agacharse to crouch, bend, stoop down

agarrado holding on

agarrar to catch, grab

agazapado hidden, crunched down

agitar to wave, agitate, move, stir; —**se** to move about

agonizante dying

agonizar to die slowly, be dying

agotado exhausted, worn out

agotarse to be exhausted; to run out (*material, food, etc.*)

agradar to please

agradecer to thank, be grateful for

agradecido grateful

agradecimiento gratitude

agrandar to enlarge

agregar to add

agremiado union member

agriarse to sour

agua: el — misma the very water; —**s arriba** upstream

aguamanil *m.* washstand

aguantar to endure, bear, suffer, stand; to wait

aguardar to wait (for)

agudo sharp

aguja needle

agujerito *dim. of* **agujero** hole

ahíto gorged, stuffed

ahogado stifled, muffled

ahogar to drown (out), stifle; —**se** to drown

ahora (bien) well now (then) — **mismo** right now

ahorrar to save

ahorro saving

ahuyentarse to run away

aire: al — libre outside

aislar (í) to isolate, put apart, separate

ajedrez *m.* chess

ajeno alien, of others

al +*inf.* (up)on + *pr. p.* (*e.g.,* **al levantarse** on getting up)

ala wing

alabado praised

alambre *m.* wire

álamo poplar tree

alardear to boast

alargado slender, long

alargar to extend, draw out, lengthen

alarido howl, scream, cry

alarma alarm

alarmante alarming

alba dawn

albergado lodged

alborotar to make noise

alcaide *m.* special guard

alcance *m.* reach

alcanzar to reach, gain; — **a** + *inf.* to succeed in, get to + *verb*

alcoba bedroom

aldaba door knocker

aldea village

alegrar to make happy, gladden; —**se
(de)** to be happy, glad (about)
alegre happy, joyful
alegría happiness, joy
alejar to take farther away; —**se (de)**
to leave, go (move, draw) away,
walk off
alelado stupefied
alentar (ie) to encourage
aleta wing, small wing
aletargado lethargic, drowsy, groggy
alfiler *m.* pin
alfombra rug, carpet
algazara din, clamor
algo: servir de — to do any good
algodón *m.* cotton
alguna parte somewhere
alhajar to adorn
alharaca clamor
aliado allied
aliento: sin — breathless
alimentar to feed, nurture, harbor
alimento food
alineados *pl.* lined up
alirroto with a broken wing
alisar to smooth (down)
aliviado relieved
alivio relief
allá there; — **arriba** up there; **más** —
far away, farther on; **más** — **de**
beyond; **el más** — *m. n.* the great
beyond
alma soul, "heart"
almohada pillow
almuerzo lunch
alocado wild, crazed
alojamiento lodging, room
alojarse to stay, take lodging
alpestre Alpine
alquilar to rent
alquiler *m.* rent
alrededor (de) around; *m. n.* **a su** —
around him (her, etc.); *pl.*
surroundings, outskirts
alteración unevenness
alterado upset
altivez haughtiness
alto high, tall; loud; **lo** — high up; *pl.*
n. upstairs **pasar por** — to
overlook, pass over

altura height
alucinación hallucination
alumbrar to light
alvéolo cell, compartment
alzar to lift, raise; —**se** to rise, go higher
ama housekeeper
amamantar to nurse (*an infant*)
amanecer *m.* dawn; *v.* to dawn, to
wake up
amante *m., f.* lover
amargo bitter
amargura bitterness
amarillecido yellowed
amarillento yellowish
amarillo yellow
amarrar to tie, fasten
ambicionar to aspire to, seek
ambos both
amenazar to threaten
amistad friendship
amoldar to mold, fashion, figure
amonedar to coin, mold, fashion
amonestador admonishing, reproving
amontonar to pile up, gather together
amoratado livid
amortajar to wrap in a shroud
amortiguado muffled
amotinado in a mob, milling about
amparado protected
amparo protection
amueblado furnished
analfabeto illiterate
anaranjado *adj.* orange
anclar to anchor
andar to walk; go; **con el** — **del
tiempo** with the passing of time
andén *m.* platform (railroad station)
anegar (ie) to overwhelm
angosto narrow
angustia anguish
anhelado longed for
anhelo desire, longing
anheloso longing (for)
anidar to nest
animal de presa predatory animal
animalejo odd-looking creature, nasty
animal
animar to encourage; —**se (a)** to get
up the energy (to), have the
courage (to), to get lively, excited

ánimo courage, fortitude, strength; mind, spirit

aniquilar to destroy, wipe out, crush

anochecer *m.* nightfall

anonadado annihilated, crushed

anotación note

ansia eagerness; anxiety, fear; **con —s de** anxious to

ansiado anxious; long-awaited

ansiedad anxiety, impatience

ansioso anxious

antaño long ago, "yesteryear"

antecámara anteroom

antecomedor *m.* small serving room (*adjacent to a dining room*)

antes: cuanto — without delay, as soon as possible, immediately

anticipo advance (*money*)

antojar: —sele a uno to take a fancy, have a whim

antojo fancy, whim

anudar to tie, bind, knot

anular to eliminate, overcome

añadido addition

añadir to add

añorar to reminisce

apacible peaceful

apaciguador comforting, pacifying

apaciguar to soften, soothe, pacify, calm, alleviate; **—se** to calm, settle down

apagado subdued

apagar to turn out, extinguish; muffle; **—se** to go out, die out

aparador *m.* sideboard, china cabinet

aparecer appear, show up

aparentar to feign, pretend

apariencia illusion, appearance

apartado isolated, retired

apartar to spread, separate, take away, push away; **—se** to move away (back)

aparte aside (*adv.*)

apellidarse to have as a last name

apellido surname, last name

apenas scarcely, barely, hardly; just as soon as

apercibirse (para) to prepare (for)

apilado piled up

apilarse to pile up

aplacar to placate, soothe

aplastar to crush, smash, flatten; to stick (against)

aplaudidor *m.* admirer, applauder

apoderamiento seizure of power

apoderarse de to overcome, take possession of, seize

apodo nickname

apoltronado lounging

apostura good looks

apoyar to support, lean

apoyo support

aprehendido arrested

aprendizaje *m.* apprenticeship; learning

apresurar to hasten, quicken; **—se** to hurry

apretado clenched

apretar (ie) to press, squeeze, pinch, grasp

aprobar (ue) to approve

aprontarse to prepare

aprovechar to take advantage of, make use of

aproximarse to approach, come closer

apunte *m.* note

apuñalar to stab

apuro difficulty, "tight spot"

aquél the former (*lit.,* that one)

araña spider; chandelier

arcano secret, mystery

arco iris rainbow

arder to burn (*intrans.*)

ardid *m.* ruse, trick

ardiente burning

ardor *m.* burning

arena sand

arengar to harangue, deliver a speech to

argumento plot (*of a book, play, etc.*)

arete *m.* earring

armadura armor

armario closet, wardrobe

armonía melody, harmony

arraigado deep-rooted, fixed, settled

arrancar to draw (pull, tear, snatch) out (off, away)

arrasar to demolish, flatten; to fill to the brim

arrastrar to drag; pull; **—se** to drag, crawl, creep

arrastre *m.* drag, pulling
arre (*expl.*) giddiyap
arrebañar to clear, clean up, off
arrebatadamente violently, excitedly
arrebatar to snatch away, wrest (from), carry off
arrebato fit of enthusiasm, passion
arreglar to arrange, fix, settle
arremangar roll up (*sleeves*)
arrendar (ie) to rent
arrepentirse (ie, i) to repent
arrestos *pl.* boldness
arriba up, upstream; **aguas —** upstream; **allá —** up there; **de — abajo** up and down, from top to bottom, from head to foot; **para —** upward; **río —** up river
arribar to arrive
arriesgar to risk; **—se** to take a chance, risk
arrimo support, attachment
arrinconado cornered
arrobo ecstasy, rapture, trance
arrodillarse to kneel
arrojar to throw; **—se** to leap
arroyito *dim. of* **arroyo** stream
arroyuelo *dim. of* **arroyo** stream
arroz *m.* rice
arruga wrinkle
arrugar to wrinkle
arrullar to lull
articular to utter
artificio: castillo de — artificial castle
artificiales: fuegos — fireworks
ascenso promotion
ascensor *m.* elevator
ascua hot coal
asear to clean up, tidy up, groom
asegurar to assure
asentar (ie) to establish, put down
asentir (ie, i) to assent
asequible available, feasible
aserrín *m.* sawdust
asesinar to murder
asesinato murder
asesino murderer
asestar to deal, strike (*a blow*)
así thus, like this (that), this (that) way; **— siendo** in that case

asiento seat; **tomar —** to be seated
asimismo in the same way
asir to grasp **—se (a)** to hold on (to), grab, grasp
asistir (a) to attend
asomar to show; **—se** to peek at; to look out (of), appear (at); to get a glimpse of
asombrar to astonish, amaze
asombro astonishment, amazement
aspecto look
áspero rough, hoarse
asunto matter, affair
asustadizo jumpy, easily frightened
asustar to frighten; **—se** to get, become frightened
atajar to cut off (short)
atar to tie
atardecer *m.* dusk, late afternoon
ataúd *m.* casket, coffin
atender (ie) to take care of, tend to, pay attention to; to answer (*door or telephone*)
ateo atheist
aterrado terrified
aterrador terrifying
aterrizar to land
aterrorizado terrified
atestiguar to witness, attest
atinar (a) to succeed (in)
atónito astonished
atracado moored
atraer to pull back; to attract
atrás back, backward
atravesar (ie) to cross
atreverse (a) to dare (to)
atrio inner courtyard
atronar (ue) to boom, play deafeningly
atropelladamente in a rush, pell-mell
atropellar (con) to knock down, over, to run over, trample
atroz atrocious
audacia boldness, daring
auditorio audience
augusto magnificent, august, majestic
aula schoolroom, classroom
aullar (ú) to howl
aumentar to increase
aún still, yet

auricular *m.* receiver (*telephone*)
aurora dawn
ausencia absence
austral southern
auxiliado helped, aided
auxilio help, aid
avance *m.* advance
avaro greedy, stingy
ave *f.* bird, fowl; — **de rapiña** bird of prey
avejentado old-looking
aventajado favored, endowed
aventurarse (a) to risk, take a chance on
avergonzar (üe) to embarass; —**se** to be ashamed, embarrassed
averiado damaged, in bad condition
averiguar to ascertain, verify
avión *m.* airplane
avisar to inform, let know, warn
aviso notice; warning
ayudante assistant
azada hoe
azar *m.* chance, luck, fate; hazard; unforeseen happening
azorado terrified, frightened
azotar to lash, whip
azucena white lily
azulado bluish
azulear to look blue (bluish)

B

baba drool
baboso drooling
badajo clapper of a bell
bagaje *m.* beast of burden
bailarina dancer
baja discharge (*from service; hospital*); **dar de** — to discharge
bajar to go (come) down; to get out (*of a vehicle*)
bajo under
bala bullet
baladí trivial
balanza scale
balazo shot; bullet wound
balbucear to babble, stammer
balde: en — in vain

baldosa paving stone
balido bleat(ing)
ballena whale
bancarrota bankruptcy
banco bench
bandada flock
bandeja tray
baño bath
barato cheap
barba beard
barbudo bearded
barcelonés *adj.* from Barcelona
barco boat
barrer to sweep
barriada district, quarter (of city)
barriga belly
barro mud, clay
barroso muddy
barrote *m.* rung, bar
bastar to be enough, suffice; ¡**Basta!** Enough!
bastón *m.* cane; stick
basura garbage, trash
bata housecoat, robe
batón *m.* dressing gown, housecoat
beato devout, pious
belleza beauty
bendición blessing
bendito blessed one; **dormir como un** — to sleep like a baby
bengala: luces de — Roman candles (*fireworks*)
bermejo vermillion
berrear to bellow, howl
besar to kiss
beso kiss
bestia beast
bicho bug, insect
bien: —mirado carefully considered; — **que** although; **ahora** — now, well then; **de** — honest; **más** — rather, more; **pues** — well then; *m. n.* good, benefit; **tener a** — to see fit, find convenient; «**No hay mal que por** — **no venga**» "Everything turns out for the best," "Every cloud has a silver lining"; *m. pl. n.* property, estate
bienaventuranza bliss

bienvenido welcome
bigote *m.* whisker, moustache
billete *m.* bill (money)
bioquímica biochemistry
bisabuelo great-grandparent
bisturí *m.* surgical knife
bizcocho pastry; cupcake
blandir to brandish
blando soft
blandura tenderness, softness
blanqueado whitewashed
blanquear to whiten
bloqueado blocked (off)
boato luxury, pomp, pageantry
boca mouth
bocado bite, mouthful
bocal *m.* jar
bocanada whiff, breath, gasp; puff of
  smoke
bofetada slap
boga style, vogue; **en** — popular
bola ball
bolear to shine (shoes)
boleto ticket
boliche *m.* general store
bolsillo pocket
bolsita *dim. of* **bolsa** bag
bolso purse, bag
bombón *m.* candy sweetstuff; "honey"
bondad kindness, goodness
bondadoso kind
borde *m.* edge
bordo: a — **de** aboard
borrachera drunkenness
borracho drunk, drunken
borrar to erase, remove
bosque *m.* woods
bota boot; leather wine bottle
bote *m.* bounce, rebound
botella bottle
botica medicine; shop
bravío wild, fierce
bravo wild, savage; mad, angry; rough,
  rugged
brazo arm
brea tar
brillante *m.* diamond
brillar to shine, gleam
brillo gleam
brincar to caper, frisk, leap, jump

brinco leap, jump; **dar un** — to jump,
  take a jump; **de un** — with a leap;
  pegar un — to jump
brindar to offer, present
brisa breeze
broma joke
bromear to jest
bronco solid, hard, rough
brotar to spring forth, sprout, appear
  suddenly
brújula magnetic needle, compass
bruma mist, fog
brusco sudden, abrupt
bucle *m.* curl, lock (hair)
buche *m.* craw (of a bird)
bueno: de —**a gana** willingly; **de una**
  —**a vez** once and for all
buhardilla garret
bulto bundle, package
bullicio uproar
bullicioso noisy, bustling
bullir to bubble, boil
burbuja bubble
burdo coarse
burla scorn, jest, mockery, taunt;
  hacer — **de** to mock
burlarse (de) to make fun of, mock,
  scorn
burlesco ludicrous
burlón mocking, teasing
busca search
buscar to look for, seek, search
butaca easy chair
buzo diver

C

cabal: a carta — through and
  through, in every respect
cabalgar to ride on horseback
caballero gentleman
cabecera head (*of a bed*)
cabellera head of hair
cabello hair, lock
caber to fit, be contained
cabestro halter
cabezal *m.* small pillow
cabo end, handle; **al fin y al** — after all
cabrita kid (*goat*)

caburé *m.* pygmy owl (*bird of prey native to southern South America*)
cachete *m.* (fat) cheek
cachorro cub; young of wild animals
cachucha cap
cada: — **cual** each one; — **vez más** more and more
cadáver *m.* body, corpse
cadeneta chain stitch
caer to fall; **dejar** — to drop; —**se** to fall down
cafetera coffee pot
cafetería coffee house, coffee shop
caída fall
caja box, case; main part of telephone
cajero cashier
cajón *m.* drawer, big box, case
calafate *m.* caulking
calafatear to caulk
calavera skull
calcomanía decal, transfer
calcular to figure, estimate
calefacción heat, heating
cálido hot
caligrafía penmanship
cáliz *m.* center of a flower (*within the petals*)
calorcillo extreme heat, nice warmth
calorífico burner, stove, hot plate
caluroso hot, warm
calvo bald
calza cord, fetter (*used on animals*)
calzado footwear; — **con** wearing (*on one's feet*)
calzar to wedge; —**se** to put on shoes, gloves
callado silent
callar(se) to be silent, shut up
calleja side street, alley
callejón *m.* alley
callejuela narrow street
camarero waiter
cambiación change
cambiar to change, exchange
cambio change; **a** — **de** in exchange for; **en** — on the other hand, on the contrary
camello camel
caminar to walk, go, travel
caminata long walk, hike

camino way, road; trip — **de** on the road to, in the direction of
camiseta undershirt
campanada ring of a bell
campanilla *dim. of* **campana** bell
campaña campaign
camposanto cemetery
canal *m.* channel
canalizar to channel
canastilla basket
canoso gray-haired
cansancio fatigue
cantaleta noisy ridicule
cántaro pitcher
cantero flowerbed
canto song, chant
caña reed, cane
cañaveral *m.* cane field
caño pipe
capa layer, coating, covering
capacitar to prepare, qualify
capataz de servicio head waiter
capaz capable
capilar: vasito — capillary
capilla chapel; **vagón** — **ardiente** funeral chapel car
capitalino *adj.* of, from the capital
capricho caprice
cara face
caramelo hard candy
carbonero coal peddler
carcajada burst of laughter
cárcel *f.* jail, prison
carcelario *adj.* jail, prison
cárdeno livid, purple, violet
cardo thistle
carecer de to lack
carga charge, load; **de** —**s** loading
cargar to carry, transport; — **(de)** to load, burden (with); — **con** to carry, haul; —**se** to become charged
cargo charge; **a** — **de** in charge of
caricia caress
carilla page (*of a manuscript*)
cariño affection, fondness, love
cariñoso affectionate, fond
caritativo charitable
carne *f.* meat; *pl.* flesh, fat (*on human body*)

carnicero *n.* butcher; *adj.* bloodthirsty, carnivorous
caro dear; expensive
carpeta table cover
carrera course; career; race; **a la —** hastily
carrero wagon driver
carretta cart, wagon
carretero driver (*of a cart*)
carretilla wheelbarrow
carroza carriage, coach
carta: a — cabal through and through, in every respect
cartera purse, wallet
casarse to get married
caserón *m.* large, ramshackle house
casilla cage, booth
caso incident, fact; case; **darse el —** to happen; **hacer —** to pay attention, listen, heed; **poner ... por — to use . . . as an example
casta breed
castillo castle
casualidad chance, chance event, coincidence
casualmente by chance, coincidentally
catarata waterfall, cataract
catecúmeno person being instructed in the Christian doctrine
catequista *adj.* pertaining to instruction in the Christian doctrine
catequizar to instruct in the Christian doctrine
caterva throng, crowd
cauda train, tail
caudal *m.* fortune, wealth, property
caudaloso of great volume, carrying a lot of water
caudillo boss, strong man, leader
causa: a — de because of
cautivador captivating, charming
cautivo captive
cauto cautious
cavilación penetrating, detailed thought; calculation
caza hunt, pursuit; **dar —** to hunt, pursue
cazador *adj.* hunting
cazar to hunt, catch, chase

cebar to brew, make
ceder to yield, give (up), give way; **— la plaza** to give up
cedro cedar
cegado stopped up
ceja eyebrow
celda cell
celeste celestial, heavenly; blue
cena supper
cenar to eat supper
ceniciento ash-colored
ceniza ash
centella flash
centenar *m.* hundred; **a —es** by the hundreds
centésimo hundredth
ceño brow
cera wax
cercanía nearness
cercano *adj.* near, nearby, close
cercar to enclose, encircle, surround
cercenar to cut, lop off, pare
cerciorarse (de) to find out (about), make sure (of)
cerco wall, fence (outside)
cerdo pig
cerebro brain
cernirse (ie) to spread against; to hover
cerrada: noche — completely dark
cerradura lock
cerrar el paso to block the way
cerro hill
cerrojo bolt, latch
certidumbre *f.* certainty
cesar to stop, cease
césped *m.* lawn, grass
cesta basket
cetrino yellow-skinned
cianuro de potasio potassium cyanide
cicatriz scar
cicatrizar to heal over
cicuta hemlock
ciego blind; sluggish
cielo: — raso ceiling; **¡Cielos!** Good heavens!
ciénaga marsh, swamp
cieno mire, slime
cifra sum total, number
cigarra locust

cinta tape; ribbon
cintura waist
cinturón *m.* belt
círculo circle
circundar to circle, surround
circunvecino neighboring, surrounding,
   nearby
cirio candle
cirujano surgeon
cisco coal dust, small pieces of coal
citarse to make an appointment (date)
ciudadano citizen
clamar to cry out
claridad light, brightness
clarín *m.* bugle; bugler
clarividencia clairvoyance
claro light (colored); of course
clausura closing
clavar to fix, nail; to stick in, pierce,
   prick, thrust with sharp instrument
clave *f.* key
clavo nail, spike
clientela clientele
coartada alibi
cobayo guinea pig
cobertizo covering
cobertor *m.* bedspread
cobrador *m.* bill collector
cobrar to charge (for), collect, take in
   (money)
cocimiento concoction
cocina kitchen; cooking
cocinera cook
cocotero coconut tree
cochero driver
codicia fervent desire; envy, greed,
   covetousness
codicilo document, codicil
cofradía religious brotherhood
cofre *m.* box, chest
coger to catch, pick up, grab
cogote *m.* back of the neck
cohete *m.* rocket
cohetón *m. aug.* of cohete
cojear to limp
cola tail
colarse (ue) to pass (steal) through,
   slip (sneak) in
colchón *m.* mattress

colear to pull an animal's tail
colegio secondary school
cólera rage
colgante hanging (down)
colgar (ue) to hang (up)
colmado complete, full
colmena hive
colmenar *m.* apiary (*group of beehives*)
colocar to place, set, put
colorado red
comadrear to gossip
comadrería gossip
comarca territory, region, district,
   neighborhood
comedor *m.* dining room
comer: dar de — to feed
comerciante *m.* businessman
comercio business
comestible *adj.* edible
cometer to commit
comida food
comisario commissioner
como: — para as if to; hacer —
   que + *indicative* to pretend + *inf.;*
   tal — just as
cómoda dresser
cómodo comfortable
compadecer to pity
compadecido showing pity, sympathetic
compañero friend, companion
compañía: hacerle — a uno to keep
   someone company
compás *m.* compass; beat, rhythm
complacencia pleasure, satisfaction
complacer to please; —se (en) to take
   pleasure (in), be pleased with
complaciente agreeable, kind
componer to fix, adjust, repair
compra purchase
comprensivo understanding
comprobar (ue) to verify, confirm,
   substantiate, prove
comprometedor compromising
comprometer to compromise
comprometerse to become engaged; to
   commit oneself
compuesto *p.p. of* componer; dressed
   up, made up; tidy
con que so (*sent. introducer*)

concienzudamente conscientiously
concluir to finish, end; — **de** + *inf.* to finish; *pr. p. (e.g.,* **Concluyó de comer.** He finished eating.)
concordar (ue) to agree, tally
concurrir (a) to attend, go (to)
concurso aid, assistance
condiscípulo classmate
conducir to lead, direct, take, conduct; to carry, drive
conductor *m.* driver, conductor (*Mex.*)
conejo rabbit
confabularse to plot, scheme
conferencia speech, lecture
confesionario confessional
confianza confidence
confianzudo confident, trusting
confiar (í) to confide, entrust
conformarse (con) to make do, get along; to decide (to), agree (to), resign oneself (to)
conforme agreed; as soon as; according to the way, accordingly; — **a** in accordance with
confundir to confuse, mix
congestionado congested, flushed
congoja grief, affliction, distress
congregar to gather together; —**se** to gather together, congregate
conjunto combination
conocedor *adj.* expert, competent (*as a connoisseur*)
conocer: dar a — to make known
conocido acquaintance, friend
conocimiento knowledge
consabido well-known, above-mentioned
consagrar to consecrate, dedicate
conseguir (i, i) to obtain, get, gain; — + *inf.* to get to, be able to, manage to + *verb*
consejo bit (piece) of advice
conservar to retain, keep
constancia record, account, proof, evidence
constar de to consist of, be composed of
consuelo consolation, comfort
contabilidad bookkeeping
contar (ue) to tell, relate

contenido *n.* contents; *adj.* prudent, careful, restrained, controlled
contiguo adjoining
continuo: acto — immediately after
contoneo swaying
contorno vicinity; outline, form
contra: dar — to hit against
contraer to contract
contrariar (í) to upset, annoy
contrario adverse; **por el** — on the other hand; **todo lo** — just the opposite
contrasentido contradiction
contratar to engage, rent
contratiempo snag, problem
contraveneno antidote
contundente forceful
conveniente desirable, suitable; —**mente** *adv.* in the right way, as one is supposed to
convenir (ie) to be desirable, suitable, fitting, proper; to agree
convento monastery
convertir (ie, i) to turn into (*trans.*); —**se** to turn into, become
convivir to coexist
convoy *m.* train
copa drink (*alcoholic*); (*lit.* wine glass)
copetudo high, lofty
copudo thick-topped (*tree*)
corazón *m.* heart
cordón *m.* cord; curb
coro chorus; **a (en)** — in chorus (unison)
corola corolla, petals
corona *type of fireworks that explodes in a shower of colors;* ring; crown
coronar to crown, top
corporeidad body weight
corredizo *adj.* moving, sliding
corredor *m.* front porch
corregir (i, i) to correct
correntón *m.* gust
correr to run; to pursue, chase; to go through, over; to undergo; —**se** to slide, move sideways
corriente *f.* current; **darle la** — **a uno** to humor someone; **llevarle la** — **a uno** to let someone have his own way; *adv.* —**mente** in the usual way

cortadera *type of sharp-bladed grass*
cortante cutting
cortar to cut (off), hang up (*telephone*)
cortejar to court, woo
cortésmente courteously
cortina curtain; — **metálica** steel
  shutter (*placed over store fronts at
  night*)
cosa thing; **gran** — much, very much;
  — **de** a matter of; about, more or
  less; — **de pensarlo** something to
  think about
coser to sew
cosmorama *m. exhibition of scenes
  from different parts of the world*
costado side; **de** — on one's side
costar (ue) to cost; to be hard,
  difficult; — **poco** to be easy
costear to go along the edge (*of a
  body of water*)
costilla rib
costoso expensive, costly
costumbre *f.* custom
cráneo skull, head
crapuloso foul
crecer to grow, increase (*intrans.*)
crecido large
creciente growing, increasing
crédito belief, faith
creencia belief
creer: ¡**Ya lo creo!** Of course!, Yes,
  indeed!
crepuscular *adj.* twilight
crepúsculo twilight, half-light
criado servant
crianza breeding
criar (í) to raise, bring up
crin *f.* mane
criollita *f. dim. of* **criolla** born in
  Spanish America of European
  descent
crispado curled, contracted, twisted
cristal *m.* glass, crystal
criterio judgment, discernment
cromo picture
crónica chronicle
crujido rustle, creak
crujiente *adj.* rustling, crackling
cruz *f.* cross, crossing
cruzar to cross

cuadrante *m.* dial
cuadrilla crew, gang (*of workers*)
cuadro square
cuajado ornately decorated,
  encrusted
cual: cada — each one; **tal o** —
  such-and-such, so-and-so
cuan how (*used only before adj. and
  adv.*)
cuando: — **menos** at least; **de** — **en**
  — from time to time; **de vez en** —
  from time to time, now and then
cuanto all that, everything that, as
  much as; — **antes** without delay,
  as soon as possible, immediately;
  en — as soon as; **unos** —**s** a few,
  some
cubierto *p.p. of* **cubrir: a** — protected
cuchichear to whisper
cuchufleta joke, wisecrack
cuello neck
cuenta: a — **de** through the fault of;
  dar — **(de)** to give an account
  (of), relate; **darse** — **de** to realize;
  por su — on one's own; **tomar en**
  — to take into account
cuentagotas *m. sing.* dropper
cuento story
cuerda rope, string; **dar** — **a** to wind
  (*a timepiece*)
cuero leather
cuerpo body; — **de policía** police
  force
cuervo crow
cueva cave, opening
cuidado care; be careful; — **con** watch
  out for
cuidadosamente carefully
cuidar: — **de** to take care (be careful)
  to; to take care of; —**se de** + *inf.*
  to take care + *inf.*
cuitado unfortunate
culpa blame, guilt; **tener la** — to be
  to blame
culpable blameworthy, guilty
culpar to blame
cultivo cultivated field
cumbre *f.* peak
cumplimiento fulfillment; performance;
  compliance

cumplir to fulfill, keep, observe;
  comply with; to keep one's word;
  — **años** to be . . . years old
cuna family, lineage; cradle
cundir to grow, flourish, expand
cuñada sister-in-law
cuota dues
curarse to get well
curiosear to look around
curtiembre *f.* tannery
cúspide *f.* tip, point
cuyo whose

CH

chacal *m.* jackal
chaleco vest, waistcoat
chapita small metal plate
chapotear to splash
chaqueta jacket, coat
charco puddle
charlar to chat
charol *m.* patent leather
chasqueado disappointed
chasquear to snap, crack; to disappoint
chicuelo *dim.* of **chico** boy, lad, kid
chichón *m.* lump, bump
chillar to shriek, scream
chiquilín *m. dim. of* **chico** child, kid
chiribitil *m.* shack, hovel
chirigota joke
chirrido squeaking
chispa spark
chiste *m.* joke
chocar (con, contra) to bump (crash,
  run) into, hit
chocarrero coarse, vulgar
chocolatín *m.* piece of chocolate candy
chorro stream, spurt
choza hut
chúcaro wild, untamed
chucho chill; fright

D

dado que given the fact that, since
dados *pl.* dice
daga dagger
dama lady; queen (*chess*)

damnificado injured party
dañino harmful
daño harm, damage, injury; **hacer**
  —to hurt
dar to give; to strike (*the hour*) (*e.g.,*
  Dieron las cinco. The clock struck
  five.); — **a** to face; — **a conocer** to
  make known; — **a entender** to lead
  one to believe, imply, insinuate;
  — **caza** to hunt, pursue; — **con** to
  come across; — **contra** to hit
  against; — **cuenta (de)** to give an
  account (of), relate; — **cuerda** to
  wind (*a timepiece*); — **de comer** to
  feed; — **de mamar** to nurse (*an*
  infant); — **en** to take to, get into
  the habit of; — **la vuelta (a)** to go
  around; — **las buenas noches** to
  say goodnight; — **lecciones** to
  recite lessons; — **que hablar** to give
  occasion for talk, comment;
  — **razón a** to confirm; — **sobre** to
  fall (hit) on; — **un brinco (salto)** to
  jump, take a jump; — **una mirada**
  to take a glance; — **un paso** to
  take a step; — **una vuelta** to take a
  walk, turn; — **voces de socorro** to
  call for help; — **vuelta** to turn
  around; — **vueltas** to walk around;
  —**le a uno por** + *inf.* to take a
  notion + *inf.;* —**le la corriente a**
  uno to humor someone; —**le la**
  gana a uno for someone to feel like;
  —**se a** + *inf.* to devote oneself to,
  take to, up + *pr. p.;* —**se cuenta de**
  to realize; —**se el caso** to happen;
  —**se por satisfecho** to be satisfied;
  —**se prisa** to hurry; —**se una**
  vuelta to turn around
dársena dock, wharf
dato fact; *pl.* information, data
deber *m.* duty, obligation, homework
  assignment; *v.* to owe; to be
  supposed to, should, ought to,
  must; — **(de)** *used to express*
  probability (*e.g.,* **Deben (de) ser las**
  ocho. It must be (is probably) eight
  o'clock.); —**se** to be due
debidamente in the proper fashion

debido due
débil weak
debilidad weakness
decible utterable
decir (i): — entre dientes to mutter; **a
— verdad** to tell the truth; **es —**
that is to say; **oír —** to hear, hear
it said; **querer —** to mean
declinación fall
dedicar to devote, dedicate
dedo finger, toe
definitivamente finally
defunción death, decease (*legal*)
deglutir to swallow
degollar (üe) to cut one's throat,
behead
dejar to let, allow, permit; to leave;
— caer to drop; **—(se) de** + *inf.* to
stop + *pr. p.* (*e.g.,* **Dejó de escribir.**
He stopped writing.); **no —
de** + *inf.* not to fail, be sure + *inf.*
(*e.g.,* **No deje de escribirle.** Don't
fail (Be sure) to write to him.)
delantal *m.* apron
delantero *adj.* front
delatar to give away, betray
delator *m.* informer, stool pigeon
deleite *m.* delight
deletrear to spell
deleznable fragile, insubstantial
delgado slender, thin
delicadeza daintiness, tenderness
delicioso delightful
delirio delirium, ravings
delito crime
demacrado emaciated
demanda: en — de asking for
demás *pl.* rest, other(s)
demoler (ue) to demolish, tear down
¡Demonios! The Devil!
demora delay
demorar to delay
denostar (ue) to condemn
deporte *m.* sport
depósito depot, warehouse
derecho *n.* right, privilege; *adj.* right
(-hand)
derramar to pour, spill, shed
derribar to destroy, raze, knock down

derroche *m.* flood, proliferation;
squandering, waste
derrota defeat
derrotar to defeat
desafiante defiant
desafiar (í) to challenge
desafinado out of tune
desafío challenge
desaforado outrageous, wild,
extraordinary, crazy
desagradecido ungrateful
desagrado displeasure
desalentado out of breath
desaliento dejection, dismay
desamargar to make less bitter
desamparado unprotected, abandoned
desangrar to drain the blood
desapacible harsh, unpleasant
desarmar to take apart
desarrapado ragged
desatar to untie
desayunar to eat breakfast
desayuno breakfast
desazón *f.* annoyance, displeasure
desbocado runaway (*horse*)
desbordante overflowing
desbordarse to come out of, overflow
descalabrarse to fracture one's skull
descalzo barefoot
descansar to rest
descanso rest
descolgar (ue) to unhook, take down;
to lift, pick up (*telephone*)
descolorido faded, pale
descomponerse to separate, come
apart, break down
descompostura *n.* upset, disorder
descompuesto upset, broken
desconcierto uneasiness, uncertainty
desconocido unknown, strange; *n.*
stranger
desconocimiento ignorance, lack of
familiarity
descosido stitches that have come out
descoyuntar to dislocate
descubrimiento discovery
descubrir to uncover, discover
descuento discount
descuidado careless

descuidar to overlook, neglect, disregard

desde from, since; *to show lapse of time with* **hacer** (*e.g.,* **Vivo aquí desde hace cinco años.** I've been living here for five years.); — **luego** of course

desdecirse (i) to retract

desdeñar to disdain, scorn; —**se de** to scorn, disdain

desdeñoso disdainful

desdichado unhappy, unfortunate

desechar to discard

desembocar to come into, flow into

desempedrar to tear up

desempeñar to perform, discharge; to redeem, take out of pawn

desenfado ease, naturalness

desenfrenado unrestrained

desengañado disillusioned, disappointed

desengaño disillusion, disappointment

desenlace *m.* conclusion (*of the plot of a story*)

desentenderse (ie) to feign ignorance, pay no attention

desentonado discordant, out of tune

desenvainar to unsheathe

desenvoltura ease, freedom, confidence, poise

desenvolverse (ue) to develop, unfold

desenvuelto free, confident, open

deseo wish, desire

deseoso desirous

desequilibrado mentally unbalanced

desesperación desperation, despair

desesperado desperate

desesperante maddening, desperate

desesperanza desperation

desesperar(se) to lose hope, despair

desfile *m.* parade

desfondado with the bottom out

desgarradura break, tear

desgarrar to tear, claw

desgraciado unfortunate

deshacer to destroy, cut to pieces; —**se de** to get rid of; —**se** to be overwhelmed, overcome; to come apart, fall off

designio plan

desistir to stop, cease

deslizar *trans.* to slip, slide; —**se** to glide by

deslumbrado puzzled, bewildered

desmayado in a faint, unconscious

desmayarse to faint

desmoronarse to crumble, fall apart

desnucarse to break one's neck

desnudo naked, bare

desocupado idle; free, vacant

desorbitado disproportionate, excessive

desordenado wild, irregular

despacito *dim. of* **despacio** very slowly, very softly

despachar to deal with, attend to; to take care of; to dismiss, put away

despacho office

desparpajo ease, self-confidence

despatarrado stupefied, motionless, dumbfounded

despavorido terrified

despectivamente contemptuously

despecho scorn

despedazado ruined, broken, crumbled

despedida farewell

despedir (i, i) to dismiss, fire, discharge; —**se (de)** to say good-by (to), take leave (of)

despegar to unglue, separate, detach, remove

despertar(se) (ie) to wake up

despilchado poorly dressed (*Arg. slang*)

despistar to throw off the track

desplegado unfolded, opened up

desplomarse to collapse, topple over

despojado free, stripped

despojo loot, war trophy; *pl.* spoils, ruins

despotismo tyranny, despotism

despreciar to scorn

desprecio scorn

desprender to remove, detach; —**se** to come (peel) off, come loose, separate, detach

despreocupar to put someone's mind at ease; —**se** to become at ease, indifferent

desprolijo untidy

desprovisto (de) bare, lacking, deprived (*of*)
desquiciarse to become unhinged, disordered
destacarse to stand out, be prominent
destartalado poorly furnished
destejer to undo, unravel knitting
destello flash
destemplado out of tune
desteñido faded
destiempo: a — at the wrong time
destreza skill, agility
destrozado ruined
destrozar to destroy
desvalido helpless
desvanecido vanished, out of sight, disappearing from sight; in a faint
desvanecimiento dizzy spell
desvelar(se) to stay awake, not be sleepy
desvestir (i, i) to undress
desviar (í) to deflect, ward off; **—se** to stray, deviate, get sidetracked
detener (ie) to stop, hold back; to arrest; detain; **—se** to stop
detenido slow, careful, thorough
determinado definite, decided
devastar to destroy, ruin
devolución return
devolver (ue) to return, give back
di *imp. of* **decir**
día: al otro — on the next day
diablo devil
diafanidad transparency, translucency
diáfano translucent; of very light texture
diario *n.* daily newspaper; *adj.* daily
diarista *m., f.* writer for a daily newspaper
dibujar to draw, sketch; **—se** to stand out, be seen, displayed, outlined
dicha happiness, good fortune
dicho *p. p. of* **decir; — y hecho** no sooner said than done; **lo —** as I (you, he, etc.) have said; *n.* saying, proverb; **mejor —** rather, I mean to say
dichoso happy, fortunate
diente *m.* tooth; **decir entre —s** to mutter
diestro right(-hand)

digitado with fingers
digno worthy; **— de fe** trustworthy
dilatar to stretch out, lengthen, widen
diluir to dilute
diminuto tiny, minute
dique *m.* dike
directorio board of directors
dirigible blimp, dirigible
dirigir to direct, send; **—se a** to turn to, go up to, go toward; to address, speak to
díscolo unruly
disculpa apology
disculparse to apologize
discurrir to pass, flow by
discurso speech
discutir to argue, discuss
disecado stuffed, mounted
disfrazar to disguise
disfrutar (de) to enjoy, benefit (from)
disfrute enjoyment
disgustado displeased
disgusto displeasure, disagreement, unpleasant occurrence
disimulado feigned, fake
disminución loss, decrease
disminuir to lessen, diminish
disolverse (ue) to disappear, to dissolve
disparar to shoot, fire
disparate *m.* nonsense
dispensar to excuse
displicencia disagreeableness, displeasure
disponer to order, command; **— de** to have available; **—se a** + *inf.* to get ready to + *verb*
dispositivo device, contrivance
dispuesto *p. p. of* **disponer;** ready, inclined, disposed
distinguir to make (pick) out, distinguish
distraer to distract
divagar to roam
divertido enjoyable, amusing
divertir (ie, i) to amuse; **—se** to enjoy oneself, have a good time
divisar to sight, see, perceive at a distance
doblar to bend (over), turn

dócil docile, meek
dolencia illness, ailment
doler (ue) to hurt, pain
dolor *m.* pain
dolorcillo little pain, twinge
dolorido sore, painful
dolorosamente painfully
domador de fieras wild animal tamer
dominar: — +*language* to
  speak + *language* + fluently
don *m.* gift, talent
dorado golden
dormitorio bedroom
dorso back
dosis *f. sing.* dose
dotar to give (*as a gift*)
dote *f.* dowry
duda doubt
dudar to doubt
duende *m.* goblin, elf
dueño owner
dulce *m. n.* piece of candy; *adj.* sweet
dulzura sweetness, softness
durar to last
durmiente *m.* railroad tie
duro *n.* dollar, peso; *adj.* hard, tough;
  a —**as penas** with great difficulty

E

¡ea! hey!
echar to stick out; to throw, toss; to
  put; to pour; to mail; — **a** to begin
  to; — **a perder** to spoil, ruin; —
  de menos to miss; — **llave** to lock;
  — **mano de** to make use of; —**se a**
  to begin to; — **una ojeada** to take
  a quick look, glance
edad age
editorial *f.* publishing house
educación upbringing, training,
  breeding
educar to raise, to bring up, train
efectivamente really, actually, as a
  matter of fact, in effect
efecto: en — as a matter of fact, in
  fact, in effect, indeed
eficacia effectiveness
eficaz effective, efficacious
efímero fleeting, ephemeral

eje *m.* axle
ejecutar to carry out
ejercitar to exercise
ejército army
elaborar to make, manufacture, work
  out
electoral: guapo — ward heeler
eléctrico: linterna —**a** flashlight
elegir (i, i) to elect, choose
elevarse to rise
emanación glow
embalar to wrap
embalsamado embalmed
embanderar to decorate with banners
  or flags
embarcar to board (*a boat*), embark
embargo: sin — however, nevertheless
embaucar to deceive, trick
embelesado charmed, delighted,
  enraptured
embobado fascinated
embolsar to pocket
emborracharse to get drunk
embotamiento dullness
embriagador intoxicating
embrujado bewitched, haunted
embrutecido depraved
embutir to imbed, force into
empalme *m.* road junction, freeway
  exit or entrance
empañado tarnished, sullied, cloudy,
  dull (*glass*)
empapar to soak
empaque *m.* look, appearance
empeñar to pawn; —**se (en)** to insist
  (on), persist (in)
empeño effort
empero nevertheless
empezar (ie) (a) to begin (to)
empinarse to rise up
emplasto poultice
emplazar to summon
empleado employee
emplear to use
empleo employment, use
emponchado with a poncho on
emponzoñado poisoned
emprender to undertake
empresa company, firm; enterprise,
  undertaking

empujar to push
empujón *m.* push, shove
empuñadura hilt, handle
en fin anyway (*expl.*)
enamorarse (de) to fall in love (with)
encaminarse a to set out (head) for
encantador charming, delightful,
  enchanting
encantar to charm, delight, enchant
encanto magic, enchantment, delight
encaramarse to climb (up)
encarcelar to jail, imprison
encarecer to promote, favor
encargado person in charge
encargar to order; —se de to take
  charge of
encargo charge, order
encarnar to embody, personify
enceguecido blinded, enraged
enceguedor blinding
encender (ie) to light, turn on
encendido bright, lit, burning
encerado waxed
encerrar (ie) to enclose; to shut (lock)
  up
encía gum (*mouth*)
encima (de) on top (of), over; llevar
  — to have on one's person; por de
  — on top of
encogerse de hombros to shrug one's
  shoulders
encogido huddled
encomendar (ie) to commend, entrust,
  put in the hands of
encomienda parcel
encontrar (ue) to find, meet; —se con
  to meet, run into
encorvado curved
encrespado curled up
encristalado *adj.* glass
encuentro meeting; al — de to meet
  (*e.g.,* Salió al encuentro de su
  amigo. He went out to meet his
  friend.)
endemoniado demoniacal, devilish
enderezar to go straight; to straighten
  out
enebro juniper
enérgico energetic
enfadarse to get angry

enfermedad illness, sickness
enfermería infirmary
enfermizo sickly
enfrentar to face
enfrente across the street
enfriamiento chill, chilling
enfundado encased, in a holster
enfurecerse to get furious
enfurecido furious
engañar to fool, deceive, cheat
engarzado joined, set in
engendro monster
engolfar to engulf, plunge
enharinado whitened with flour
enhiesto erect, lofty
enjambre *m.* swarm
enjugar to wipe dry
enlazar to join, unite, link, bind
enloquecer to drive crazy, madden
enmascarado masked
enmohecerse to get rusty
enmohecido rusty
enmudecer to become silent
ennegrecido blackened
ennoblecer to ennoble, embellish
enojarse to get annoyed, angry
enorgullecerse to become proud
enredadera vine
enrojecido reddened, reddish
ensangrentado bloody
ensayar to test, try (out); to rehearse;
  —se to try
enseñanza teaching
enseñar (a) to teach, show how (to)
ensillar to saddle
ensombrecido shaded, in shadow
ensueño illusion, fantasy, daydream
entablado herded (*Arg.*)
entablar to initiate, start, begin
ente *m.* being, entity
entender (ie) to understand; —se to
  imagine, understand; —se con to
  handle; to get along with; dar a —
  to lead one to believe, imply,
  insinuate
entendimiento understanding,
  knowledge
enterarse (de) to find out (about), be
  informed
entero entire, full

enterrar (ie) to bury
entonar to sing, intone
entonces: en ese — at that time
entornado ajar, half-open
entrada entrance; admission ticket
entraña intestine, entrail
entrañable strong, deep, intense
entreabrir to open halfway
entrecerrado half-open
entrecruzar to criss-cross, interlace
entrega delivery
entregar to give up, surrender, hand
over, deliver; **—se a** to give oneself
over to, lose oneself in
entrelazar to intertwine
entrenamiento training
entretanto meanwhile
entretener (ie) to entertain
entrevisto *p.p. of* **entrever** glimpsed
entristecer to sadden
entrometerse to intrude, interfere, butt
in
entusiasmado enthusiastic
envenenar to poison
enviar (í) to send
envidiar to envy
envidioso jealous, envious
envoltura covering, wrapping, "skin"
envolver (ue) to wrap
envuelto *p.p. of* **envolver**
equivaler (a) to be equivalent (to), be
worth the same
equivocar to mistake; **—se** to make a
mistake
érase (*imperfect of* **ser** + **se**) once
upon a time there was (*used to
begin a story*)
erguirse (ye, i) to straighten up
erigir to erect
erizado raised
errante *adj.* wandering
esbelto slender, well-built
escala stop, stopping place
escalera stairway
escalinata set of steps
escalofrío chill
escalón *m.* step
escándalo tumult, improper conduct
escaparate *m.* display window

escarmentar (ie) to take warning,
learn one's lesson
escasear to be scarce
escena scene
escolar *m. n.* schoolboy; *adj.* school,
academic
esconder to hide
escondidas: a — secretly
escribir: máquina de — typewriter
escrito *n.* writing
escritorio office
escudero page, squire
escupir to spit (out)
esforzar (ue) to exert, strengthen; **—se
(por)** to make an effort (to)
esfuerzo effort
esfumar to soften, blur
esguince *m.* slight movement, jerk
esmaltado enamelled
esmalte *m.* enamel
esmerado careful, neat, fastidious
esmeralda emerald
eso: en — just then, at that moment;
por — therefore
espada sword
espalda back (*of a person*)
espantado frightened, terrified
espantar to frighten, shoo off
espanto fright, terror
espantoso frightful, dreadful
esparcirse to spread
especie *f.* kind, type
espejismo mirage, illusion
espejo mirror
espera wait, waiting, expectation
esperanza hope
espetar to quiz, grill
espía *m.* spy
espina fishbone; thorn
espinazo spinal column
esposas *pl.* handcuffs
espuma foam
espumarajo froth (*at the mouth*)
espumoso foamy
esquila bell
esquina corner
esquivo aloof, unsociable, shy
estación season; station
estada stay, sojourn

estadística statistics
estallar to explode, break out (*war*)
estallido explosion
estampa picture
estampido crack, report of a gun
estante *m.* shelf
estar: — para (por) to be about
    (ready) to; **—se** to be, stay, remain
estatura figure; height
este *m.* east
éste the latter (*lit.,* this one)
estelar stellar
estilo: de — usual, customary; **por el
    —** like that
estirar to stretch
esto: en — just then
estómago stomach
estorbar to disturb, get in the way
estrado stage platform, dais
estragar to despoil, ruin
estrago havoc, ruin
estrechar to shake (*one's hand*)
estrechez austerity, poverty
estrecho *adj.* close, narrow
estrella star
estrellado starry
estremecer(se) to shake, tremble,
    shudder, shiver
estremecimiento chill, shudder
estrépito noise, ruckus
estrepitosamente noisily
estribo running board
estridente harsh, strident
estropear to injure, cripple
estruendo noise, racket, din
estrujar to wring, squeeze
estrujón *m.* squeezing, pressing
estuario estuary, meeting of the mouth
    of a river and the sea's tides
estuche *m.* box, case
estupefacto stupefied
estupidez stupidity
etéreo ethereal, delicate, airy
eterno eternal
etiqueta label
evasiva evasion
evitar to avoid
exangüe bloodless, anemic
exánime lifeless
exigencia demand

exigir to demand
éxito success
expectativa expectation
expedición sale
expediente *m.* means, resource, device
expender to sell
experiencia experiment; experience
explicar to explain; **—se** to
    understand, see
expuesto *p.p. of* **exponer;** liable, exposed
expulsar to expel, get rid of
extender (ie) to draw up (*a document*)
extenuarse (ú) to languish
extorsionar to extort
extranjero foreign; **al —** abroad
extrañar to surprise, seem strange; to
    miss
extrañeza strangeness, oddness; surprise
extraño strange
extraviarse (í) to get lost, misplaced
extravío aberration, deviation
extremo: en — a great deal
exvoto votive offering

F

fabricación manufacture
fabricar to make
fabril *adj.* manufacturing
facción feature; *pl.* face
facultad college, school (*of a university*)
fachada facade
falange *m.* bone of the finger
falda slope
falsa: llave — passkey
falta lack, need; **hacer —** to be
    necessary, needed
faltar to be lacking, missing, needed;
    — a to be absent (from), miss
falla defect, failure, handicap
fallar to fail
fallecer to pass away, succumb
fallecimiento death
fallo mistake
fama fame
fanfarrón *m.* boaster, loudmouth
fango mud
fantasma *m.* ghost, spirit, phantom
farol *m.* street light, lamp
fastidio arrogance, nuisance

fastidioso annoying, bothersome
fastuoso pompous, lavish
fatiga fatigue, weariness
fatigar to fill (*figurative*)
fatigoso tiresome; **—amente** *adv.*
   laboriously
fauna the animals from a given region
favor: a — de with the help of; **por**
   — please
faz *f.* face
fe *f.* trust, faith, credence; **digno de —**
   trustworthy
fecundo fertile, fruitful
felizmente happily
feo ugly
feria fair, festival
ferrocarril *m.* railroad, railway
ferrocarrilero *adj.* railroad
ferroviario *adj.* railroad
festejar to celebrate; admire, praise
feúcho ugly, homely
fiambre cold food (*as cold cuts*)
fichero file (*for records*)
fidedigno trustworthy, creditable
fiebre *f.* fever
fiel faithful
fiera beast, wild animal; **domador de**
   —s wild animal tamer
figa fig
figurar to have the shape of; **—se** to
   imagine
figurilla *dim. of* **figura** shape, form,
   figure
fijamente steadily, unwaveringly
fijar to fix, establish; **—se (en)** to
   notice, observe
fijo fixed
fila row, line
filiación description
filo line; edge of a blade
fin: al — finally, after all; **al — y al**
   cabo after all; **en —** anyway
   (*expl.*); **por —** finally, at last
finca farm
fingir to feign, simulate, pretend
finura refinement
firmar to sign
fiscal *m.* prosecuting attorney
fisgón *m.* snooper

flaco thin, skinny
flamante brand new; bright, polished
flamear to flutter
flanco side, flank
flaquear to get weak, weaken
flaqueza weakness
flecha arrow
florecer to blossom, flower; to flourish
florero flower vase
florido flowery, showy
florón *m.* big flower
fluctuante floating, fluctuating
follaje *m.* foliage
fonda inn
fondo bottom, depth; background;
   back, rear (*of a house*); **telón de —**
   backdrop
forastero stranger (*from another city*
   or town)
forense *m.* coroner
forjado wrought, built, constructed
fornido husky
fortuna: por — fortunately
forzado compelled, forced
forzar (ue) to break open
fosa grave, hole, ditch
fósforo match
fracaso failure
fracasar to fail
fraile friar, monk
franquear to open, clear, pass, get
   through
frasco bottle, flask
frasquito *dim. of* **frasco**
frenar to check, restrain
frenesí *m.* frenzy
frenético frenzied
freno brake
frente *f.* forehead; *m.* front; **— a**
   opposite; in front of; **al —**
   opposite, across the street; **en —**
   opposite, in front
fresco *n.* cool, coolness; **tomar el —**
   to get some fresh air; *adj.* fresh,
   cool; ruddy, healthy
frescura coolness, freshness
fresquito very fresh *dim. of* **fresco**
frialdad coldness
frotar to rub

fruncir to pleat, gather
fruncido wrinkled
fuego fire; **—s artificiales** fireworks
fuente *f.* fountain, stream; large
  serving dish
fuera away; off (with); **— (de)** outside
  (of), out (of)
fuertemente tightly
fuerza(s) force, strength; **sin —**
  exhausted
fuga flight
fugazmente fleetingly
fulgor *m.* brilliance
fulgurar to flash
fullero "shady," dishonest
fumar to smoke
funda slipcover, case, cover
funesto fatal, disastrous
furgón *m.* railroad car
furor *m.* rage, fury

G

galantear to court, pay attention to
galería hall
galpón *m.* shed
gallardo gallant
gallina hen
gana desire, whim; **darle la — a uno**
  for someone to feel like; **de buena**
  — willingly; **de mala —**
  unwillingly; **tener —s (de)** to feel like
ganarse el pan to earn a living
gansa female goose
garabatear to scribble, scrawl
garbo jauntiness, grace
garboso jaunty, graceful
garganta throat
gargantillo *South American songbird*
garra claw, talon
gastar to waste, spend, wear out; **—se**
  to wear out
gasto expense
gaveta small drawer
gemido moan, cry, groan
gemir (i, i) to moan
genial brilliant
genio genius

germencito seed
gesto gesture
gira trip, visit
girar to spin, turn, swing, rotate
gis *m.* chalk
globo balloon
glutinoso gluey, sticky
gobernar (ie) to rule, direct
goce *m.* joy
golosina sweet, "goody"
goloso greedy, "sweet-toothed"
golpe *m.* blow; **de —** suddenly
golpear to hit, knock, strike, beat
golpecito tap, rap
golpeo beating
goma: faja de — girdle
gota drop
gotera leak
goterón *m.* large drop, glob
gozar (de, con) to enjoy
grabadora tape recorder
gracia: hacer — to be funny
gracioso funny
gradas *pl.* gallery (*of an amphitheater*)
grado degree
granate garnet, deep red
gran cosa much, very much
grandullón *m.* big brute
grasoso greasy
gresca uproar, row
griego Greek
gris gray
gritar to cry out, shout, scream
gritería shouting
grito cry, shout
gritón loud-mouthed
grosería rudeness, boorishness; coarse
  word *or* action
grosero rude, crude, boorish, coarse,
  rough
grúa crane, derrick
grueso thick, heavy
gruñir to growl
gruta cavern, grotto
guante *m.* glove
guapo *adj.* good-looking; *n.* **—**
  electoral ward heeler
guardagujas *m.* switchman
guardar to keep; to put away

guarida lair, den
guía guide, guidebook, directory,
  telephone book
guiar (í) to guide, lead
guijarro pebble, stone
guiñapo tattered rag
guiño wink
guisar to cook
guiso cooked dish
gula gluttony, greed
gusano worm
gusto pleasure; taste

H

haber to have *aux.;* — **de** to be
  supposed to, be to, have to; — **que**
  to be necessary to
habilitación backing (*business*)
habitación room
habituarse (ú) (a) to become
  accustomed (to)
hablar: dar que — to give occasion
  for talk, comment
hacendado rancher, landowner
hacer to do, make; *to show lapse of
  time* (*e.g.,* **Vivo aquí desde hace
  cinco años.** *or* **Hace cinco años que
  vivo aquí.** I've been living here for
  five years. **Llegué hace pocos días.**
  I arrived a few days ago.); *to
  express weather* (*e.g.,* **Hace calor.**
  It's hot.); — **burla de** to mock; —
  caso to pay attention, listen, heed;
  — **como que** + *indicative* to
  pretend + *inf.;* —**le compañía a
  uno** to keep someone company; —
  daño to hurt; — **falta** to be
  necessary, needed; — **gracia** to be
  funny; — **llegar** to convey, send;
  — **saber** to inform, notify; —**se** to
  "play," pretend (*e.g.,* **No se haga
  el tonto.** Don't play dumb.); to
  become; —**se el sordo** to turn a
  deaf ear
hacia toward
hacienda estate, ranch

hacha axe
hachar to chop
hachazo blow with an axe
hada fairy
hallar to find; —**se** to be, be found
hallazgo find, discovery
hambre *f.* hunger
hambriento hungry
hartarse to get one's fill, be satisfied
harto full, fed up
hastío weariness, tedium
hazaña feat, deed
hebra string, thread (*of yarn*)
hechicero sorcerer, wizard
hecho *p.p. of* **hacer; dicho y** — no
  sooner said than done; **lo** — that
  which was done; *n.* fact, deed; —
  de sangre crime, bloody deed
helado frozen, icy
helarse (ie) to freeze
hembra female
hendija crevice, crack
herboristería herb shop
heredar to inherit
herencia heredity
herida wound, injury
herido wounded, injured, struck
herir (ie, i) to wound
hermanar to harmonize
herrumbrar to rust
hervir (ie, i) to boil, seethe
hiato hiatus, gap, interval
hidalgo nobleman, gentleman
hiel *f.* gall
hielo ice
hierro iron, piece of iron
higo fig
hilacha fiber; "true colors"
hilarse por to filter through
hilera file, row
hilo thread, wire
hinchado swollen
hinchar to swell (up)
hipócrita: a —**s** hypocritical(ly)
hipotensión insufficient tension
historieta comic strip
hito: de — **en** — from head (top) to
  foot (bottom)
hogar *m.* home

hoja leaf; page, sheet
holgazán *m.* idler, loafer
holgazanería idleness, laziness
hollar (ue) to tread, trample
hombro shoulder; **encogerse de —s** to shrug one's shoulders
homicida *f.* murderess
hondo deep
hongo mushroom
honradez honesty
honrado honest
hormiguear to swarm
hormiguero anthill
horno oven
hosco sullen, grumpy
hoy: de — en adelante from this day on
hoyuelo little hole
hubo *3rd pers. pret. of* **haber** there was (were)
hueco *n.* hollow, open space; *adj.* hollow; **a —as** hollow
huella trace, print
huérfano orphan
huerto orchard
hueso bone
huésped *m.* guest; host
huida flight
huir (y) to flee
humear to smoke (*intrans.*)
humedecer to wet, moisten
humedad dampness, humidity
húmedo damp, wet, humid
humilde humble
humildoso excessively humble
humillar to humiliate
humo smoke
humor *m.* mood, humor
hundir(se) to sink
húngaro Hungarian
hurgar to handle, move, agitate
hurto theft

I

ida: — y vuelta round trip; **boleto de — one-way ticket
idear to conceive the idea of
idilio idyll

idioma *m.* language
ignorar not to know, to be ignorant of
igual: por — equally
igualado equalized, the same
ilusionista *m.* magician
imagen *f.* statue, image
imborrable indelible, unremovable
impar odd, unequal
impedir (i, i) to prevent
imperioso overbearing, haughty, urgent, overriding
impermeabilizar to make waterproof
impermeable *m.* raincoat
implacable relentless
imponente imposing
imponer to impose
impracticable rough, impassable
imprecisable unforeseeable
imprevisto unforeseen
imprimir to press; to print
impropio inappropriate, unsuited
imprudencia indiscretion
impulso impulse
inadvertencia accident, oversight
inadvertido unnoticed
inapreciable invaluable, inestimable
inaudito unheard of, inconceivable
incapaz incapable
incendiado ruined by fire
incendio fire, blaze
inclinado bowed, tipped
incluso even, including
inconsciente unaware, unconscious
inconveniente *m.* objection; disadvantage, obstacle, difficulty, problem; **tener — (en)** to mind, object (to)
incorporarse to stand, sit up
incorpóreo bodiless, intangible
increpar to rebuke, chide
inculcar to inculcate, ingrain
indagar to ascertain
indecible inexpressible, indescribable
indefenso defenseless
indemnizar to pay for, compensate (damages)
índice *m.* index finger
indicio hint, clue
indigesto undigested

indistintamente indifferently, without distinction
inerte paralyzed
infaltable everpresent, unfailing
infamación infamy
infamar to dishonor, slander, defame
infamia disgrace, insult
infausto unlucky, ill-starred
infeliz unhappy
informe *adj.* formless; *m. pl. n.* information
infortunio misfortune, bad luck
infranqueable impassable
infundir to infuse
ingeniero engineer
ingenio talent, skill, cleverness
ingenuo candid, ingenuous
ingestión eating
ingrato unpleasant
ingravidez lightness, weightlessness
ingresar to enter, enroll
injuria insult, slander
inmóvil motionless
inmovilidad motionlessness
inmutarse to become disturbed, lose one's composure
inopinado unexpected; **—amente** unexpectedly
inquietar to make uneasy; **—se** to worry, become uneasy
inquieto restless, anxious, uneasy
inquietud uneasiness
inquilino tenant
inquina ill will
inquieto uneasy
insano unhealthy
insidia snare, trap; sneakiness, treachery
insobornable incorruptible
insoportable insufferable, unbearable
instante: por —s continuously
íntegro whole, complete; **—amente** wholly, completely
intemperie *f.* bad weather
intempestivo sudden, unexpected, inopportune
intentar to try
intercalar to insert
interlocutor *m.* interlocutor (*one who takes part in a conversation*)

internarse to go into
interponer to interpose, place between
interrogatorio interrogation; questioning, grilling
intimar to order, require
intransitable impassable
inútil useless; **—mente** *adv.* in vain
inutilizar to disable, render useless
inverosímil unlikely, implausible
inversión investment
inyectar to inject
ir to go; **¡Vaya!** *imp.* Well! (*to express surprise*); **—** + *pr. p.* to be gradually + *pr. p.*
irrespetuoso disrespectful
irrumpir (en) to burst (into)
isla island
itinerario schedule, timetable
izquierdo *adj.* left

J

jactarse to brag, boast
jadear to pant, gasp
jadeo panting, heavy breathing
jamás never
jaque mate checkmate (chess)
jaqueca severe headache
jardín *m.* yard, garden
jaula cage
jazmín *m.* jasmine (*shrub with fragrant flowers*)
jefatura police station
jinete *m.* rider (*horseback*), cavalryman
jirón *m.* shred, piece
joya jewel
jubilado retired
juego game
jugada move (*chess*), play
jugar (ue) to play; to gamble
juguete *m.* toy, plaything
juguetear to frolic, gambol
juicio senses, judgment; **poner en tela de —** to question
juicioso wise, prudent
juncal *m.* field of reeds, rushes
juntar to gather, join
junto together; **— a** next to, against
jurar to swear, take an oath

justamente just, exactly, right; to be
precise
justicieramente fairly, justly
justipreciar to evaluate
justo exact
juzgar to judge

L

laberinto labyrinth
labio lip; sellar los —s to silence
labrador *m.* farmer
lacrimógeno: gas — tear gas
ladear to tilt, tip
ladino sly, crafty
lado side
ladrar to bark
ladrillo brick
ladrón *m.* thief
lago lake
lágrima tear
laja rock protruding out of the water
lambiscón *adj.* "boot-licking," fawning
lamentarse (de) to be sorry (about)
lamento wail, lament
lámina sheet, layer, plate
lámpara lamp
lana wool
lancha launch
languidecer to be weak, languish
lanzallamas *m.* flame thrower
lanzar to launch, fling, throw; to
issue, let out, emit
lápida gravestone
lares *m. pl.* home
largar to release, launch
largo *n.* length; *adj.* long; a lo — de
along (the length of)
lástima pity, sorrow; tener — de, a to
feel sorry for
lastimosamente painfully
lastre *m.* steadiness, good sense; ballast
lateral *adj.* side
latigazo crack, blow of a whip
látigo whip, lash
latir to beat, pulsate
lavandera laundress
lavar to wash
lavatorio lotion; lavatory
lazo tie, band, bond

lecciones: dar — to recite lessons
lectura reading
lechería dairy bar
lecho bed
lechoso milky
legista: médico — criminal pathologist
lego lay brother, friar
legua league (*distance of about three
miles*); a la — a mile away
legumbre *f.* vegetable
lejano *adj.* far, distant
lejos: a lo — in the distance
lengua language; tongue
lente *m.* lens; —s eyeglasses
lentitud slowness
lento slow
leña firewood
leño timber
lepra leprosy
lesionado injured
letanía litany
letargo lethargy
letra letter (*of the alphabet*);
handwriting
letrero sign
levantar vuelo to take off (*as a bird or
a plane*)
leve light (*in weight*); slight
levita frock coat
levitar to float
ley *f.* law
libar to sip
librarse (de) to be free (from), get rid
of
libre: al aire — outside
librería bookstore
libreta memorandum book, notebook
licencia leave, vacation
licenciar to license; to confer a degree
(on)
ligado bound, fastened
ligadura bond, tie
ligar to tie, join
ligero quick, fast; light (*in weight*)
lijado ground, worn down
lila lilac
limitar to border, bound
limonero lemon tree
limpiar to clean
limpidez cleanness, purity

limpieza cleaning, cleanliness
limpio clean, neat; **sacar en —** to gather, conclude
lindar con to border on
linde *f.* border, edge
lindo pretty; nice
linfa stream
linterna lantern; **— eléctrica** flashlight
liquidación sale
lirio lily
liso smooth, flat
lisonjero flattering
listo ready
liviandad lewd, immoral behavior
liviano light (*in weight*)
lo: — + *adj.* the + *adj.* + part (*e.g.,* **lo milagroso** the miraculous part)
lobo wolf
lóbrego gloomy, somber, dark
locura madness, insanity
lodo mud
lograr to win, succeed; **— +** *inf.* to manage (get) + *inf.*
loro parrot
losa stone, flagstone
losange *m.* diamond-shape
lote *m.* lot, group
loza china
lucecita little light (*dim. of* **luz**)
luciérnaga firefly
lucir to shine
lucha fight, battle, struggle
luchar to fight
ludión *m.* Cartesian devil (*device used in physics*)
luego then; immediately, soon; afterward; **— de** after; **desde —** of course
lugar *m.* place; village
lúgubre mournful, gloomy
lujo luxury
lujoso luxurious, lavish, fancy
luna moon
lustro period of five years
luto: de — (dressed) in mourning
luz *f.* light; **luces de bengala** Roman candles (*fireworks*)

LL

llaga wound
llama flame
llamado call
llamarada flame, blaze
llanos *pl.* plains, flatlands
llanura flatland
llave *f.* key, electric switch;— **falsa** passkey; **echar —** to lock
llegada arrival
llegar (a) to arrive, get (to); **— a +** *inf.* to manage (get) + *inf.;* **hacer —** to convey, send
llenar (de) to fill (with)
lleno full
llevadero bearable
llevar to carry, take; to lead; **— +** *time + gerund* to be + *gerund +* for + *time* (*e.g.,* **Lleva dos años trabajando aquí.** He's been working here for two years.); **— encima** to have on one's person; **—le la corriente a uno** to let someone have his own way; **—se** to take away, carry off; **—se con** to get along with; **—se una sorpresa** to be surprised
llorar to cry, weep
lluvia rain

M

macilento pale, dim
macizo *n.* flower bed; *adj.* solid, massive
madeja skein (of yarn)
madera wood
maderero lumberman
madriguera den
madrugada dawn, early morning; **muy de —** at daybreak
maduro grown-up
magia magic
mágico magician
mago magician, sorcerer
majadería nonsense

mal *m.* sickness; evil, wrong; «**No hay — que por bien no venga.**» "Everything turns out for the best." "Every cloud has a silver lining."; *adv.* badly, poorly

maldad evil

maldecir (i) to curse, damn

maldición curse

maldito *p.p. of* **maldecir** cursed, damned

malear to spoil, sour, corrupt

malecón *m.* pier, jetty, sea wall

maleficio curse, spell

malentendido misunderstanding

malestar *m.* indisposition

malgastar to waste, squander

malo: de —a gana unwillingly

maltrecho battered

malva mallow (*plant*)

malvado evil, wicked

mamar: dar de — to nurse (*an infant*)

mamarracho grotesque figure

mamífero mammal

mamotreto huge, imposing book or volume (*slang*)

mañanita bed jacket

mancebo young man

manco one-handed; crippled in one hand or arm

mancha stain, spot

manchar to stain

manchón *m.* large stain, spot

mandadero errand boy, office boy

mandar to send; to command, order

manejar to drive (*vehicle*); to manage, handle

manejo use

manera way; **de — que** in such a way that, so; **de otra —** otherwise; **de todas —s** anyway

manga sleeve

mango handle

maniatar to tie one's hands

maniático crazy, eccentric

manicura manicurist

manifestar (ie) to declare, reveal, show, make clear, indicate; **—se** to appear

manivela crank

mano: — de pintura coat of paint; **echar — de** to make use of; **untar la —** to grease the palm

manotada blow with paw, hand

manotear to cuff, flail

manotón *m.* slap with the paw

manso meek, tame

manta blanket, poncho (*Chile*); **a —s** by the dozen, in abundance

mantenerse (ie) to stay, continue

manuscrito handwritten

manzana apple

maña skill, art

mañana *f.* morning; *m.* tomorrow; **— mismo** tomorrow at the latest; **pasado —** day after tomorrow

máquina machine; car; **— de escribir** typewriter

maquinalmente automatically, mechanically

mar *m.* sea, ocean

maraña trick, ruse

maravilla wonder; marvel

maravillado in wonderment, marveled, amazed

maravillar to amaze, surprise

marca brand

marco picture frame, window case

marcha motion, walk, course, way, journey, route, advance; **en —** moving, going; **poner en —** to start (*a vehicle or machine*)

marchar to go

marcharse to leave

mareado dizzy, slightly nauseated; dazzled

marfil *m.* ivory

marido husband

marino *adj.* sea

mármol *m.* marble

martillar to hammer

martirizar to torture, torment

mas but (*literary*)

más: — allá far away, farther on; **— allá de** beyond; *m. n.* great beyond; **— bien** rather, more;

a — de besides; **no — que** only; **no poder —** not to be able to go on (stand anymore), to be all tired (worn) out, to be "all in"; **poder — to** win out, overcome; **sin —** without further ado; **valer — to** be better
máscara mask
mascullar to mumble
matadero slaughterhouse
matinal *adj.* morning
matiz *m.* shade, nuance
matizado colored, tinged
matrimonio married couple
matutino *adj.* morning
mayólica plaster wall decorations; china covered with metal
mayor *m. n.* adult; *adj.* older, oldest; greater, greatest; **persona —** adult
mayordomo butler
mecha wick, fuse
mediado halfway through
mediano average
mediante by means of
medias *pl.* stockings
médico legista criminal pathologist
medida measure; **a — que** while, at the same time as
medio *n.* way, manner; middle; means; *adj.* half
medrar to thrive, prosper
mejilla cheek
mejor better, best; **— dicho** rather, I mean to say; **a lo —** when least expected; probably, as likely as not
mejorar(se) to improve, get better
melífluamente sweetly, like honey
mellizo twin
memoria: de — by heart
mendicante *m.* beggar
menos less, least; **a — que** unless; **cuando —** at least; **no poder — de** + *inf.* not to be able to help but + *v.* (e.g. **No se podía menos de imaginarlos.** One could not help but imagine them.); **por lo —** at least
menosprecio scorn
mensaje *m.* message
mensajero messenger
mensualidad monthly payment

mentecato idiot
mentir (ie, i) to lie (*tell a falsehood*)
mentira lie (*falsehood*)
menudo small; **a —** often
mercado market
merced favor, benefit
mercería dry-goods store
merecedor *m.* deserving person
merecer to deserve
merienda luncheon, light meal (*taken in the afternoon*)
meter to put into; **— la pata** to butt in; to stick one's foot in it, "goof"; **—se** to enter, slip into
meticulosidad meticulous care
mezclar to mix (up)
mezquite *m.* cactuslike shrub
miaja bit
miedo fear; **tener — de** to be afraid of
miel *f.* honey
mientras while; **— tanto** meanwhile
milagrería miracle-making area
milagrero miraclemaker
milagro miracle
milagroso miraculous
millar *m.* thousand
mimar to spoil, indulge
mimbre *m.* wicker
mimo spoiling, pampering
mimosidad indulgence, solicitousness
minar to sap, weaken
mío: a pesar — against my wishes
miope nearsighted
mirada glance, gaze, look; **dar una —** to take a glance
mirado: bien — carefully considered
mirador *m.* bay window
misa mass (*church service*)
misántropo misanthrope, hater of mankind
misericordia pity, mercy
mísero miserable
mismo same, -self, very; **ahora —** right now; **el — rey** the king himself; **mañana —** tomorrow at the latest; **por lo —** by the same token; **yo —** I myself; **el agua —a** the very water
misto *South American songbird*

mitad half, middle
mito myth
mobiliario furniture
mocedades *pl.* youth, younger days
mocetón *m.* lad
mocoso brat
modales *m. pl.* manners
modo way, manner; **a — de** in the manner of, like; **de (tal) — que** in such a way that, so; **de todos —s** anyway, at any rate
mohino peeved
mojar to wet; **—se** to get wet
moler (ue): — a palos to give a severe beating to
molestar to bother; **—se (en)** to bother, take the trouble (to)
molestia bother, trouble
molesto annoying, bothersome, bothered
momento: al — at once; **de —** for a (the) moment
moneda coin
monja nun
mono monkey, ape
monstruo monster
montar to ride (*horseback*)
moño topknot, crest
morada abode, dwelling
morder (ue) to bite, gnaw
mordida payoff (*lit., "bite"*)
moreno dark (*skin or hair*)
morfología structure, morphology
moribundo dying
morir(se) (ue, u) to die
morisco Moorish
mortífero deadly, lethal
mosca fly
mosquitero mosquito netting
mostrador *m.* counter, bar
mostrar (ue) to show; **—se** to appear, look
mote *m.* nickname
motivo reason, motive; occasion
movedizo shifting, moving
moverse (ue) to move (*intrans.*)
movimiento motion
mozo boy, lad; waiter
mucama maid (*Arg.*)
muchachada group of children

muchacherío group of children
muchedumbre *f.* crowd, multitude
mudar to change
mudo mute, silent
mueble *m.* piece of furniture
mueca grimace, grin, "face"
muelle *m.* wharf, pier
muerte *f.* death
muestra example, sign; sample
mugir to moo, bellow
mugriento dirty, grimy
multa fine (*traffic*)
mundo world; **todo el —** everyone
muñeca wrist
muñeco manikin, dummy
muralla wall
murmullo murmur
murmurar to gossip; to murmur
muro wall
muslo thigh
mustio withered

N

nacimiento birth
nadar to swim
naftalina naphtalene
naranja orange
nariz nose, nostril
naturaleza nature
náufrago castaway, shipwrecked person
navideño *adj.* Christmas
neblina fog, mist
neblinoso foggy, misty
necesitado needy person
negar (ie) to refuse, deny; **—se (a)** to decline, refuse (to)
negocios *pl.* business, commercial affairs
negrura black(ness)
ni siquiera not even
niágara stream (*poetic*)
nido nest
nieto grandson
niquelado nickel plated
noche: — cerrada completely dark; **de — ** at night
Nochebuena Christmas Eve

nombre: poner un — to name
noticias *pl.* news; **recibir — (de)** to hear (from)
novedad something new
noveno ninth
novia bride
novio boyfriend, fiancé
nube *f.* cloud
nubecilla *dim. of* **nube**
nublado cloudy
nuca back of the neck
nudo knot
nuevamente again
nuevas *pl.* news
nuevo: de — again
numen *m.* deity
nupcias *pl.* wedding
nutrirse to be nourished

O

obispado bishopric (*office or diocese of a bishop*)
oblicuamente slanting, obliquely
obra work, deed
obrar to work, operate, to behave
obrero *n.* worker; *adj.* working, labor
obscurantismo ignorance
ocaso setting sun, sunset
occidente *m.* west
ocultar to hide (*trans.*); **—se** to hide (*intrans.*)
oculto hidden
ocuparse de to take care of, pay attention to
ocurrencia witticism
ocurrir (a) to have recourse (to), apply (to); **—sele a uno** to get an idea
odiar to hate
odio hate, hatred
odioso hated, hateful
oeste *m.* west
ofrecer to offer
oído ear (inner)
¡oiga! *imp. of* **oír** Hey!, Listen!
oír decir to hear, hear it said
ojalá may, I hope, God grant (*e.g.,*
  Ojalá que te acompañe siempre.
  May He always be with you.)

ojeada glance; **echar una —** to take a quick look, glance
ojeroso having circles under the eyes
ola wave
óleo oil; oil painting
oler (hue) to smell (*trans. and intrans.*)
olfatear to smell (*trans.*)
olor *m.* smell, odor
olvidarse (de) to forget
olvido forgetfulness, oblivion
onda ripple, wave
opaco opaque
opinar to have an opinion, judge
oponerse (a) to oppose
oprimir to press down, oppress
optar (por) to choose (to)
oración prayer
orar to pray
orbe *m.* earth
orden *f.* order, command; **a sus —es** at your service; *m.* order (*arrangement*)
ordenadamente in an orderly manner
oreja (*outer*) ear
orfeón *m.* singing society
orgullo pride
orgulloso proud
orilla shore, bank, edge
oro gold
orondo serene (*Arg.*)
osar to dare
o(b)scurecer to get dark
oso bear
otoño autumn, fall
otorgar to grant, give, authorize
otro: —a parte elsewhere; **—a vez** again; **al — día** on the next day; **de —a manera** otherwise; **por —a parte** on the other hand; **unos a —s** each other, one another
ovillo ball of wool, string
oyente *m., f.* listener

P

pábulo food
pacífico peaceful
padecer to suffer

padrino godfather
página page
paisaje *m.* landscape, view
paja straw
pajarera bird cage
pájaro bird
paladear to savor
palanquita *dim. of* **palanca** lever
palidecer to turn pale
palidez paleness, pallor
pálido pale
palito stray mark (*in handwriting*)
palma palm tree, palm
palmada pat with the hand
palmera palm tree
palmotear to clap, slap
palo stick; **moler a —s** to give a
   severe beating
palpar to feel (*touch*)
palúdico noxious, malarial
pan: ganarse el — to earn a living
panal *m.* honeycomb
pandilla gang
pañoleta woman's triangular shawl
pantalla lamp shade; screen (*movies,*
   TV)
pantera panther
pantalón *m.* pair of pants
pantuflas *pl.* slippers
pañuelo handkerchief
papagayo parrot
papel de plata tinfoil
papeleta ticket, slip of paper
par *m.* pair, couple, few; **a la — de**
   even with; *adj.* even (*numbers*)
para: — abajo downward; **— arriba**
   upward; **— que** so that; **— siempre**
   forever; **como —** as if to; **estar —**
   to be about (ready) to
parábola parable
parada stop
parado standing, stopped
paraguas *m. sing.* umbrella
pararse to stop (*intrans.*)
parecer to seem, look like, appear;
   —se a to look alike, resemble
parecido similar
pared wall
paredón *m.* thick wall

pareja couple
pariente *m.* relative
párpado eyelid
párrafo paragraph
parroquiano customer
parsimonia sparingness
parte: alguna — somewhere; **de — de**
   on the side of; **otra —** elsewhere;
   por otra — on the other hand;
   todas —s everywhere
particular private
partida game, match; departure;
   shipment; group, party
partir to leave, depart; to break, split,
   share
parvada flock
pasada pacing
pasadizo passageway, corridor
pasado: — mañana day after tomorrow
pasador *m.* bolt
pasajero passenger
pasamano *m.* railing
pasar to spend (*time*); to pass,
   happen; to enter, come (go); to
   swallow (*food or drink*); **— por**
   alto to overlook, pass over; **¿Qué**
   pasa? What's the matter?
Pascua Easter; *any one of several*
   important Church holidays
paseante *m.* stroller, passerby
pasear to walk, stroll; to pass; to go
   on a pleasure trip
paseo walk, stroll, outing; wide street,
   boulevard, avenue
pasillo hall
pasmo wonder, astonishment
paso passage, passing, way, crossing,
   path; step, footstep; **abrir —** to
   clear the way; **cerrar el —** to block
   the way; **de —** in passing, by the
   way; **dar un —** to take a step;
   vedar el — to block the way
paspado chapped
pasto fodder
pastoso pasty
pata paw, foot, leg (*animal*), **meter la**
   — to butt in; to stick one's foot in
   it, "goof"
patalear to kick, thrash around

patente obvious, evident
patitieso stupefied
patito duckling
patraña story, hoax
patria country, homeland
patrimonio heritage
patrón *m.* boss
paupérrimo very poor
pausadamente slowly, deliberately
pavor *m.* fear, terror
paz *f.* peace; **en —** alone
pebete *m.* fuse
pecado sin
pechera breast; front
pecho chest, breast
pedazo piece
pedrada blow from a stone, stoning
pegado attacked, stuck
pegar to stick, attach; to hit, strike; **— un brinco** to jump
pelea fight
pelear to fight
peligroso dangerous
pelo hair
pelota ball
peludo hairy, furry
pellejo skin (*animal*)
pellizcar to pinch
pena pain, sorrow; **a duras —s** with great difficulty; **valer la —** to be worthwhile
penacho crest
pender to hang
pendiente *adj.* waiting
penoso painful
pensamiento thought
pensar: cosa de —lo something to think about
pensativo thoughtful, pensive
penumbra shadows, semidarkness
penumbroso shadowy
peón *m.* farm worker
percance *m.* misfortune, mishap
percatarse (de) to be aware (of), to notice (take note of)
percha hat rack
perder (ie) to lose; to waste; **— el pie** to lose one's footing; **echar a —** to spoil, ruin; **—se** to lose one's way, get lost; to disappear, end
pérdida loss

perdonar to excuse
perecer to perish
peregrinación pilgrimage
perfil *m.* profile, outline
periodismo journalism
periodista journalist
perito expert
perjudicado damaged, injured, "bested"
perjuicio damage
permanecer to stay, remain
pernoctar to spend the night
perplejo perplexing
persa Persian
persecución pursuit
perseguir (i, i) to chase, pursue
persiana slatted shutter; **—s** Venetian blinds
persona mayor adult
personaje *m.* person, character
personal *m.* personnel
perspicacia shrewdness
pertenecer to belong
pesadilla nightmare
pesado heavy, weighty
pesadumbre *f.* grief, sorrow
pesar to weigh, have weight; *m. n.* grief, sorrow; **a — de** in spite of; **a — mío** against my wishes
pesaroso sorrowful, sad
pescado fish (*after it is caught*)
pescante *m.* driver's seat
pescar to fish
pescuezo neck (animal)
pese a despite
peso weight; peso
petirrojo robin
pétreo stony
pez *m.* fish (*before it is caught*)
piadoso pious, merciful
pica lance
picado perforated
picaflor *m.* hummingbird
picardía: con — roguishly
pico beak
pie: de — standing up; **perder —** to lose one's footing; **ponerse en (de) —** to stand up; **puntas de —** tiptoes
piedad pity
piedra stone
piel *f.* skin

pierna leg
pieza part (*of a machine*), piece; room
pila heap, pile
pillar to catch, grab
pillo rogue, scoundrel
pinchar to prick, puncture, pierce
pino steep
pintoresco picturesque
pintura paint; **mano de** — coat of paint
piropeador *m.* admirer (*one who makes remarks at passing women*)
pirueta pirouette (*a whirl on the toe while dancing*)
pisapapeles *m. sing.* paperweight
pisada footstep; hoofbeat
pisar to step on; to set foot on
piso floor
pisotear to trample
pistolero gunman
placa plaque, sign
placer *m.* pleasure
plano blueprint, plan, map
planta sole (*foot*)
plata money, "dough"; silver; **papel de** — tinfoil
platanar *m.* group of banana trees
plateado silvered, silver(y)
playa beach
plaza: ceder la — to give up
plazo term, period of time
plazuela *dim. of* **plaza**
plegada fold
plegar (ie) to fold, bend
plegaria prayer
pleito lawsuit
pleno full, complete; **en —a selva** right in the middle of the jungle
pliego sheet of paper
pliegue *m.* line, wrinkle, crease
plomo lead (*metal*)
pluma feather; pen
población town
poblar (ue) to populate, inhabit
pocillo demitasse
poco: a — in a little while; **costar** — to be easy
poder *m.* power; *v.:* — **más** to win out, overcome; **no** — **más** not to be able to go on (stand) anymore, to be all tired (worn) out, to be "all in"; **no** — **menos de** + *inf.* not to be able to help but + *v.* (*e.g.,* **No se podía menos de imaginarlos.** One could not help but imagine them.); **puede que** maybe
poderío power
poderoso powerful, mighty
podrido rotten
policía: cuerpo de — police force
polvo dust
pólvora powder
polvoriento dusty
pomada ointment
pomo fist (*figurative*)
poner to put, place, set; — **... por caso** to use . . . as an example; — **a prueba** to put to the test; — **en marcha** to start (*a vehicle or machine*); — **en tela de juicio** to question; — **reparos (a)** to find fault (with); — **un nombre** to name; —**se** to become, get; —**se** + *article of clothing* to put on; —**se a** to begin to; —**se de acuerdo** to come to an agreement; —**se en (de) pie** to stand up; —**se en ridículo** to look ridiculous, make a fool of oneself
por: — **el contrario** on the other hand; — **eso** therefore; — **favor** please; — **lo visto** apparently; — **si acaso** just in case; — **su cuenta** on one's own; **estar** — to be about (ready) to
porfía persistence, stubbornness
portador *m.* bearer
portátil portable
portazo door slam
portentoso prodigious, marvelous
portezuela small door (*often in a vehicle*)
pórtico hall, portico
portón *m.* gate
portoncito little door
porvenir *m.* future
posarse to land, (a)light
postergar to delay, postpone
postizo artificial
postre: a la — at last
postrero last, final
potasio: cianuro de — potassium cyanide

potrero pasture, field
potro colt
poyo stone seat
pozo well, pit
precipitado hasty, wild, hurried
precipitar to hasten; —**se** to rush,
  race, charge
preciso necessary
predilecto favorite
prefijar to determine beforehand
premiar to reward
premio prize
prenda article, garment
prendarse (de) to become attracted
  (to), fond (of)
prendedor *m.* pin, brooch
prender to light; to attach
prendido (de) grasping, holding on (to)
prensa press
preocupar to worry
presa capture, catch; prisoner, captive;
  animal de — predatory animal
presagiar to foretell
prescindir de to do without, do away
  with
prescribir to indicate
presenciar to witness
presentarse to show up
presente present
presentir (ie, i) to sense, have a
  premonition
presidio prison
presión pressure
preso prisoner
préstamo loan
prestar to lend; to pay (*attention*); to
  provide
pretender to claim; — + *inf.* to
  try + *inf.*
pretendiente *m.* suitor
preterido left out, ignored
prevalecer to prevail
prevenir (ie) to warn, caution
prever to foresee, anticipate
previsible foreseeable
previsión foresight
previsor foresighted
primera: de — first class
primogénito first-born
primor *m.* beauty, elegance

principiar to begin
principio: al — at first
prisa hurry, haste; **darse** — to hurry;
  de — hurriedly; **tener** — to be in
  a hurry
privar to deprive
proa prow, bow (*ship*)
probar (ue) to prove; to try out, test
procacidad insolence, indecency
proceder (de) to come (from),
  originate (in)
prodigar to lavish
prodigio prodigy, marvel
producirse to happen, occur, take place
proferir (ie, i) to utter, speak
prófugo fugitive, escapee
profundidad depth
progresista progressive
prometer to promise
pronto: ready; **de** — suddenly; **por de**
  — in the meantime; **por lo** —
  meanwhile, for the present
propicio favorable, right, propitious
propiedad: con — properly
propietario owner
propio own; characteristic; -self (*e.g.,*
  la propia botella the bottle
  itself)
proponer to propose; —**se** to plan,
  intend
proporcionar to furnish, provide
propósito purpose, end; **a** — on purpose
proseguir (i, i) to go on, continue
prospecto brochure, pamphlet
prosternarse to prostrate oneself
protegido protected
provisto (de) provided (with)
prueba proof, test, trial; **poner a** — to
  put to the test; **viaje de** — trial
  run; *pl.* evidence
¡puaf! bah! (*or any similar
  exclamation of exasperation*)
puchuela trifle, insignificant sum
puente *m.* bridge
puerto waterfront, harbor
pues well *expl.;* since, because; —
  bien well then
puesta de sol sunset
puesto *p.p. of* **poner**; on (wearing, *as
  with clothing*); — **que** since;

n. post, position, job; place-setting; stand (*in market*)

pulcro neat, clean

pulgar *m.* thumb

pulmón *m.* lung

pulsar to feel one's pulse

pulsera bracelet; **reloj de —** wrist watch

punta tip, end; point; **—s de pie** tiptoes

puntapié *m.* kick

puntería marksmanship, aim

punto dot, point; popular song, stitch; **al —** at once, instantly

puñado handful; **a —s** by the handful

puñal *m.* dagger

puñalada stab

puño fist; handle

puro pure (*when after the noun*); nothing but, only (*when before the noun; e.g.,* **puras tonterías** nothing but foolishness)

Q

quedar to remain, be, be left; **— en** to agree to, on; **—se** to stay, remain

quedo quiet, still

quehacer *m.* task, chore

queja complaint

quejarse (de) to complain (about)

quejido moan, groan

quejumbroso plaintive

quemadura burn

quemar to burn (*trans.*)

querella quarrel

querer (ie) to want, wish try; to love, like; **— decir** to mean; **sin —** unintentionally

querida mistress

querido dear, beloved

quiebra bankruptcy

quieto still, motionless

quimera chimera (*unreal creature of the imagination*)

quimérico fanciful, hopeless

quinta farm; villa, countryhouse

quitar to take off, away; **—se** + *article of clothing* to take off

quizá perhaps, maybe

R

rabia rage, fury

rabiosamente furiously

racha gust, streak

ráfaga small cloud, a gust of wind

raicilla little root

rajar to cleave, slit

rama branch

ramalazo gust, lash

ramo bouquet, bunch

rapaz *m.* lad; bird of prey

rápido express train

rapiña: ave de — bird of prey

rapto impulse

raro strange

rascacielos *m. sing.* skyscraper

rascar to scratch, scrape

rasgar to scratch vigorously, tear

rasgo feature

raso satin; **cielo —** ceiling

raspar to scrape, scratch

rastro track, trace

rato time, while; **al —** in a little while

raudamente rapidly

raya line, streak, stripe

rayado striped, lined

rayar to emit rays; **— en** to border, verge on

rayo streak of lightning

raza race

razón *f.* reason; **dar — a** to confirm; **en — de** with regard to, as regards to, due to; **tener —** to be right

razonamiento reasoning

real real; royal

realizar to carry out, make, do

reanudar to resume

rebatir to refute

rebozo shawl

rebullir to stir, move about

rebuscar to search carefully

recargo extra charge, new charge

receloso suspicious

receso recess

receta prescription; recipe

recibir noticias (de) to hear (from)

recinto enclosure, place

recio tough, robust

reclamación claim, demand
reclamar to claim, demand
recobrar to recover; —**se** to recover, recuperate
recoger to gather, take in, collect, pick up; —**se** to crouch
recogimiento withdrawal, quietness
recomenzar (ie) to begin again
recompensa reward
recóndito obscure, profound
reconocer to recognize
reconquistado regained
reconvenir (ie) to reproach, reprimand
recordar (ue) to remind (of), remember
recorrer to travel (go) through (over, across)
recorrido search, check; journey, route, course
recortado outlined
recostado reclining
recostarse (ue) to lie down, recline, lean back
recova street market
recreo play, recreation
recruzar to recross
rectángulo rectangle
recto straight
recuerdo memory
recuperar to recover, regain
recurrir a to resort to
recurso means, resort, recourse
rechazar to turn away, down, reject, refuse
red net; network, system
redacción composition
redactor *m.* editor
redondel *m.* circular area
redondelito little circle, ring, disc
redondo round
reencender (ie) to rekindle
referir (ie, i) to relate, tell; —**se a** to refer to
reflejo reflection
reflexionar to reflect
refrán *m.* proverb
refuerzo reinforcement
refugiarse to take refuge (shelter)
refunfuñar to growl, mutter
regalar to present, give as a gift

regaño scolding, reprimand
regazo lap
registrar to search
registro record
regla: en — in order, in proper form
regocijo joy, elation
regresar to return
regreso return
reguero trickle, stream of drops, line left by liquid
rehuir to shun, avoid
rehusar to refuse
reina queen
reino kingdom
reírse (í, i) (de) to laugh (at)
reiterado repeated
reja grill, bars
relamer to lick
relámpago lightning, flash of lightning
relato story, narrative
relieve *m.* importance
reloj de pulsera wrist watch
reluciente glittering, gleaming
relucir to glitter, glisten
rellano landing (*of a stairway*)
relleno stuffed
remanso quiet place, haven, oasis
remedio solution, remedy, choice
remendar (ie) to patch, repair, fix up
remero boatman
remordimiento remorse
removerse (ue) to move around
remudar to change
rencor *m.* ill-will, hatred
rendija crack
rendir (i, i) to produce, achieve, give to; —**se** to give up, surrender
renegrido very black
renguear to limp
renovarse (ue) to be renewed
renuevo shoot (*plant*)
reojo: de — suspiciously
reparar (en) to notice; to repair
reparo: poner —s (a) to find fault (with)
repartir to divide, distribute
reparto distribution
repasar to go over, through
repaso review
repechar to go uphill

repente: de — suddenly
repentinamente suddenly
repentino sudden
repicar to ring out, resound
repique *m.* peal, ringing
repleto crowded, full
replicar to reply
reponer to repair; to reply
reposado relaxed, rested
reposición recovery, recuperation
reprobar (ue) to blame, condemn
resabio bad taste
resbalarse to slip, slide
rescatar to rescue
resecar to dry thoroughly
resentir (ie, i) to weaken, damage
resolver (ue) to solve; to resolve
resonar (ue) to resound, echo; to ring
resorte *m.* spring
respirar to breathe
resplandecer to gleam, shine
resplandeciente shiny, luminous
resplandor *m.* glow
respuesta reply, answer, response
restablecido recovered, recuperated
restante remaining
restar to subtract
restos *pl.* remains
restregar (ie) to rub
resuelto *p.p. of* **resolver;** determined, prompt, resolute
resultado result
resultar to be, turn out (to be), end in
resultas: de — as a consequence
retaceo misgiving, hesitation
retirado remote
retirarse to withdraw, retreat, leave, go away, retire
retocar to adjust
retomar to take again, regain, go back to
retorcer (ue) to twist (*trans.*); —**se** to twist, writhe, squirm
retozar to frolic, caper
retrato portrait
retroceder to retreat, move backward, back up
reunir (ú) to gather, collect
revelar to reveal; to develop (*film*)
reventar (ie) to burst

reverencia bow; nod
revés *m.* reverse, back; **al** — in reverse, backward; **al** — **de** just the opposite from
revisar to examine
revolcarse (ue) to roll about, turn over and over
revoloteo fluttering
revolver (ue) rummage, to go through, turn over; —**se** to move back and forth
revuelto *p.p. of* **revolver;** intricate, tangled, mussed up, topsy-turvy
rey: el mismo — the king himself
riachuelo stream
ribera bank (*river*)
ridículo: ponerse en — to look ridiculous, make a fool of oneself
riesgo risk
rincón *m.* corner
río: — **abajo** downstream; — **arriba** upstream
riqueza wealth
risa laugh, laughter
risita giggle
risotada loud laugh, guffaw
roble oak
robo robbery
roce *m.* poise, ability to get along with others; brushing, rubbing
rodar (ue) to roll, tumble; to travel
rodear to surround, circle, cover
rodeo: sin —**s** without "beating around the bush," straight to the point
rodilla knee
rogar (ue) to beg, request
rollizo sturdy, stocky
rombo diamond-shaped parallelogram, rhombus
romper to break, tear; — **a** + *inf.* to begin to + *verb*
roncar to snore
ronco hoarse; rough
rondar to patrol, prowl
ronronear to purr (also **runrunear**)
ronroneo purring, whirring, humming
ropero wardrobe
rosa rose; pink

rosado rose-colored, pink
rosal *m.* rosebush
rostro face
rozar to brush, rub against
rubor *m.* blush, flush
ruborizado blushing
rudeza roughness
rudo hard, vigorous
rueda wheel
rugido roar
rugir to roar
ruido noise
ruidoso noisy
ruin weak, miserable
ruiseñor *m.* nightingale
rumbo course, destination, direction; "way out"; — **a** bound (headed) for, on the way to
rumor *m.* noise, sound
runrunear to purr (also **ronronear**)
rutilante sparkling

S

sábana sheet
sabandija nasty insect, vermin
saber to know; — **con** to have to do with; **hacer** — to inform, notify
sabiduría knowledge, wisdom
sabio wise; *n.* wise man, sage
sabor *m.* flavor
saborear to relish, enjoy
sacar to take out; — **en limpio** to gather, conclude; —**se** to take off (*hat*)
sacerdote *m.* priest
saco suitcoat
sacristán *m.* sexton (*of a church*)
sacudida shake
sacudir to shake
sacudón *m.* violent jerk, shake
sagrado sacred
sal *f.* salt
salado salty
salida exit; departure, outing; an errand to run; **trampa de** — trapdoor
salitre *m.* saltpeter
salobre salty
salón *m.* room, living room; theater

salpicado sprinkled
saltadura nick, chip
salto jump, leap; **dar un** — to jump, take a jump
salud health
saludar to greet, hail
saludo greeting
salvador *m.* saviour
salvaje *m.n., adj.* savage
salvar to save; to cross (*an obstacle*)
salvo except; **a** — safe, out of danger
sangrante bleeding
sangrar to bleed
sangre *f.* blood; **hecho de** — crime, bloody deed
sangriento bloody
sano sound, healthy, well; harmless
santiaguino *adj. pertaining to Santiago*
santidad: Su S — His Holiness
santiguarse to cross oneself
santo *n.* saint; *adj.* holy, saintly, sainted
sañas *pl.* fury
sastrería tailor shop
Satanás Satan
satisfecho: darse por — to be satisfied
saya skirt
sayuela petticoat
secar to dry
seco dry
secuestrar to kidnap
sed thirst
seda silk
seguida: en — right away, at once, immediately
seguir (i, i) to follow, continue, keep on
según according to; as, while
segunda: de — second class
seguridad safety
selva jungle, forest; **en plena** — right in the middle of the jungle
sellar to seal; — **los labios** to silence
semejante similar, such a
semilla seed
sencillo simple
sendero path
seno bosom, breast
sensible sensitive
sentar (ie) to seat; —**le a uno** to look good on someone; to agree with

(suit) someone; —**le mal a uno** to disagree with one, not suit one
sentenciar to pass judgment, decide
sentido meaning, sense
sentimiento feeling
sentir (ie, i) to feel, note; to regret; —**se** to feel
señal *f.* signal, sign
señalar to show, point out
señas *pl.* distinguishing marks; **por más** — to be exact, more specific
señor mío my good man
señorío stateliness, elegance
separado: por — separately
sequía drought
ser: como es de imaginar as one might imagine; **así siendo** in that case; *m. n.* being
seráfico Franciscan (*religious order*)
serenar to calm
sereno calm
seriedad seriousness
serpentina streamer
servicio: capataz de — headwaiter
servidumbre *f.* staff of servants
servir (i, i) to serve; — **de algo** to do any good; — **para** to be good for; —**se** to do business
sesos *pl.* brains
sí: volver en — to come to (*regain consciousness*)
siempre: para — forever
sien *f.* temple (of the head)
siervo slave
sigilo secrecy
sigilosamente secretly, stealthily
siglo century
significado meaning
signo sign
siguiente following, next
silbido whistle (*sound*)
silla chair
sillón *m.* chair, easy chair
simpatía liking, friendly feeling
simulacro image, idol; fake, sham
sin: — **embargo** however, nevertheless; — **fuerzas** exhausted; — **más** without further ado; — **querer** unintentionally; — **tregua** unceasingly

síncope *f.* failure (medical)
sindical *adj., from* **sindidicato** labor union
siniestro sinister; left (*opp. of right*)
sino but, except; — **que** but, rather
siquiera at least, even; **ni** — not even
sirviente, —a servant
sitio place, spot
sobrar to be more than enough, exceed, be left over
sobre *m.* envelope; *prep.* — **todo** especially; **dar** — to fall (hit) on
sobrecoger to startle, take by surprise
sobrellevar to bear, endure
sobrenatural supernatural
sobrepasar to exceed, surpass
sobreponerse to recover
sobresaltar to startle, frighten, alarm; —**se** to be startled
sobresalto start, scare, sudden fear
sobrevenir (ie) to take place, follow, to come along unexpectedly
sobrio plain, ordinary
sobrino nephew
socavar to undermine
socio member, partner
socorro help, aid; **dar voces de** — to call for help
soga rope
sol *m.* sun; **de** — **a** — from sunup to sundown; **puesta de** — sunset
solas: a — alone
solazo hot sun
soleado sunny
soledad solitude; lonely place
soler (ue) to be in the habit of, to be accustomed to
solidez solidity, weight
soltar (ue) to let go of, loosen, set free, release
soltero unmarried
solterona "old maid"
solucionar to solve
sollozar to sob
sollozo sob
sombra shade, shadow; **a la** — in the shade
sombrío dark, shadowy, brooding, gloomy
son: en — **de** by way of

sonajero rattle
sonar (ue) to sound, ring
sonido sound
sonoramente loudly
sonreír(se) (i, i) to smile
sonriente smiling
sonrisa smile
sonrosado pink
sonsonete *m.* mocking sing-song
soñador dreamy
soñar (ue) (con) to dream (about)
sopa soup
sopapo punch on the chin
soplar to blow
soplo puff, breath
soporífero boring, sleep-inducing
soportable bearable
soportar to stand, endure, bear
soporte *m.* support
sorber to sip
sordidez meanness, nastiness
sordina: a la — very quiet, muffled
sordo deaf; muffled, quiet, silent, dull;
   hacerse el — to turn a deaf ear
sorna sarcasm
sorprendente surprising
sorprender to surprise
sorpresa surprise; **llevarse una —** to
   be surprised
sospecha suspicion
sospechar to suspect
sospechoso suspicious
sostenerse (ie) to hold on, endure
sótano cellar
suave soft
subalterno subordinate
subir to rise, go up; to raise; **— a** to
   get on (in) (*a vehicle*)
súbito sudden
subrayar to underline
subrepticio surreptitious
subvenir (ie) to provide, supply
succionar to hold by suction
suceder to happen, occur; to turn
   out
suceso event
sucio dirty, filthy
sudor *m.* sweat
sudoroso sweaty
suela shoe

suelo floor; ground
suelto *p.p. of* **soltar;** loose
sueño sleep, sleepiness; dream
suerte *f.* luck, fate, destiny; type, kind;
   way, manner, fashion; **de — que** so
   that; **por —** luckily, fortunately;
   tener — to be lucky
sugerir (ie, i) to suggest
suicida *m., f.* one who attempts or
   commits suicide
suizo Swiss
sujetar to hold (down, tight); **—se
   (de)** to hang on (to)
sumamente exceedingly, highly
sumar to add
sumir (se) to sink
superchería trick, fraud
superior upper
superpuesto superimposed
súplica entreaty, plea
suplicante pleading
suplicar to ask, beg, entreat, plead
suplicio torture, torment
suponer to suppose, assume
supuesto *p.p. of* **suponer;** supposed
surco furrow, row
surgir to come into existence; to
   come out (forth)
surtir to supply
suscribir to sign
suspirar to sigh
suspiro sigh
sustento livelihood
sustraerse to withdraw, elude
susurrar to whisper
susurro murmur, hum (of voices)
sutil subtle
sutileza subtlety
suyo: de — naturally; **los —s** the
   members of his family (*lit.* his)

T

tablero chessboard; board, panel
taciturno taciturn, silent
taco heel (*shoe*)
taconear to strut, put one's heels
   down hard
tacha defect

tahur *m.* gambler

tal such, such a; — **como** just as; — **o cual** such-and-such, so-and-so; — **vez** perhaps; **de — modo que** in such a way that

taladrar to drill, bore into

talante *m.* will, mood

talismán *m.* amulet, charm

talón heel (*foot*)

tamaño size

tamarindo tamarind (*large tropical tree*)

tambaleante staggering

tambalear(se) to stagger

tamborilear to drum, pound

tangente bordering

tanque *m.* reservoir, tank

tanto so much (many), as much (many); **de — en —** every so often; **en —** meanwhile; **en — que** while; **mientras —** meanwhile; **un —** somewhat

tapa cover, top

tapar to stop up, plug; to cover

tapia wall

tardanza slowness, delay

tardar to delay, be late; to last, take (time); **— en +** *inf.* to take time + *inf.* (*e.g.,* **Tardó un día en terminar.** It took him a day to finish.)

tarea task

tarifa fare

tarima low bench; platform

tarjeta card

tarlatán *m. shiny-surfaced thin cloth*

tartamudear to stammer, stutter

tartamudeo stammering, stuttering

taza cup

techo roof; ceiling

tecla key (*piano, typewriter, tape recorder,* etc.)

teja roof tile

tejer to weave

tejido knitting

tela cloth, fabric; **poner en — de juicio** to question

telaraña spider web

telón *m.* curtain; **— de fondo** backdrop

temblar (ie) to tremble, shake, shiver

temblor *m.* tremor

tembloroso trembling

temer to fear, be afraid

temerario reckless, bold

temeroso afraid, fearful

temor *m.* fear

tempestad storm

templar to harden; to temper, moderate

tenaz tenacious

tender (ie) to spread (hold) out, to make (bed), extend, lay down; **—se** to stretch out

tendero shopkeeper

tener (ie) to have, hold; to be; to be wrong with one (*e.g.,* **¿Qué tienes?** What's wrong with you?); **— a bien** to see fit, find convenient; **— ganas (de)** to feel like; **— inconveniente (en)** to mind, object (to); **— la culpa** to be to blame; **— lástima de, a** to feel sorry for; **— miedo de** to be afraid of; **— prisa** to be in a hurry; **— que** to have to; **— que ver con** to have to do with; **— razón** to be right; **— suerte** to be lucky; **—...años** to be . . . years old

tentar (ie) to tempt

tentativa attempt, try, effort

tenue thin, light, delicate

teñir (i, i) to tinge, stain, darken, dye, tint

terminantemente absolutely, definitely, strictly, flatly

ternura tenderness

terraza terrace

terreno earthly, terrestrial; *n.* lot (property)

terrón *m.* clod (*of earth*)

tesoro treasure

testarudo stubborn

testigo witness

tez *f.* skin

tibio warm

tiempo: con el andar del — with the passing of time

tientas: a — feeling around, groping

tierno tender

timbrazo ringing of a small bell or buzzer

timbre *m.* tone, quality; bell, buzzer
tímpano eardrum
tinieblas *pl.* darkness
tinta ink
tinto stained
tiple *m. stringed instrument similar to guitar*
tipludo falsetto, sopranolike
tipo "guy"; type
tirador *m.* marksman
tirante tight, clutching
tirar to pull; to throw; to shoot
tiro shot
tirón: de un — all at once, without a break, straight through
tiroteo shooting
titubear to hesitate
título: a — de by way of, in the capacity of
tiza chalk
tizne *m.* soot
tocadiscos *m. sing.* juke box, record player
tocador *m.* dressing table
tocar to touch, knock; to ring (bell, buzzer); to sound, play (*musical instrument*); **—le a uno** to be someone's turn (*e.g.,* **Le toca a él.** It's his turn.)
todo: —as partes everywhere; **— el mundo** everyone; **— lo contrario** just the opposite; **a — trance** at any cost; **de todas maneras** anyway; **de —s modos** anyway, at any rate; **del —** completely; **sobre —** especially
todopoderoso all-powerful, omnipotent
tomar to take; to eat, drink; **— asiento** to be seated; **— el fresco** to get some fresh air; **— en cuenta** to take into account; **—lo a la tremenda** to be surprised, get excited; **—sela con** to have a grudge against, pick on, quarrel with
tomo volume
tonelada ton
tonito tone of voice
tontería foolishness, nonsense
torcer(se) (ue) to twist

tordo thrush
tormenta storm
tornar to return; **— a +** *inf.* to do again; **—se** to turn, become
tornasolado iridescent
torno: en — de around
torpe clumsy, slow
torpeza clumsiness, slowness
torre *f.* tower; rook (*chess*)
torrentera ravine
torta loaf
toser to cough
tozudo stubborn
trabajosamente with great effort
trabar to block, trip, tie (the tongue)
tráfago hustle-bustle
tragar(se) to swallow
trago swallow, gulp; drink (alcoholic)
traición betrayal
traicionar to betray
traje *m.* suit; dress
trajeado well-clothed
tramar to plot, scheme
trámite *m.* step, stage, transaction; *pl.* procedure
tramo section, link, division
trampa trick, trap; **— de salida** trapdoor
trance: a todo — at any cost
tranquear to bound, take long strides
transcurrir to pass, elapse, transpire
transeúnte *m.* passerby
transigir to compromise, give in
transitar to travel, pass through
tránsito passage, way; traffic
transitoriamente temporarily
translúcido translucent
transportarse to be carried away
transporte *m.* rapture, ecstacy; transportation
tranvía *m.* streetcar
trapo rag
tras after, behind; **— de** behind
traslado act of moving
trasnochar to stay up (out) late
traspasar to transfix, penetrate, go through
trasponer to go behind, over; to pull, go across, over
traspirar to perspire

trastienda back room
trastornar to upset, confuse
trastorno discover, disturbance
tratar to treat; to discuss, deal with;
— (de) to try (to); —se de to be a
question (matter) of
través: a — de through, across
travieso mischievous
trazado outline, shape
trazar to draw, trace
trayecto section, stretch
trébol *m.* clover
trecho space, stretch, lapse
tregua: sin — unceasingly
tremendo terrible, tremendous (*with
unfavorable connotation*); tomarlo a
la —a to be surprised, get excited
trémulo trembling
trepar to climb
tricota knitted sweater
trigésimo thirtieth
tripulante *m.* crew member
tristeza sadness
trocarse (ue) (en) to be transformed,
changed (into), be exchanged (for)
trompa proboscis (*of an insect*)
tronco tunk
tropezar (ie) (con) to stumble (against,
over), trip (over)
tropilla herd
trueno thunder
tuerca nut (*metal*)
tugurio slum
tupido dense, thick
turbación confusion
turbar to disturb, upset
turbio turbulent, muddy; misty,
cloudy, murky
tutear to speak in the familiar tú form

U

u or
ubicar to locate
ufano conceited, haughty
últimamente lately
ultrajado outraged
umbral *m.* threshold

unir to join, unite; —se to join (*intrans.*)
unísono: al — all together, as one
unos: — a otros each other, one
another; — cuantos a few, some
untar to grease, oil, smear; — la mano
to grease the palm
uña claw, fingernail
urbanidad politeness, manners
usurero money lender

V

vacante *f.* vacancy
vaciar (í) to empty
vacilación hesitation
vacilante hesitating, stumbling, hesitant
vacilar to hesitate
vacío empty
vagabundo vagrant
vagar to roam, wander
vago *n.* bum, tramp; *adj.* lazy, idle
vagón *m.* railroad car; — capilla
ardiente funcral chapel car
vahido dizziness
valer to be worth, be of value; — la
pena to be worthwhile; — más to
be better; —se de to make use of
valija suitcase, valise
valimiento benefit
valioso valuable
valor *m.* courage; worth, value
válvula valve
valla barrier
vanagloria excessive pride in one's
accomplishments
vano empty
vapor *m.* steam
vaqueta *type of cow leather*
varilla stick, bar
varón man, male
vasito: — capilar capillary
vaso glass (*container*)
vaya *imp. of* ir Well! (*to express
surprise*)
vecindad neighborhood, vicinity
vecino *n.* neighbor; *adj.* nearby,
neighboring
vedar el paso to block the way
velador bed lamp

velar to stay awake, keep watch over
veleidad whimsy
velo veil
veloz swift, fleet, rapid
vello fuzz, down, hair
velludo hairy
venalidad corruptibility
vencer to conquer, defeat
venda bandage
vendar to bandage
vendedor *m.* clerk
veneno poison
venganza revenge
vengarse to take revenge, avenge
venida coming
venta sale
ventaja advantage
ventajoso advantageous
ventanilla *dim. of* **ventana** window (*of a vehicle*)
ventura happiness
venturoso lucky, successful, prosperous
ver to see; **a** — let's see; —**se** to find oneself (*in a particular situation*); —**se (con)** to have it out (with), have a talk (with); **tener que** — **con** to have to do with
veras *pl.:* **de** — really
verdad truth, true; ¿—? isn't it?, aren't they?, *etc.,* **a decir** — to tell the truth; **de** — **que** really
verdadero real, true
verdoso greenish
verdugo executioner
verdura vegetation, foliage, greenery; *pl.* green vegetables
vergüenza shame, embarrassment
vericueto difficult terrain
verja iron railing (fence)
verosímilmente understandably, logically
verter (ie) to pour, spill
vértice *m.* tip, apex
vertiginoso dizzy
vértigo dizziness, dizzy spell
vestíbulo hall
vestido dress
vestimenta dress, clothing
vestirse (i, i) to dress, get dressed

vete *imp. of* **irse** Go away!, Get out!, Leave!
veteado streaked
vez time; **alguna** — ever, sometime; **a la** — at the same time, simultaneously; **a su** — in turn; **cada** — **más** more and more; **de** — **en cuando** from time to time, now and then; **de una (buena)** — once and for all, finally; **en** — **de** instead of; **otra** — again; **tal** — perhaps
vía track, line (*railroad*)
viajar to travel
viaje *m.* trip, journey; — **de prueba** trial run
viajero traveler; *adj.* traveling
víbora viper, snake
victimario person responsible for someone else's misfortune or suffering
vida: con — alive
vidriera large window
vidrio glass; pane of glass; glass case
viejecillo *dim. of* **viejo**
viento wind
vientre *m.* belly, innards
vigésimo twentieth
vigilante *m.* watchman, guard
vigilar to watch over, stay on guard
vigilia wakefulness
vilano down of a thistle
vilo: en — up in the air
vinagre *m.* vinegar
vincular to link, connect
vínculo link, bond, tie
virrey *m.* viceroy
virtuosismo virtuosity
viruela smallpox
víscera also *pl.* inner organ; entrails, bowels
visita caller, visitor (*lit.,* visit)
visitante *m.* visitor
vislumbrar to glimpse, catch a glimpse of
víspera eve, night before
vista sight; **a la** — in sight, before you
visto *p.p. of* **ver**; **por lo** — apparently
vistoso showy, attractive

vitral *m.* panes of stained-glass
vitrina china cabinet
viuda widow
viudo widower
víveres *m. pl.* food, provisions
viveza cleverness
vivo alive; lively, active; **—amente**
  quickly; deeply, intensely
vocablo word, expression, term
vocación calling, vocation
vocecita weak voice
volandas: en — in the air, as if flying
volante *m.* balance wheel
volar (ue) to fly; **—se** to fly away
volcar (ue) to overturn
voltear to overturn, demolish, knock
  down
voluntad will
volver (ue) to return, go (come) back;
  to turn; **— a** + *inf.* to do again
  (*e.g.,* **Volvió a ocupar su asiento.**
  He sat down again.); **— en sí** to
  come to (*regain consciousness*);
  —se to turn around; to become; to
  return
voto vow
voz *f.* voice; shout, call; the "word";
  voces rumors, news, **dar voces (de**
  socorro) to call (for help)
vuelo flight; **levantar —** to take off
vuelta return; turn; **a la — (de)**
  around the corner (from); **dar —**
  to turn around; **dar —s** to walk
  around; **dar una —** to take a walk,
turn; **dar la — (a)** to go around;
darse una — to turn around; **estar**
de — back (return); **ida y —**
round trip
vuelto *p.p.* of **volver;** turned
vulgar common, ordinary

Y

ya already, now, then; **¡— está!** there!
  expl. O.K.!; **— lo creo** of course!,
  yes, indeed!; **— no** no longer, not
  anymore; **— que** since
yacente reclining
yacer to lie
yermo *n.* wasteland; *adj.* deserted,
  barren
yerno son-in-law
yerto stiff

Z

zafar to dislodge; to untie
zafiro sapphire
zaguán *m.* entrance hall
zampar to gobble, wolf down
zángano drone
zapateo stamping, foot-tapping
zarpazo blow with the paw
zorro fox
zozobra sinking, floundering
zumbar to buzz
zurcir to mend
zurdo left-handed, clumsy

PERMISSIONS AND ACKNOWLEDGEMENTS

We wish to thank the authors, publishers, and copyright holders for their permission to reprint the stories in this book.

Jorge Luis Borges, *Los dos reyes y los dos laberintos*, by permission of Emecé Editores, S.A.

Vicente Riva Palacio, *El buen ejemplo.*

Enrique Anderson Imbert, *El leve Pedro*, by permission of the author.

Isaac Aisemberg, *Jaque mate en dos jugadas*, by permission of the author.

Amado Nervo, *El ángel caído.*

Juan José Arreola, *Un pacto con el diablo.*

Horacio Quiroga, *Juan Darién.*

María Elena Llana, *Nosotras* from *Cuentos cubanos de lo fantástico y lo extraordinario* (Colección Escuela Social, 1968).

Alfonso Ferrari Amores, *El papel de plata*, by permission of the author.

Marco Denevi, *Las abejas de bronce*, by permission of the author.

Marcos Victoria, *Un suicida*, by permission of Carmen Aguirre de Victoria.

Pepe Martínez de la Vega, *El muerto era un vivo*, by permission of Ediciones de Andrea, Mexico City.

María de Montserrat, *El pajarito de los domingos*, by permission of the author.

Rubén Loza Aguerreberre, *El hombre que robó a Borges*, by permission of the author.